Cool Cat II

Hell on Route 666

Cool Cat II

Hell on Route 666

by
Dan Leissner

Midnight Marquee Press, Inc.
Baltimore, MD, USA

This story is entirely fictitious and all characters are imaginary and have no relation to any persons living or dead. This also includes places, names, companies, religious orders or any other names whatsoever.

For Cat's first thrilling adventure
see *Cool Cat* also published by Midnight Marquee

Copyright © 2016 Dan Leissner
Back Cover Artwork: Jeff Duke
Front Cover Artwork: Jeff Duke
Front Cover Design: Susan Svehla
Copy Editor: Linda Walter

Midnight Marquee Press, Inc., Gary J. Svehla and A. Susan Svehla do not assume any responsibility for the accuracy, completeness, topicality or quality of the information in this book. All views expressed or material contained within are the sole responsibility of the author.

Without limiting the rights under copyright reserved above, no part of this publication may be reproduced, stored in or introduced into a retrieval system, or transmitted, in any form, or by any means (electronic, mechanical, photocopying, recording or otherwise), without the prior written permission of the copyright owner or the publishers of the book.

ISBN 13: 978-1-936168-63-7
Library of Congress Catalog Card Number 2007922772
Manufactured in the United States of America

First Printing by Midnight Marquee Press, Inc., November 2016

Dedicated to Roger Corman, Russ Meyer, Modesty Blaise, Honey West, Emma Peel, Coffy, Cleopatra Jones, Foxy Brown…

…and to my parents, my friends and Cool Cats everywhere

CONTENTS

CHAPTER 1: SACRIFICE — 9

CHAPTER 2: HELL'S ANGELS — 26

CHAPTER 3: GOING UNDERCOVER — 43

CHAPTER 4: ON THE ROAD AGAIN — 62

CHAPTER 5: CAT-FIGHTING — 73

CHAPTER 6: BLACK — 95

CHAPTER 7: TRUCKIN' — 112

CHAPTER 8: HIJACK — 131

CHAPTER 9: BAD MOON RISING — 150

CHAPTER 10: THE DISCIPLES — 160

CHAPTER 11: MEDICINE MAN — 171

CHAPTER 12: AN EVIL IN THE LAND — 181

CHAPTER 13: THE GATES OF HELL — 192

CHAPTER 14: MONSTERS — 204

CHAPTER 15: A HARVEST OF SOULS — 211

CHAPTER 16: DRUMS OF WAR — 220

CHAPTER 17: THE ONE — 231

CHAPTER 18: BLACK AND GOLD — 240

A Tribute to those glorious Blaxploitation movies of the '70s

The Time: 1970s
The Place: Somewhere in the United States

CHAPTER 1

SACRIFICE

The girl screamed.

"N-NN-N-NOOO-OOO...!!!"

The desert shone like silver in the moonlight, every wrinkle and fold picked out in stark clarity. High above, the sky was ablaze with stars, sizzling and scintillating like sparks of ice.

"O-Ooohh...hh...N-NN-OOO-OOO...!!!"

There was a strange light in the desert that night, an angry red glow. A supernatural sound drowned out the rustle of predatory reptiles or the scuttle of a desert rat; the drone of human voices chanting.

"We hear and obey you, oh Master...!"

The fire formed a towering cone, feeding vigorously on a pyramid of stacked wood. The chanting came in rhythmic gusts that fanned the tall flames. The firelight was reflected in the red eyes that ringed the pyre in deep and densely packed ranks, swaying figures cloaked and hooded.

The flames crackled viciously, spitting and hissing.

The girl screamed again.

"OOOO-OOO-OOOOO-HH-Hhh...hhh...hhh...!!!"

She was pretty, the kind of girl one saw every weekend tending the barbeque by the pool; her sturdy body stripped down to a T-shirt and panties.

"P-P-pp-plee-eee-zzz...zze...!!!"

Strong hands gripped her arms down to the bone, twisting them up behind her back. Her body writhed, held between two burly figures shrouded in grey, as they cuffed her wrists together behind her back.

The chanting quickened and increased in volume. Within the shadow of the hoods, there was the pale glimmer of faces turning upwards, the red sparks glinting in their eyes.

They were dragging her to a wooden platform set on tubular metal scaffolding. The platform supported a steel crane, with ropes and pulleys connected to a mechanical winch.

"D-D-dd-d-don't...!!!"

A hook dangled from the long arm of the crane. They secured the hook to the cuffs that bound the girl's wrists. Her eyes were enormous. Her whole body shook, her legs trembling.

There was a great up-swell of noise from the crowd. A strange form had materialized on the platform, tall and broad-shouldered, robed in billowing black lined with scarlet. It was masked in black with slit slanting eyes rimmed in red, crowned by long and curving horns.

"Aaaaaaaa...hhhh...!!!" the crowd sighed. The girl moaned in terror. Her legs sagged but the hooded men supported her.

As the commanding figure advanced to the edge of the platform, the sound of the crowd took on a shape and a rhythm and the chanting rose up again.

An imperious gesture had the hooded men jumping to man the winch.

"AAAIIEEE-EEE-EEEE...!!!"

The girl rose into the air. Her face contorting, she screamed in pain as her bound arms were jerked up behind her. The arm of the crane extended, lifting her out and over the lip of the wooden platform, towards the blazing pyramid.

There was a sudden surge in the crowd ringing the fire, thrusting forward until forced back by the intense heat, a tide rushing in and then receding.

Twisting at the end of the cable, the girl's body jerked and juddered, her legs thrashing.

"EEEEE...AAIIEEEE...!!!"

The figure in black motioned again and the winch began to lower her. Her twitching body descended slowly. Long tongues of flame stretched up greedily, reaching for her dangling limbs.

The crowd was a heaving mass, ebbing and flowing towards the fire. The chanting became feverish.

The girl's eyes were bulging with horror. She screamed until her voice cracked hoarsely. The flames were licking at her toes.

"AAAAAAA-AAA-AAAA...aaa..aa...hhh...hh..."

She fainted, her head lolling down. A great groan burst from the crowd.

They continued to lower her until she had vanished entirely into the roaring fire. The crowd was dancing, a crude shuffle, packed tight together, their palms outstretched towards the flames.

On the platform the tall black specter flung its arms up to the stars, now mingled with red sparks thrown up by the fire.

"Take this our offering, oh Master...!"

The night was psychedelic. The fires were tall fountains of sparks and the smoke was a creeping fog generated by dry ice, aglow with pulsing light. The air was thick with sweet illicit smells and suffused by the ever shifting rainbows cast by whirling multi-colored gels and iridescent oil slides.

"Let's hear it, people…the guys you've been waitin' for…!"

"*YEEEEEEEEEEEEEEE…*"

"…here they are…!"

"*…EEEEEEEEEEEEEEEEEEEEE…*"

"…Six-Six-Six!"

"*AAAAAAAAAAAAAAAAAAAAAAAAAAAAAAA…*"

Silhouetted against the light, figures waded through the artificial fog, jogging onto the stage.

"*AAAAAAAAAAAAAAAAAAAAAAAAAAAAAAAAAAAAAAAA…*"

They raised their hands in salute and, raked by the beams of traversing spotlights, a forest of arms shot up in reply, hands shaped into the twin horns of the beast.

"*AAAAAAAAAAAAAAAAAAAAAAAAHHHHHHHHHHHHHHHHHH…!!!*"

The great exhalation was an escalating scream like the engines of a jet plane, carrying the audience forward until it washed up against the stage. The lights shone on a sea of bright upturned faces with wide eyes and open mouths; teenage boys and girls, bedecked and bejewelled in tribute to their heroes. Hair dyed jet black, black eye shadow and glossy black lips in corpse-white faces. Black leather, black T-shirts sliced and shredded with great deliberation, emblazoned with the numbers in blood-dripping red—"**666**".

"Y'all know it!" screamed the lead singer as he seized the mike stand. "Go To The Devil!"

The scream peaked on a note of recognition.

"*HAAAAAAAAAAAAAAAAAAAAAAAHHHHHHHHH…!!!*"

Behind the lead singer, the band was plugged in and ready to go. The opening riff rode the scream in a crazy warped harmony.

Up front, "Snake" was lean and lanky, with startling blue eyes and an untamed mane of hair so fair it was almost white. Capering and wind milling, he twirled the mike stand like a giant baton, narrow shoulders draped in black satin, his impossibly long and thin legs encased in skin tight silver, tucked into shiny black boots. As he prowled the front of the stage, inciting the crowd, his voice dipped and soared outrageously, now a bull bellow, now a glass-shattering shriek.

"Cannibal" laid down the beat, producing rolling thunder from his drum kit. Stripped to the waist, his muscle-bound torso was already drenched in sweat, decorated by lurid tattoos of daggers and skulls. His long black hair flailed in soaked rat-tails, spraying beads of sweat in a halo caught by the lights.

"Tank" played the bass, with a skull-crushing, subterranean sound, a hulking figure armored by studded black leather down to his Frankenstein boots, shoulders hunched, head down, long dark hair hiding his face.

"Chainsaw" was the rhythm guitarist, wiry and hyperactive. Sheathed in a black and silver jumpsuit, he stalked the length and breadth of the stage, running and jumping, pausing to strike a pose; legs wide apart, bent over the neck, head bobbing, long black hair flailing as he ground out his trademark buzz saw flaying chords.

"The Axe" played lead guitar, on an instrument custom-made for him, shaped like a skull-and-crossbones. He dressed in style, sporting a heraldic leather jacket presented to him by the genuine Hell's Angels, shredded blue jeans and heavy biker's boots. His left hand was a blur on the ebony fret board inlaid with runic symbols, his right flicking out flurries of notes like shards of jagged metal.

"The Axe"'s solo, as ever, prompted a synchronized display of "air guitar" theatrics from the boys, while the girls all raised their hands in the "horns" salute. When "Go To The Devil" crashed to its typically apocalyptic conclusion, the kids went crazy, rocking the hall, a seething mass bathed by the swirling rainbows.

To the side, where the wall streamed with condensation, two boys were standing stock still amidst all the leaping and gyrating. Their faces were blank, their eyes staring, unseeing.

When they built a new High School, in a nice neighborhood that was preyed on by the bad neighborhood, they built it like a fortress. They built it out of concrete and put in barred windows. They ringed it with a tall fence of steel mesh, topped by curls of razor wire. They mounted floodlights on high poles, so at the dead of night, when the nice neighborhood slept and the bad neighborhood came creeping, the main buildings and outbuildings and yards and playgrounds were exposed by a garish glare that penetrated everywhere.

Footfalls padded softly on the slumbering suburban streets, past the identical front lawns and the identical houses. Teenage feet, laced into high-topped sneakers with thick rubber soles.

There were two of them, boys, fifteen going on sixteen. They were typical of the breed, slim with a shock of long brown hair and a smattering of spots on their pale faces. One wore faded blue jeans, bell-bottoms flapping, the other baggy black track suit bottoms with a white racing stripe. The one wearing jeans had a short shiny black windbreaker draped over his ripped black cotton T-shirt with the "**666**" in blood red; the other a ragged denim jacket held together with skull and dagger patches. The boy wearing blue jeans carried a bulky canvas sports bag, slung over his shoulder.

The High School was set at the crest of a shallow slope, a little way off from the grid of identical streets with their identical houses. The boys walked briskly across a broad area of neatly mown grass that framed the School all the way round, pushing through a knee-high hedgerow in order to reach the steel fence where it bordered the playground.

Between them, they swung the heavy bag back and forth and then up and over the fence. It landed with a thud on the grey asphalt of the deserted playground, gleaming dully under the floodlights.

The boys found finger and toeholds in the mesh and scuttled swiftly up to the top of the fence. Deftly, they slipped off their jackets and laid them over the coils of razor wire. They hardly made a sound as they dropped down into the playground. Leaving their jackets snagged on the wire, they lifted the bag between them and made a swift dash across the floodlit playground.

"Hey!" said the Security Guard, leaning towards the flickering screen of his TV monitor. "We got company!"

The boys knew which window to go to. The one in the boys' locker room, a rectangular block attached to the sloping barn of the gymnasium.

"C'mon!" the Security Guard was buckling on his gun belt. "Let's go!"

The empty spaces of the gym still tingled with tiny echoes left over from the day's activities, evidenced by the dangling ropes and rings and the squat vaulting horses, all picked out by the silvery half-light flowing down from the skylights in the ceiling.

Without a word, the boys walked quickly to the middle of a carpet of dark blue rubber matting, laid down for the benefit of the gymnasts, partially obscuring the multi-colored basketball and volleyball courts marked out on the polished wooden flooring.

They put the bag down and zipped it open. The zipper made a sudden loud sound.

"Hold it right there!"

The doors crashing open made another, louder sound, a hot electric light bursting in on the cool blue and silver.

The two Security Guards came in shoulder to shoulder, chunky middle-aged men in pale blue uniforms. They had guns in their hands.

The boys were hunched down over the open sports bag, speared by the shaft of yellow light that lanced all the way across the floor of the gym. The Security Guards relaxed. Just kids. Local white kids. Probably broke in to spray paint something bad about their gym teacher. Nothing to worry about.

"Okay, guys," said one of the guards, holstering his gun. "You've had your dare. So now why dontya just––"

The boys had their hands delving deep in the bag. When their hands came out they were holding their fathers' big blue-black pistols, too big for them, too heavy for their slim wrists.

"Jesus!"

The boys opened fire. Their faces blank and eyes unblinking, they went on firing until their guns were empty. The detonations reverberated back and forth. A haze misted the pale moonlight pouring down from the skylights.

"UH-H-H-hhh...hhh...hh..."

The Security Guards were sprawled in a lake of black blood, one on top of the other, across the path of yellow light that stretched from the open doors.

The guns slipped from the boy's fingers, thudding on the rubber carpet. They turned slowly to look at each other. Solemnly, without a word, they reached back into the bag and pulled out two large heavy-duty plastic containers; the contents made a muffled sloshing sound.

Unscrewing the plastic caps, the boys swung the containers, splashing the rubber matting and the leather padding of the wooden vaulting horses, the twitching bodies of the guards. The smell of gasoline choked the gym, the light made wavering by the vapors.

They returned to the center of the flooded rubber carpet, their feet squelching. They knelt slowly, facing each other. Expressionless, they emptied the remainder over themselves.

One of them took a cigarette lighter from his pocket.

"Take this our offering, oh Master...!"

The choir sang lustily, in stacked ranks robed in blue velvet.

"Heed the word of the Lord...!!!"

Under the glare of the TV lights, the faithful swayed in their seats, clapping their hands to the beat. Some jumped to their feet and danced in the aisles. They were dancing in the balconies. The theater was rocking, making the ushers with their brass buttons and braid glance at each other nervously.

"...of the Lord...!!!"

The choir finished on a note intended to soar all the way up to heaven. The crowd came slowly off the boil and was simmering, an excited murmur of anticipation rippling around the stalls and up to the back of the balconies.

The conductor of the choir was a perspiring butterball with horn-rimmed spectacles and floppy red hair, all tossed out of place by the vigor of his conducting. Breathing heavily and mopping the sweat from his brow, he stepped up to a polished wooden lectern and tapped the microphone to make sure that it was switched on.

"Ladies and gentlemen..."

He had to speak up to be heard above the chatter.

"My friends...!"

The murmur faded.

"We are honored to have with us once again..."

And then swelled up eagerly.

"...the Reverend Thaddeus P. Calhoun!"

There was a great shout. The choir let loose a fanfare of hallelujahs. The TV cameras were panning and zooming to follow the progress of the man who made his entrance onto the stage with long swift strides.

"...the Reverend Thaddeus P. Calhoun!"

He was tall and broad-shouldered, tanned and handsome. He had the head of a lion, with electric blue eyes over classical cheekbones, a long aristocratic nose and a strong jaw. As he entered, he doffed his snow white Stetson with a flourish, the silver band twinkling, to reveal steel grey hair combed back from his high forehead in luxuriant waves that brushed the collar of his pearly silk shirt. In the glare of the TV lights, his white suit was blinding. His gold rings and watch chain flashed and sparkled as he raised his hands to acknowledge a thunderous ovation.

"Thank you! Thank you, my friends!"

The portly choirmaster retreated, bowing and scraping. Reverend Calhoun waited with his large hands resting on the wooden lip of the lectern. When he finally gestured for the ovation to cease, it did, instantly.

The Reverend shifted slightly, to ensure that the cameras would be able to admire his patrician profile. He held a long pause, until the pin-drop silent tension of the audience was stretched to breaking point.

"My friends," he began, in a voice that resonated with authority. "I have come here to warn you of the danger to your children...!"

Concern was etched upon every upturned face, shining under the bright lights. And an eagerness, an eagerness to be told, to hear the message.

"Do you know what your children do, when they are alone? Do you know where they go?"

He was pointing, at something above and beyond them, something lurking behind them.

"They go to the Devil!"

He jabbed with his pointing finger and the crowd rocked back, a shudder that rippled to the back of the hall, all the way to the rear of the balconies.

"They listen to the Devil's music! They hear Satan's siren song!"

His mighty fist slammed down on the lectern. There were gasps. Some cried out.

"They are seduced by heathen Rock Music!"

At dawn, she liked to walk along the beach.

Beneath a glowing, champagne-colored sky, the glittering surf was all froth and bubbles, lapping at her ankles. The sun was a huge disk of pale gold, hanging low above the horizon and the undulating sea sparkled as the tide came rolling in.

"Da...da...da...da-da-da...da....."

A little pink plastic transistor radio dangled by a strap from her wrist. Sweet Soul sounds merged with the soothing rhythm of the surf.

"Mmmm...da...da-da-da...dee...dee....."

She was young, in her early 20s. Her straight, silken fair hair hung down to the small of her back, framing green eyes over high cheekbones, eyes like a cat's, slanted just a little, just enough to be bewitching. Her lips were ripe and pouting, just a little, just enough to make her ravishing.

Her bare toes tickled by the bubbling surf, she was wearing a skimpy, fringed chamois leather halter-top and cut-off faded blue denim shorts. She was tall, not too tall, but tall enough to make her formidable. Her shoulders were strong and supple and her breasts filled the daring halter-top to perfection. Lightly tanned and golden, her bare midriff was superbly trim and toned. Her splendid hips swung with a lazy insolence, as she strolled along the fringe of the ocean with a lithe, athletic swagger.

She turned and walked into the sea, towards the rising sun, until she was thigh deep in the sparkling water.

"Ooops!"

The plastic radio burbled when she accidentally dunked it. Laughing, she raised her hands, tossing out her long blonde hair like a shining cape, to drape her strong shoulders. In the early morning light her body was glowing. She was golden.

Beep! Beep! Beep!

Eyes closed, she was dancing in the water, her arms wafting, embracing the luminous sky.

Beep! Beep! Beep!

She was hip swaying, her body in synch with the undulations of the ocean.

Beep! Beep! Beep!

"Aw…!"

Frowning, she rolled her eyes and waded back towards the shining sand.

Beep! Beep! Beep!

"Okay, okay! I'm coming!"

Beep! Beep! B——!"

Parked at an angle on a tilting down slope; a pert yellow dune buggy. She reached in and plucked out the handset of the CB mounted below the dash.

"Hello…?"

The voice that came from the speaker had a lilt like an exotic bell.

"Good morning, Cat. Sleep well?"

The blonde girl pouted.

"Good morning, Aiko," she yawned extravagantly. "No, I didn't."

The voice was laughing.

"Oh honestly, Cat! Who was he? Did you actually get round to asking him his name?"

The blonde snorted.

"Hah!"

Then she burst out laughing. Her voice was the sound of the sun and the sand and the surf.

"He had a groovy car…"

She could almost hear the voice shaking its head.

"Oh, Cat!"

And the voice was laughing too.

"Well, when you've woken up, Selena wants to see you."

The blonde stopped laughing and looked eager.

"Far out! Work?"

"Yes, work."

The handset was returned to its hook. Leaning her rump against the fiberglass flank of the dune buggy, she deftly rolled herself a joint; a mild, mellow morning joint.

"Mmmmm...mmm.......!"

Tilting her face to the champagne sky, she let the morning breeze and the sounds of the surf and the sweet Soul music wash over her like warm honey.

She hung the little radio on the rear view mirror.
"Da...da...da...da-da-da...dee...dee....."

In its element, the yellow buggy buzzed along the beach, where the ocean met the sand, framed by a glowing halo of spray.

She licked her lips, savoring the salty tang.
"Da...da...da-da-da...dee-dee.....!"

Brown fingers blurred, making gemstones flash and sparkle. Long gold-glitter fingernails clicked rapidly on the keys.

Glowing green characters marched out onto the blank screen, forming ranks and filling it with information:

PERSONNEL FILE
(Classified Level 1)

"Field" name—Cat
Real name—*classified*
Age—24
Nationality—American
Base of operations—Bay City Office
Place of residence—*classified*

· · · · · · · · ·

Cat took the road that ran by the beach, where she could taste the salty tang in the wind that washed her face, and watch the golden ball of the morning sun race parallel to her and the inviting, glittering froth of the surf rolling onto the glowing sand.

The road was the long way to anywhere and in a world where everyone was in a hurry to get somewhere important it was almost deserted, in the middle of a working day. She enjoyed the luxury of taking her time, of having this road all to herself, detached from the workaday hustle.

Thank you, Uncle John.

She felt benign. She could afford to be. She had a five-million-dollar trust fund, and her Uncle's orders not to spend a penny of it wisely.

Thank you! Thank you! Thank you!

She didn't have the road entirely to herself. There was a shape expanding in her mirror.

Shit

A salesman, in an anonymous beige sedan. In a big hurry. Cat could see his bland face quite clearly, greasy with sweat, his eyes big with anxiety. He'd taken the wrong road and was going to be late for his meeting.

He was pushing her. His ugly front bumper was closing in on the rear of the dune buggy, with its exposed engine and blaring exhaust curled like the tubing of a trumpet. He obviously wanted to pass and began to edge out nervously.

Cat laughed.

Fuck off

Cruising, she kept the buggy's rear end in his face. Whichever way he tried to go, she was there in front of him.

It was just a woman. His blood boiled. He was bigger and faster.

"Bitch!"

PERSONNEL FILE
(Classified Level 1)

Special skills—all-collegiate heptathlon champion: can swim, ski, ride, fence and shoot; proficient in several of the martial arts; speaks nine languages.

Weapons—authorized: Colt .25 automatic carbine; Smith & Wesson .357 Magnum

        unauthorized: no information available.

· · · · · · · · · ·

He tried to be clever. He slowed, hanging back, then hit the pedal and accelerated, feinting to go outside, then swinging in.

No way man!

He was no match for her reflexes. Cat made him think that he'd fooled her. Then she shut the door. His brakes squealed, tires smoking. The blunt tail of the dull sedan swung wildly and then the car performed a full revolution, sliding sideways down a gentle slope onto the beach in a cloud of sand.

PERSONNEL FILE
(Classified Level 1)

Education: all the best schools—*classified*
Was inevitably expelled from most of them; dropped out of college in her final year in search of excitement and adventure.

· · · · · · · · · ·

"Wooo!"
Cat whooped. In a haze of gas fumes, the sedan's engine was grinding, wheels spinning uselessly in the deep sand. She heard the staccato shrilling of his horn.
"Chill out, square. Don't get so uptight..."

PERSONNEL FILE
(Classified Level 1)

Homes—a fashionable penthouse apartment - *classified*
    but tends to live at the beach—*classified*

Transport—*classified*
Made an impressive debut and considerable impact on the local racing circuits at the age of 19 but was banned after only four races for over-aggressive driving

· · · · · · · · · ·

She shifted gear and the dune buggy's engine changed key, climbing a notch in intensity. The sun slipped behind her shoulder.

PERSONNEL FILE
(Classified Level 1)

Status—agent has now passed probation. Has performed all of her assignments with conspicuous success. Agent is cool and resourceful. However, her flair for improvisation has a tendency to spill over into reckless self-indulgence

· · · · · · · · · ·

She passed some kids hanging out on the beach, teenage boys and girls in Bermuda shorts and bikinis. They were huddled around a psychedelic VW Beetle with surfboards strapped to the roof, peering anxiously under the raised rear engine hatch.

Cat slowed and brought the buggy to a rolling stop. The kids waved and she grinned and waved back.

"What's the trouble?"

The kids were so cute. At 24, Cat suddenly felt very old.

"Dunno," one of the boys shrugged, his long hair swinging. "It was fine a minute ago. Now it just won't go."

Smiling, Cat sauntered across the sand to join them. The boys were awestruck, their wide eyes rolling all over her. Her smile disarmed the girls, who smiled back shyly.

"Bummer, man..."

The kids stepped aside to let her look at the motor.

"Hmm...yeah...thought so....."

Delving in, Cat fiddled and twiddled for a second or two. Then she stood back, wiping a dark smear from her palm.

"Try it now."

It started first time. The kids cheered. Cat took a bow.

The kids all piled into the dune buggy and were yelling with delight as Cat drove them up and down through the surf and performed spectacular, dizzying 180-turns that raised fountains of spray, until everyone was soaked.

The boys wanted to show off for their girlfriends and Cat let them, watching, shaking her head and laughing as they drove the buggy around and around, tracing great loops and figure-eights in the wet sand.

"Okay, people, that's enough. I got to have enough gas to reach the City".

She shared a joint with them, as they sat around cross-legged on the sand. They just sat and rapped until the sun had almost climbed to midday. The kids were thrilled by her, and their faces sagged with disappointment when she glanced at her watch and said she had to go.

"Hey, don't worry", she chuckled. "I'll be back. I live on the beach".

She snuck into the city by the back way, with the sun at high noon beating like a brass gong on a grim tableau of destruction and dereliction. An industrial wasteland, empty warehouses, vandalized with spray cans, every window shattered, silent factories rotting slowly or reduced to charred bones, gutted by fire.

Waste paper swirled in the wake of the yellow buggy as she weaved nimbly down the alleys that ran between the hollow warehouses, swerving to avoid heaps of tumbled bricks and lumps of concrete with rusted spars jutting from them. The smell of decay made her wrinkle her nose, longing for sea breezes.

The light at the end of a long dark tunnel expanded with blinding abruptness into a broad plain of glaring concrete with tall weeds spiking its cracks, strewn with rubbish and rubble.

Rolling to a halt, she let the motor idle. On the far side of the bleak expanse of concrete, there was the towering, corrugated frontage of a massive warehouse. Its high windows were sightless pits, its bristling hoists and cranes scabbed and scarred with rust. The bankrupt corporate banners emblazoned on its vast doors were faded and ghostly, their livery blistered and flaking.

Cat shook her head, frowning. The lightweight buggy bounced on its wide tires across the broken concrete, bits of debris crunching under its wheels. Her rear bumped in the deep bucket seat. Her teeth rattled.

Jeee-zus!

She let it roll on and on and just when it looked like there was going to be a collision a section of the corrugated wall swung inwards and the buggy vanished into the inner darkness. The wall swung shut behind it.

The dune buggy rolled into a huge steel cage. She switched off the engine. Iron shutters descended with a clang that made her flinch.

The cage was lit by an unflattering yellow light. Cat made a face at herself in the rear view mirror. She felt the swift descent in the pit of her stomach. It lasted for a full minute.

There was a slight jolt as the cage stopped. She heard a muffled beeping and the front gates of the cage rose quickly. The beeping was suddenly louder, insistent.

"Okay, okay!"

With a last glance in the mirror, pausing to tease her windblown hair a bit, Cat vaulted lithely out of the low-slung buggy. Striding out of the elevator, she advanced into a large semi-circular area with stark white walls and a white carpet, from which long white corridors, punctuated at regular intervals by white doorways, radiated like the spokes of a wheel, as far as the eye could see.

All that whiteness made her blink, as it always did, but she quickly got used to it.

"Ah, Cat. Here you are."

There was a woman walking towards her, down one of the corridors to her left. A young Oriental woman with a face like a dangerous kitten, neat and crisp in a pale blue blouse and dark blue skirt, carrying a thick box file under her arm.

"Oh, hi, Aiko," Cat looked appropriately apologetic. "Sorry I'm late."

The Japanese girl shook her head, smiling.

"It just wouldn't be you, Cat," she said. "If you were on time."

Veering off at right angles, Aiko set off rapidly down the central corridor that ran straight ahead of the exit from the elevator, tapering to a far distant vanishing point.

"The Boss is waiting for you."

Cat had to jump to catch up with her. The white corridor was very bright. Young women in pale blue blouses and dark blue skirts were exiting one door and entering another, laden with files and documents. They gave the new arrival a long, interested look as she passed by, looking her up and down, in her revealing halter top and bold, cut-off denims.

"Lap it up," Aiko chuckled. "You're a living legend."

"Aw shucks!" Cat replied, laughing.

At the end of the long corridor, there was a door that wasn't like the others. It was sheathed in padded green leather, with sparking brass studs.

Aiko pressed a brass button. A buzzer sounded and the door opened inwards.

"In you go."

The office was immense, with a plush maroon carpet and a carnival of exotic tapestries on the walls. There were fearsome tribal masks and warrior's shields, hung above leopard skin rugs.

Cat entered to the old familiar greeting.

"There you are. Nice of you to join us."

The voice was a slow, Southern drawl, rich like golden syrup. Her face, framed by a flourishing afro, was the color of fine mahogany. Hers was a proud, fierce beauty, with slanting eyes that burned with a dark fire; high, broad cheekbones, a strong nose, full lips and determined chin. A beauty that belonged to an ancient, royal race, a culture that built stone cities and cultivated and wrote songs and fought and conquered, on an undiscovered continent, while Europe still sat and scratched itself in its mud huts.

"Sorry, Selena. I got distracted."

The office was dominated by a massive desk, lavishly carved with animal's heads and tribal scenes. On the wall behind it there was a panoramic map of the United States and a battery of TV screens. In front, a semi-circle of high-backed conference chairs, upholstered with zebra-skin.

"As always...."

The woman rose from behind the desk. Cat gazed at her in frank admiration. She was magnificent, and ageless. She was straight and tall, taller even than Cat, and powerful, dressed in a green robe that draped down to her golden sandals, gold thread trimming its collar and billowing cuffs.

"You're easily distracted, child..."

Cat looked serious.

"Only when I'm off duty."

She watched the woman called Selena as she left her desk and walked across the office. The strength of her body was evident in the way that she moved, the long robe flowing. Framing the beautiful blonde head between her long brown fingers with their golden nails, she looked deep into Cat's jade-green eyes.

"I know, honey. But I do worry about you sometimes."

Cat sighed.

"I'm sorry."

Selena stroked her cheek, smiling.

"Don't be. That's why I love you."

Cat's eyes were suddenly very moist. Selena returned to her desk and made a motion with a gold-tipped finger. Cat and Aiko settled into the zebra-striped upholstery.

Selena opened a buff-colored file that lay on the carved desk top.

"Now, let's get busy."

Aiko had the box file on her lap. She lifted the lid and handed a replica of Selena's file to Cat. The top page, as usual, was a potted summary; Selena sat back in her chair and gave Cat a chance to peruse it.

Cat looked up from the folder.

"Weird!"

Selena nodded soberly.

"Yeah, the kids are going crazy."

Aiko was leafing through her copy. She made her seat swivel towards Cat.

"And we're not dealing with your typical delinquents here," she expanded.

"That's right," added Selena. "These ain't street gangs from the ghetto..."

"These are nice kids," Aiko continued. "Nice white kids from the 'burbs, killing and burning."

Cat nodded, her features creased into a wry smile.

"Oh, I see. So when it was just blacks and Hispanics from the 'hood, it was simple just to come down on them. But when it's the nice kids, the Power gets confused; it doesn't know what to do."

Selena was smiling too.

"Right on. They can't turn the riot squad and the SWAT teams loose on the sons and daughters of the doctors, the lawyers, politicians, police chiefs and business leaders."

"So we get a call," said Aiko. "We can go where they can't."

Cat was turning over the pages. Her brow furrowed when she came to a glossy 8x10.

"What's this?"

Long-haired, guitar-toting men in black, their faces contorted in an evil leer, and one at the back poised over his massive drum kit, with the twin bass drums emblazoned with the numbers in blood red—**666**.

"Freaky-lookin' dudes," Cat commented.

"Heavy Rock," said Selena.

"With an emphasis on the heavy," added Aiko.

Cat made a face.

"Not my bag. I like it fun-kay!"

"Rock 'n Soul not Rock 'n Roll," Aiko chuckled.

Laughing, Cat raised a clenched fist.

"Solid!"

Raising her eyes to the ceiling, Selena rapped her long fingernails on the desk top.

"Okay, can the double act, children…"

Cat and Aiko stifled their grins and turned to her attentively. Selena slid a copy of the photo from her file.

"What this is," she explained. "Is our only clue."

She frowned at the photograph.

"Maybe."

CHAPTER 2

HELL'S ANGELS

"*Come! Come! Come to the Sabbath...!*"

It was an intoxicating incense—of exhaust fumes and rubber on hot sunlit asphalt.

"*...Come to the Sabbath...!*"

The sound of the engine was a bestial chorus for the buzz saw guitar and nerve-drilling vocals.

"*...Satan's there...!*"

The bulky cassette that projected from the slot of the eight-track had a label that said "**666**".

"*Come! Come...Come to the Sabbath!*"

They were burning rubber in a stark yellow Roadrunner with glossy black racing stripes. The desert blew by in brown and orange streaks; the long strand of telegraph poles that lined the highway became a flickering blur.

The kids were in uniform: slashed black T-shirts, chains with pentangle pendants and belts made out of bullets. In the back seat, a chunky boy with a mop of brown hair did a sit-down dance, pounding invisible drums. Beside him, a lanky companion with a straggly blond fringe was making like a claw with his hand, ripping at the strings of his imaginary bass.

"*...Come to the Sabbath...!*"

In the passenger seat, a chubby youth with freckles and a carrot-colored thatch that flopped over his eyes held his fist up to his mouth for a microphone, screeching the words.

"*...SATAN'S THERE...!*"

The guitar solo peaked on a frenzy of notes like a spray of shredded metal. The driver, a well-built, good-looking kid with straight, jet-black hair and piercing blue eyes, took his hands off the wheel to play air guitar.

"*...SATAN'S...!*"

Suddenly, the driver grabbed the wheel, slamming on the brakes. Tires squealing, the Roadrunner skidded to a halt.

The yellow car stood sideways, straddling the line of faded white dashes that divided the two-lane highway. The primal beat was pumping from its rolled-down windows.

The boys were sat up straight, rigid, eyes fixed and unblinking.

There was a shapeless dark blob in the distant heat haze, where the highway tapered to its vanishing point. As it approached it took on form and substance and revealed itself to be an enormous, red and silver truck, hauling its long articulated trailer.

The driver saw the yellow car idling on the center line.

"What the——?"

He hit the horns, making the silver trumpets blare.

"Get the fuck outta——!"

Wheels spinning and smoking, the Roadrunner exploded off the blocks. Engine howling, it was a spear of light, making straight for the oncoming truck.

"AW......"

The trucker tried to swerve, but his bulk was sluggish.

"........SHH...HH....HHHEEEE....EEEE...TT...TTTT....!!!!"

The metal guitars were shrieking.

"...*COME TO THE SABBATH*..."

The drums and bass thundered.

"...*SATAN'S THERE*...!!!"

The guitars merged into the rending shriek of crumpled metal. Bass and drums became the **"BOOM!"** that echoed dully across the flat desert as a rolling mushroom cloud of violent black and orange rose above the scorched highway, up into the bright blue sky.

Cat heard it.

"Huh...?"

Not so much heard it. She sensed it. She felt it, like a sudden feeling of compression all over her body, pressing on her eardrums.

She was truckin'; she was cruisin', rolling down the desert highway, with the sun on her face and the wind in her long blonde hair, dressed for driving in white rubber-soled high-tops and a pale blue brushed denim jumpsuit with the ring pull on the zipper tugged all the way down to her navel.

The Meters were pumpin' out the Funk. The engine was humming.

"Woo! Woo...oooo...!"

It had the power and poise of a big cat. Bright "rally red" with white go-faster stripes on the hood and along its muscular flanks. Heavyweight chrome and racing wheels, gleaming white upholstery and all the wood grain trimmings on the glittering dash and inside the doors, more like a luxury yacht than a motor car.

1970 Oldsmobile 442 convertible, with the W-30 badge which boasted that under that bulging hood lurked the total package.

"....Woo!...ooooooo...!"

BOOM!

Cat pulled over and the 442 came to a stop, tires crunching on the gritty fringe of the highway. Twisting a chrome-plated knob, she turned the music down and leaned sideways, listening.

"Wha...?"

She pulled the sunglasses with the big round lenses down the bridge of her nose, peering over the top of them.

"Shit!"

Beyond the bend was the crumbly red ochre slope of a low hill, tufted by scraps of dry grass. A writhing fiery mushroom cloud rose high above the ragged ridge.

Her jaw dropping, Cat watched as the boiling mushroom's crown became detached from its twisted stem, like a bubble of fire that grew paler as it escaped into the singing blue sky.

"Christ!"

The red Olds roared and sprang away in a spray of dirt and pebbles. Cat hurled it recklessly around the bend.

"OH!"

She slammed on the brakes.

The big truck was astride the two-lane highway, the cab folded back on its long trailer at right angles. The red and silver livery was seared and blackened. The front and left side of the tall cab was all buckled and stove in, by the blazing mangled ruin of the yellow Roadrunner, imbedded in it.

Cat was grabbing the CB handset from under the dash. She called the Emergency numbers. Then she got out of her car and ran towards the great tangle of flaming wreckage.

"T-they c-c-came...straight...at m-m-ee....."

The truck driver was sitting in the dirt by the side of the highway, his legs splayed out straight. His left arm was broken and he held it crookedly across his body. His face was black and laced with crusted blood, much of his hair burnt down to the scalp. His dark green overalls hung in tatters.

Cat dashed across and crouched down beside him.

"...I t-t-tried t-t-t-to...get out...of the...way...," he mumbled through blistered lips. "B-b-but...they just...k-kept...c-coming..."

There was a metal creaking, and then a crash and fountain of sparks, as the imbedded wreck of the Roadrunner shifted downwards, fanning the flames.

Cat jumped up and ran towards it. The heat on her face made her stop and step back.

"Oh, no...!"
Through the flames, she could make out the charred husks of bodies trapped in the wreckage. One had been thrown clear and lay across the dotted center line of the highway, a dark stain seeping onto the grey asphalt.

"...no...!"
He was just a kid, maybe 17. There wasn't a mark on him. Except that his head had rolled over at a strange angle. Tears rolled down Cat's cheeks as she bent over to look into his face. The light had gone out of his clear blue eyes.

Scrubbing her eyes with the back of her hand, Cat ran back to her car. Heaving open the trunk, she took out a plastic water bottle and a folded Indian blanket. Slamming the trunk shut, she returned to the truck driver.

"...just...k-k-kept...c-coming....."
She unfurled the blanket and draped it around his quaking shoulders. Gently, she tugged off his red bandanna. Unscrewing the bottle cap, she poured cool water onto the cloth and dabbed his burnt lips tenderly.

"It's okay," she murmured. "It's okay..."
She heard the whirring clatter of the Search and Rescue helicopter and tilted her head back, with her hand for a visor, looking up into the bright sky.

Her wheels were spinning.
The highway was humming again, but the music was turned off. The engine's song had an edge to it and the wind on her face was abrasive.

Cat's thoughts were jangled, rattling around and disconnected. She didn't know what to think. She kept on seeing the dead boy's flawless face with his bright blue sightless eyes.

The tang of smoke and spilled gasoline had impregnated the fibers of her brushed denim jumpsuit, pricking her nostrils. She could taste it and smell it in her hair.

Shit!

She shifted gear. The engine notes changed pitch and the needle climbed towards 90...

...95...

Oh you poor babies...!

...100...

Her eyes were misting. The blur of the highway and the desert became watery. Shivering, Cat took her foot off the pedal, slowing down.

She pulled over and parked. She switched the engine off. Flipping open the glove compartment, she delved about till her fingers closed around the small plastic container. The cap came off with a twist and she poured three small white pills onto her palm.

Cat opened her mouth and tossed the pills down. The water bottle was lying on the front passenger seat beside her. She took deep gulps from it, wiping her mouth with the back of her hand.

She sat in the car and waited. She waited until the white hot disk of the sun was sizzling, till the blue of the sky was ringing like a bell and every rock and pebble and grain of sand in the desert was like a diamond in its clarity and everything was more real than real and she was supernatural.

She could see the blood coursing in the veins and the moving bones in the hand that reached for the CB handset. She could hear a voice that sounded like hers, coming out of the sky.

"Uncle John...?"

"Hi, Princess. What's happening?"

The voice that sounded like hers was speaking very quickly, the words tumbling over each other. It was talking about cars and trucks and fire and dead boys. The deep voice that was speaking back to her sounded concerned.

"You sit tight, Princess. I'll be there..."

She was coming down.

Fuck!

Reality sucked.

"Fuck! Fuck! F--!"

There was a glittering in her rear view mirror, a distant humming like a swarm of angry bees that grew in volume as it came nearer.

"Oh great!"

The glittering was a mass of chrome, on spokes and long, long forks and high hanging handlebars.

"That's just what I need!"

She counted five of them, straddling their chopped and customized hogs, in their livery of ripped jeans and heavy leather, spiked with metal studs.

They halted in line abreast across the two-lane highway, adjacent to the bright red Olds parked on the edge of the desert.

"Hey there Momma!"

Get lost!

They were dismounting and ambling towards her, thumbs hooked into their belts, their steel shod boots ringing on the tarmac. Cat was still coming down and her reflexes were dull. Before she could start the engine, two of them were in front of the car, leaning down to leer at her through the dusty windshield with their palms resting on the hood.

They had surrounded the car, two at the back to stop her reversing out of there.

You're lucky, motherfuckers. I've seen enough dead people for one day...

The leader of the pack was standing by the driver's door. He was a big man with a battered, brawler's face full of old scars showing through three days of stubble and a large hairy beer belly spilling over his death's head belt buckle.

"Hey, pretty thang, why dontya..."

His voice was a whiskey-soaked rasp. It trailed off as Cat surprised him by swinging open the door and stepping out of the car.

"...ya......"

She was as tall as he was. There was a sharp, collective intake of breath from the men standing around the red Olds.

"SSSS...ssss....sss.....!"

Cat stood in front of the leader, in the jumpsuit that clung to her spectacular curves like a second skin, with the zipper at half mast.

"Woo-eee...!"

Mesmerized by the pale golden globes of her cleavage, the leader looked like a kid in a candy store. His men were licking their lips audibly. One groaned out loud.

"OOooo––ooohh...hhh...!"

The leader hooked a grubby finger into the ring pull on Cat's zipper. It began to descend below her navel.

Cat's mouth was curved into the shape of a smile, but her eyes were blank. Her eyes gave no warning as her knee came up like a hammer and impacted on his crotch with all the force of her powerful thigh.

"GU-UUUGG-GGHH-HHH...!!!"

His face went beet red, then white, then a pale shade of green.

" UUUU-UUURGHH...G-GG-GGHHH...HHHH....!!!!"

He sank to his knees, clutching himself, his face contorted, long strands of drool dangling from his stubbled chin. Cat took a quick step forward. Her fist traveled a short distance and landed behind his ear.

"UH!"

His eyes revolved like glass balls. He toppled onto his face and lay still.

"Bitch!"

The two leaning on the hood came running round the front of the car, rushing her, pushing and shoving to get at her. The one in front was swinging a length of bicycle chain. Cat feinted and ducked and felt the wind of it fanning her hair.

"Hah!"

Feet planted firmly, she took her strength from the ground. Short punches, one-two, aimed at his chest.

"UGH!"

Jolted backwards, the biker banged the top of his skull hard on the side of the car and slid down to sit with his legs folded under him and his head lolling down.

His partner had a knife, an evil switchblade. It flashed in the sunlight as he made flourishing passes with it, his mouth twisted in a vicious grin.

"I'm gonna slice that pretty face up bad, bitch...!"

Cat was moving sideways in a slow circle. She faked a move towards him and then a hesitation, drawing him on. As he lunged for her, thrusting with the knife, Cat pivoted smoothly in a high turning kick that shattered his jaw, spinning him round and rolling him over and over on the sand.

"YAAAA!!!"

Cat felt hot breath on the back of her neck and long arms were wrapping around her.

"Ha-yah!"

She was razor sharp now. Twisting her body in a fluid hip throw, she let her assailant's weight do all the work. The fourth biker executed a looping somersault, arms and legs flailing. He landed hard on the asphalt and as he struggled to sit up Cat's fist detonated on his chin and everything went black.

"Yew's dead, whore...!"

The fifth biker was still standing behind the red 442. He was holding a blue-black revolver in his hand.

Shit!

It was a Saturday Night Special with the barrel hack sawed down to a stub, but it could still do damage at that range. And her gun was in its secret place in the car.

"First the kneecaps...then one in the belly..."

Stay cool...you've been here before...

Cat prepared her mind and body for swift and decisive action. She was coiled to spring.
BANG!
"Yow!"
There was a sound like a dull bell as the pistol was jarred from the biker's grasp.
"Yowowowowowowowoowo....!!!"
He was hopping around, clutching his bloody fingers.
BANG! BANG!
Spurts of dust sprouted around his dancing feet. The ricochets chased him as he ran to his parked Harley, clambered on board and roared off.
"owowowowowowowowowowowo...!!!"
A horn tooted in the middle distance. Amazed, Cat turned and looked and burst out laughing.
"Uncle John!"
It crouched menacingly on the opposite lane of the highway, aimed right at her. A beast of prey, stripped down to its bare aluminum, adorned by faded racing numbers.
"Oh my!" she groaned out loud.
An evil gleam highlighted the aggressive contours of a low-slung Shelby Cobra 427, fine-tuned for the racetrack.

Oooh, come to mama...!

Cat ran all the way there, her arms flung out wide. Cooing, she was all over it, caressing it, pressing her body to its pugnacious curves, leaning in and inhaling the perfumes of its businesslike black cockpit.
Her Uncle stood beside the car, shaking his head and laughing.
"Well, it's nice to see you too, Princess."
John Warburton had the face of a middle-aged cherub, lit by a hearty glow, blue eyes twinkling behind little round lenses. Long greying hair flowed down to his wide shoulders, complemented by a flourishing walrus moustache.
He was powerfully built, his chest mighty and belly big but firm, with forearms like great hams, projecting from the copious sleeves of the striped burnoose that flapped around his sandal-shod feet.
Like a twig in his big hand, he was holding an M-16 fitted with a long sniper scope.
"Hullo, Uncle John!"

He nearly dropped the rifle as his niece sprang to wrap him in an enthusiastic embrace. Sobering, he held her out at arm's length, looking into her smiling face.

"Are you okay? You sounded out of it when you called before."

Cat was embarrassed.

"Um...yeah...I guess I kind of freaked, y'know...I..."

Her Uncle stroked her shining hair.

"I don't blame you. What you said...bad scene."

Cat's eyes clouded.

"It was. Those kids...it was awful."

John Warburton was looking over her shoulder, at the forms sprawled around the parked Oldsmobile.

"Trouble sure has a way of finding you, Princess."

Cat was laughing again.

"It's a gift, Uncle John."

They walked over and looked down at the unconscious bikers.

"Five against one," said Cat. "That wasn't fair."

Uncle John grinned, his huge hand ruffling her hair.

"No, the poor dumb assholes didn't stand a chance."

Cat started laughing. Suddenly she stopped, bending down to take a closer look.

"Hm!"

Her Uncle hunkered down beside her.

"What is it?"

"Dunno...maybe just a coincidence..."

The bikers' leathers were encrusted with faded and peeling patches; the customary tribal emblems and skulls and daggers. One caught Cat's eye: on a black ground, the dripping red numbers "**666**".

She ripped the patch off and stowed it in her pocket.

"...and maybe not..."

She rounded on her Uncle with big saucer eyes and her best little girl voice.

"Uncle John...?"

She dangled the car keys with the Olds logo on a little leather tag.

"Here. You take my car...can I drive the Cobra...?"

By the time they were halfway to Free Town it was late afternoon. The sun was mellowing as it commenced its long glide towards the glowing horizon. The blue of the sky was starting to pale.

"Wooo...ooooo..........!"

The Cobra was a bright spark a long way ahead of the cruising red Olds.

"...oooooo...oooo.....!"

Cat slowed to let her Uncle catch up, till he could see her huge grin filling the Cobra's mirrors. Then she put her foot to the floor and was gone, like a shell from a gun.

"...eeeeeeeeeeeeee...eeeeee........!!!!"

When people heard the tales about Free Town, they pictured wigwams and campfires, or a kind of Woodstock in the desert. But it was a real town. It had three parallel main avenues, connected by a grid of side streets, all bathed, as the purple dusk fell, in the soft orange radiance of old-fashioned gas lamps. Simple houses, like whitewashed wooden cubes, dotted the streets at regular intervals, their small windows lit by the same vintage glow. Old West-style false-fronted stores lined the broader avenues. There were barns and stables and a water tower and a wooden church with a steeple. There was even a town square with a circular bandstand, a Civil War cannon and a flagpole—only the cannon had a bunch of flowers in its muzzle and the flag bore a large peace symbol and a picture of a dove.

The rumble of all that horsepower made the ground tremble as they drove slowly down a gas-lit avenue, side by side. The storefronts were dark, but an old-fashioned saloon was all lit up and alive with the sound of song and laughter. Down every side street, music was floating from open windows.

Young couples were out strolling, their arms around each other: boy and girl, girl and girl, boy and boy.

"I still say you should have called it Free Love, Uncle John," Cat called out, smiling at the young people, who all smiled back at her.

They parked in front of a small white wooden church.

"Welcome, Cat," said John Warburton.

"Thank you, Uncle John."

Cat pushed the doors wide and stepped through.

Instead of pews and a pulpit she saw a luxury apartment that went all the way up to the wooden beams of the pointed roof. The floor was a sumptuously gleaming parquetry of polished woods, the walls hung with iridescent oriental tapestries. At ground level it was one long, enormous lounge, with richly hued Persian rugs and embroidered cushions tossed around.

Hanging from the beams, brass lamps from Marrakech cast a golden glow. Incense burners stood on slender tripods, wafting their honeyed musk. At the far end, where the altar would have been, the raised area had been converted into a place for dining, with cushions around a long, low table.

Cat was hugging herself with delight.

"I love this place!"

Her Uncle put his strong arm around her shoulders.

"There's always a home for you here, Princess."

A twisting iron wrought staircase spiraled up to a floor that, supported on flying buttresses, made a platform that projected almost halfway into the body of the church, creating a huge loft.

"Hello...?," said a voice from up above.

Cat skipped up the twisting stairs so fast it made her dizzy, her Uncle following at a more mature pace. The loft was split in two. To the right were the sleeping quarters and a great big brass bed.

"We're in here..."

To the left was the bathroom, constructed around a large circular sunken bath, lined with marble, fit for a Roman Emperor. The bath was occupied by two beautiful Chinese girls, the one with the round face of a perfect doll, the other more angular and exotic. Their tawny skin was gleaming, firm breasts bobbing on the water. There was a rainbow of soothing oils on the water and the steam was perfumed.

"Hello, ladies."

"Hello, Papa John."

In an instant John Warburton was naked, kicking off his sandals and hauling the burnoose off over his head. Water slurped over the lip of the bath as he waded in.

"Come and join us, Princess."

John Warburton sat with the steaming water up to his navel, pearls of moisture glinting in the hair on his broad chest and big belly, his mighty arms spread out along the marble rim of the basin. The Chinese girls were snuggled close to him, their heads pillowed on his massive biceps.

"So, how's my favorite niece?"

Cat reclined opposite him, the scented water tickling her chin.

"I hope that you're still enjoying your trust fund. I forbid you to spend a penny of it wisely."

Laughing, Cat rose lithely, the water cascading down her spectacular contours, her skin gleaming. She waded thigh deep in the water. The warm scented vapors caressed her. John Warburton savored the slow roll of her hips as she advanced across the basin, the supple muscle play of her midriff, the surge of her perfect breasts.

The Chinese girls studied her with admiring eyes. Uncle John was beaming.

"I'm so proud of you, Princess."

"Thank you, Uncle John."

Kneeling in front of him, Cat dipped her body down into the water, up to her chin, her golden hair spread out on the surface. Her Uncle looked deep into her eyes.

"Selena told me," he said.

"Yes."

"About the kids."

Cat was frowning.

"It's horrible," she said. "They're doing terrible things. They're hurting themselves..."

"And they're hurting other people."

Her eyes were huge and brimming over.

"They're just kids, Uncle John! What's happening to them?"

He reached out and pulled her close to him. Smiling, the Chinese girls made a space for her.

"That's why you're here, Princess."

By day, the ROAD HOUSE was just another pit stop on the long dusty highway, a bar and diner offering cold beer and fast food, fuel for the truckers and other long distance drivers.

A squat, single-story structure with a skin of bleached pale yellow plaster and a shallow sloping roof tiled with green shingles, it made up for its lack of height by spreading out wide, a haphazard sprawl of additions tacked onto it over the years: rest rooms; bigger kitchens; a pool room with five tables; a separate bar and a restaurant; and a dance hall with a stage for live bands.

"Here we go, sweetheart," Cat patted the chrome-spoked steering wheel.

At night, the ROAD HOUSE came alive. Its windows pulsed with multi-colored strobe light, in time with a throbbing, inciting beat. It was bursting with sound.

"Woo! We're making the scene!"

There was a tail-back of traffic, snaking slowly towards the sound and light, a chain of headlights and impatient horns. It was a while before Cat rolled the red Olds onto the smooth tarmac of the car park and found a space she could squeeze into. The car park was jam packed and some were already pulling out of the waiting line, to park at a distance, on the edge of the fathomless darkness of the desert.

The car park was full of people, slamming car doors and threading their way quickly towards the glowing slab-sided floodlit bulk of the concert hall. Young people, bright-eyed girls all belled and bangled, in their tie-dyed T-shirts and flapping bell-bottoms; grinning long-haired boys in fringed jackets and scuffed denim adorned with slogans.

"Groovy!" Cat laughed.

The kids made her smile, as she sat in her car and watched them skip by. Heads turned as she stepped out to join them. She was a spectacular sight, in a snakeskin bra-top with fringes fashioned from multi-colored beads; skin tight blue jeans secured perilously low on her hips by a chain-link belt of silver and turquoise, its billowing flares extended by inserts made from an Indian blanket, flapping around the pointed silver toecaps of high-heeled suede boots.

The teenagers were awestruck, as they looked at her, standing next to her car. They parted, clearing a path for her, as she set off for the tall doors of the concert hall. Some of the boys lingered around the red Olds, looking it over, peering at the glinting dials on the polished dash.

Inside, the concert hall was a large empty shell. It glowed with shifting patterns of light, ever-changing rainbows that washed its walls and made luminous pools on the wooden floor.

Onstage, the local support was already playing, long hair swaying as they chugged out a down 'n dirty boogie with all the earnestness that a high school rock band could muster. In a bunch, their supporters jostled and bumped up against the lip of the stage, heads bobbing, stomping. Behind them, the hall was filling, a crowd come to see the main attraction, a band big enough to have made it state-wide.

Cat wandered through the milling throng, heading towards the stage. In mid-solo, the lead guitarist saw her approaching, a vision of teenage lust bathed in rainbows, and lost it completely, playing a flurry of piercing bum notes.

"Sorry...," Cat mouthed silently, grinning up at him. The adolescent axe man shrugged and grinned back at her.

Cat moved off to the side and stood with her back against the wall, watching the kids do their thing, some dancing, some pushing and shoving and play fighting, some with their arms wrapped around each other kissing. She saw little bags of pills being offered furtively and the light was fuzzy with a thick sweet smoke.

"Hey......?"

Their allotted slot completed, the support band trouped offstage to the cheers of their teenage fan club. As the crowd began to press forward expectantly, young men with beer bellies straining their T-shirts were clearing the stage and replacing the support's drum kit with a much bigger, more professional one.

"uh......?"

It was the apprentice lead guitarist, wearing a faded US Army surplus T-shirt two sizes too big and ragged jeans. He stood a little way off, looking up at her shyly and then down at his battered sneakers.

He was a pleasant-looking youth, barely 16, with pale, smooth cheeks and a mop of dark hair down to his shoulders. Cat's smile made his knees turn to water.

"Hi, man. Good set."

The kid looked bashful.

"I...I kinda fucked up...."

Cat laughed.

"No way, man, I though you had your chops together pretty good."

Over his narrow shoulder, Cat saw what she was looking for. Three boys; all in black. She saw the emblems. In blood-dripping red––"**666**".

There was a big noise from the crowd. Men holding guitars were coming out onto the stage.

They knew their stuff and the crowd was roaring them on. The teenage lead guitarist was looking depressed.

Cat tapped him on the shoulder. He almost died when she leaned close, putting her lips to his ear. His eyes popped wide in disbelief, his Adam's apple gulping.

The boys in black were looking surly, shaking their heads with disappointment as they watched the band on the stage.

Cat was leading the young guitarist by the hand, towards the doors of the hall. He seemed to be in a trance. When they reached the doors, Cat glanced back at the stage, at the boys in black, who looked disgusted.

The Olds had its snow white top down. The windows were steamy.

"Mmmm...," said Cat. "That was nice....."

The boy couldn't speak. He was gasping, slumped on the white vinyl of the back seat, the T-shirt rumpled up under his chin, his ankles snagged in his underpants.

"Oh...G-God...," he croaked at last. "No one's g-gonna be...lieve m-me...!"

Sitting beside him, Cat was spooning her breasts back into the cups of the snakeskin halter.

"Aw, c'mon," she chuckled. "Guitar players get all the girls."

He stared at her, his eyes enormous.

"T-that was my...f-f-first...," he panted, tugging his T-shirt down and his underpants up. "I mean...the f-first t-time anyone's...d-done that... that thing...you....d-did...with...your...!"

Cat slipped a ready-made joint between her smiling lips.

"Oooh, really?"

Reaching over the front seat, she plucked the lighter from its socket in the dashboard.

"Did you like it?"

The boy just stared at her, gulping.

"Oh...hh...G-G-God...!"

Laughing, Cat helped him back into his pants. Then they sat for a while side by side on the back seat, passing the joint back and forth.

"You're amazing!" the boy blurted.

"That's true," Cat grinned at him.

Suddenly, the boy was relaxed and they were both laughing. Then he stopped laughing and, with reverence, bent across and kissed the cupped swell of her breast.

"Thank you," he said.

"You're welcome."

They smoked another joint. The lights of the hall were throbbing to the thud-thud-thud of the band.

"Heavy sounds," the boy commented.

Cat's brow furrowed.

"Tell me about Six-Six-Six."

"Huh?"

"The band. Six-Six-Six."

The kid frowned.

"Too heavy."

"Oh yeah?"

"Not my bag. They get all the freaks, y'know?"

"Uh-huh."

"Real weird. A bad vibe..."

Cat rolled down the window and inhaled the cool night air.

"Mmmmmm...!"

Spontaneously, the boy reached out and touched her. She turned back and looked at him, her face very close to his. Her eyes were warm and melting.

"Have you ever made love in the desert at night? Under the stars?"

In a school classroom, time always seemed to run backwards.

"Pay attention at the back there..."

The land of daydreams lay outside the classroom windows, beyond the empty grey expanse and wire fences of the playground. It was irresistible, and a geography lesson was no competition at all.

"...you can expect a pop quiz on this topic in the very near future!"

The door at the back of the classroom clicked open quietly. The boy entered, his rubber soles making a soft squeak on the wooden floor. He was slightly built, and round shouldered, wearing a plain black T-shirt and faded jeans. Approaching 17, he had lank blond hair with fringe flopping over his forehead and the first hint of pale peach fuzz on his chin.

All the bored young faces at the desks turned to look at him.

"Huh!" someone sniggered.

" Dweeb...."

The teacher was a stocky, plain woman in a roll neck sweater and tweed skirt, with a few streaks of premature grey in her combed back brown hair. Holding her chalk like the cigarette she badly needed, she stood by the blackboard, frowning at the new arrival.

"Well, Mr. Grunner, so nice of you to join us..."

The boy had a long brown leather sports bag slung across his narrow shoulders. Without looking at anyone, he put it down on the floor, just inside the door. Squatting down, he hauled on the heavy brass zipper.

The teacher glowered.

"Mr. Grunner, if you would kindly be seated so we can proceed with––!"

When the boy stood up, he was cradling a single-barreled pump action shotgun.

There was total silence. Then a girl screamed.

In the confines of the classroom, the roar of the shotgun was a physical sensation. The front of the teacher's sweater became a ragged, bloody mess. Arms out flung, she was hurled backwards and smashed into the blackboard, sliding down to the floor with a look of wide-eyed surprise frozen on her face.

"OH MY GOD––!"

There were shouts and screams and the crash of desks tumbling. Terrified, the pupils flung themselves flat on the floor, cowered behind their overturned desks, or scrambled over each other, trying to find shelter in the far corners of the classroom.

The boy went on firing, working the sliding pump action until the gun was empty. The room was full of smoke, and groans and shrieks of pain. Streams of red blood ran across the floorboards.

Calmly, the boy delved into the bag and produced a box of shells. Tucking the shotgun into the crook of his arm, he turned and walked out of the classroom.

He strolled down the corridor with a slow measured tread, carefully thumbing the shells into the breach of the shotgun. Some boys came running around the corner towards him. Pop-eyed, they saw the gun, scrabbled to a sliding halt, turned and ran away, yelling.

The boy watched them go. His face was blank, his eyes fixed and lightless.

He stopped walking. The empty cartridge box slipped from his fingers.

There was the thin wail of sirens, approaching fast from a distance.
The boy knelt down in the middle of the corridor. He turned the shotgun around and put the muzzle in his mouth.

CHAPTER 3

GOING UNDERCOVER

"More...on the forehead..."

The make-up girls were fussing around the Reverend Calhoun like harem slaves attending to their Sultan. Two dabbed with sponge and powder puff, while a third held up a large oval hand mirror, so he could supervise the proceedings.

"Enough!"

Irritated, the Reverend waved the girls away. Whisking the towel from the wide shoulders of his cream colored suit, they retreated hastily. Seizing the mirror girl's wrist in a grip that made her wince, he took a last long look at himself.

"Hm!"

His patrician profile was perfect and there was no danger of any unsightly glare.

"That will have to do".

He released the girl and she exited, running backwards, barely suppressing the urge to bow to him. Crooking his finger, the Reverend summoned the Floor Manager into his presence. A freckle-faced, podgy young man with curly red hair tickling the collar of his denim shirt, he crossed the floor of the TV studio, nimbly avoiding the tangled coils of electric cable.

Shrugging past the cameramen, hunched over their bulky cameras with bristling lenses mounted on rotating turrets, the Floor Manager approached the long curved blue desk where the Reverend was enthroned, bearing his trusty clipboard.

"Yes, Sir?"

Immaculate in his crisp white suit, the Reverend frowned upon the young man's faded denims.

"Are you ready?"

The Floor Manager gulped, rattling his clipboard.

"Er...just four minutes...Sir..."

Until now, the Reverend had completely ignored the man sitting a few feet away from him along the shallow crescent of the desk.

"It won't be long now, Senator."

Senator Tom Jarvis hated going on TV. He knew that the cameras didn't love him. A lean, slope-shouldered man in his early 40s, with close-cropped dark hair and small eyes in a long thin face, he knew that the cameras made him look cadaverous and gave him a distinct six o'clock shadow even when he was freshly shaven.

"Fine...fine..."

He looked like a shadow, insubstantial, a grey man, in his sober suit and tie, next to the Reverend, in his vanilla ensemble and all that flashing gold. He fidgeted irritably as a studio assistant pinned the tiny microphone to his lapel.

The red light was on. The cameramen were poised, like gunners waiting for the order to fire.

The Floor Manager raised his hand. Mouthing the numbers silently, he made "one, two, three" with his fingers and then brought his arm down quickly to point at the men behind the desk.

"Good evening, ladies and gentlemen," the Reverend began. "And welcome to *The Time Is Now*..."

The cameras pulled back to reveal the man sitting beside him.

"My guest tonight is a man whose concerns for the fate of this Christian nation are, I am certain, shared by many of you who watch this program, Senator Thomas W. Jarvis..."

The Senator sat up a little straighter. His collar felt very tight and already he could feel shiny sweat prickling on his forehead.

"...ah...good evening, Reverend Calhoun, it's...a privilege...to be here."

The Reverend made his chair swivel slightly towards his guest; his three-quarter view was always very flattering.

"Now Senator, I am sure that like me, many of our viewers will have been delighted by your decision to put your name forward in the ballot for your Party's selection of its next Presidential candidate..."

In the control booth, surveying a bank of monitors, the Director recoiled in horror.

"Jeez! No close-ups on Jarvis, medium shot only. Number Two, zoom in big on the Reverend!"

"...perhaps you would summarize for us your reasons for entering the race".

The Senator cleared his throat. His voice had a sharp pitch to it.

"Well, Reverend Calhoun, I believe that I have identified a growing concern amongst honest and industrious Americans everywhere at the cancer of moral degeneration that is infecting our great nation."

Big close-up of the Reverend nodding gravely.

"Indeed, Senator, as our viewers well know, this is an issue which has been a crucial topic of mine for some considerable time now. We are engaged in a struggle for the moral salvation of our people. And we need leaders like you to take up the fight..."

Out of the corner of his eye, the Senator could glimpse an overhead monitor. Seizing this off-camera moment, he grabbed a sip of water and swabbed his brow with a handkerchief tugged from his breast pocket.

"...but how to begin this great struggle? What is your strategy, Senator?"

The Senator hid the handkerchief on his lap.

"...ah...well, Reverend...I believe that we must start with the children. Young minds are being corrupted by the perversion that likes to call itself the 'counter-culture', that revels in a self image of 'sex and drugs and rock and roll' and promotes the flouting of authority and the rejection of all decent moral values..."

"Hmph!" John Warburton snorted. "These guys sure like to use the word 'moral' a lot don't they?"

Cat laughed.

"Yeah, and then they get caught with their pants down getting a blow job in some massage parlor."

They were sitting side by side in the big sunken bath, smoking a joint and caressed by fragrant oils that scented the steam. A small white plastic, battery-powered TV, shaped like a globe, was anchored to a ledge above them.

"Aw, I can't take any more of this," Cat frowned. "Try another channel."

Her Uncle reached for the remote.

"Yeah, maybe there's a football game..."

They got the news headlines, on a local station.

"Oh shit, now what?"

They were talking about the boy who had taken a shotgun to school.

"Hey...?"

They were showing his picture, a picture chosen by his grieving parents, a picture in which his hair wasn't dyed jet black and he wasn't wearing the T-shirt with the big red "**666**".

"Hey what?"

"I know him...I mean I saw him. He was at the gig..."

Cat stood up and was wading out of the bath.

"I have to call Selena."

When Cat rang the bell it chimed Perry Como's "Magic Moments".

Oh Christ...

The house was like all the other houses in a street that was like all the other streets. The car parked on the gentle slope of the drive that led to the garage was the only car parked in the street because all the other cars were at the office, in the middle of a Monday morning.

Bracing herself, Cat rang the bell again. Pushing her horn-rimmed glasses down the bridge of her nose, she peered over them, surveying the dull suburban landscape. The homes of Mr. and Mrs.. Ordinary, living in their ordinary homes, with their ordinary children and their ordinary cars and their ordinary cats and dogs.

Only this kid wasn't so ordinary...this one took a gun to school...

The spectacles were a costume prop, with plain glass lenses. They went with her hair tied up in a coil on top of her head and her neat pale grey suit with its knee-length skirt and sensible shoes. The kind of shoes that someone who might have to do a lot of legwork wore, the kind of shoes a reporter would wear.

As she reached for the bell push again the door clicked open quietly.

"Oh...yes...I was expecting you..."

The woman was slender, with shoulder length dark hair combed back from her forehead. There were enormous dark circles around her eyes, stark in her pale face.

"Please...come in..."

Her voice was little more than a whisper. She looked exhausted. Suddenly, Cat didn't want to be there.

Come on, you have a job to do...

"Thank you."

The woman led her through the narrow hallway and into the living room. It was exactly what Cat expected. Matching sofa and armchairs on the deep pile carpet, aimed at the TV. The coffee table with the "TV Guide" on top of a pile of magazines. The cocktail cabinet and shelves with knick-knacks and snapshots in cheap frames.

"Yes...that's Lonnie..."

He was younger in the picture, maybe nine or ten, kneeling on green grass with a huge grin on his chubby face and his arms wrapped around a shaggy dog.

"That was taken a long time ago..."

The woman's voice faded away. She seemed terribly fragile, as if she was about to crumble. Cat wanted to put her arms around her. But she didn't. She had a job to do.

"...although it only seems like yesterday..."

Glass doors looked out onto the predictable crazy paved patio, and the barbeque and the lawn. A man sat in a striped deckchair on the patio. Unshaven and in his undershirt, he sat slumped with his head hanging down, staring at the ground between his feet. A half-drained whiskey bottle stood beside the chair.

The woman's whisper made Cat start, as she stood staring deep into the innocent eyes that smiled at her from the photograph.

"That's my husband...George...he just can't..."

Cat nodded.

Come on! Get it done!

She looked hopefully to the door that led out of the living room, and the glimpse of a passageway and stairs going up.

"Oh yes...you wanted to see Lonnie's room..."

The woman led Cat up the stairs.

"We appreciated what you said...in your letter...about wanting to write about Lonnie as he really was, and not just about what he did...everyone else talked about him as if he was some kind of...monster..."

Cat hated herself.

"Thank you."

It was a typical teenager's room; organized chaos, with overflowing shelves and things tumbling out of cupboards. Dirty socks and discarded underpants were tossed about casually. There was stuff crammed under the bed, the blankets thrown aside in a tangle. On the stained top of a small desk standing in the corner, a stack of dog-eared school books was shoved aside to make way for an empty pizza box.

"Sorry..."

Cat's toe nudged a stash of well-thumbed girlie magazines, badly hidden under the bed. The woman managed the ghost of a smile.

"That's alright..."

Tears welled in her eyes.

"He was just a normal healthy boy...but then he changed...I don't know...I just don't..."

Cat stood there remembering those happy kids on the beach, and the dead kids on the road. Taking a deep breath, she turned about, looking around the room.

Thought so...

The record player was on a small table next to the bed. An LP was still on the turntable. Yellow plastic headphones lay on the pillow, the jack plug in the socket in the side of the deck.

Cat bent down to retrieve the empty sleeve from the carpet flecked with crumbs and cigarette ash.

"Hm!"

They stood shoulder to shoulder, their guitars wielded like weapons, framed by the blood red letters:

666
RIDE WITH THE DEVIL

"So...when will your piece be...in the...paper...?"

Leaning in the doorway, the housewife spoke as if she was in a dream, her thoughts in and out of focus. She was pale and fragile, as though the slightest breeze could blow her away.

Backing down the strip of crazy paving that divided the front lawn and made a path from the street to the door, Cat was scrubbing with a tissue, pretending to clean the false lenses of her glasses. She stood and scrubbed, looking down.

"I...don't know much...about these...I expect it takes a...while...?"

Cat couldn't put it off any longer. She shoved the glasses back onto the bridge of her nose and looked the woman in the eyes.

"Uh, oh it'll be a few days. Maybe next week. It, um..."

She hated herself.

"...it depends on my Editor...."

The woman nodded and faded away into the gloom of the hallway. The door swung shut behind her.

With a heavy heart, Cat walked slowly down the path, to where the red Olds stood gleaming in the suburban sunshine. She wrenched open the door and almost threw herself into the driver's seat.

Cat turned the key and the mighty V-8 rumbled, like some great beast aroused.

Come on, baby. Let's get out of here!

Despite herself, she looked back at the house. She saw the pale glimmer of the woman's face at a chink in the drawn curtains. She saw the flicker of the woman's hand and forced a smile, waving back limply.

Oh I'm never going to have children!

The house was being watched. And Cat was watched as the Olds surged forward and seemed to span the length of the street in an instant, its growl making the ground tremble, taking the bend with a tight squeal, gone in a flash.

The desert chilled at night but Cat kept the top down and let the cold air wash over her.
"Wooo-ooo-ooo…!"
The cold was part of the rush. And the funk, pumping from the speakers.
"oooo-hooo-hooo-oooo…!"
And the uppers. All mixed in a cocktail of 90 mph.
"oooo-ooooooo-hooo-oooo…"
The chill wind was a *whooshing* blackness, fanning her long hair, like an electric thrill on her face. The sky was a vastness full of stars that tumbled down like sparks, cascading all around her.

"…95…"

She was surfing on drum and bass and waves of wah-wah laden guitar.

"…100…"

Those soul sisters with their voices like spooned honey were "oooh-oooh-ing" and Cat "ooh-ooh-ed" right back at them, her whole body moving, doing a sit-down dance in the driver's seat.

"…110…"
The brass section kicked in and the horns made her sigh and moan.

"…120…"

When the sax solo peaked she screamed out loud.

Jeez! These guys suck!

Tuning up was obviously not in this band's vocabulary. But they knew how to strut, wading knee-deep in a dry ice fog suffused by a spectral luminosity.
Their shredded metal guitars were like fingernails scraping on a blackboard. Cat's whole body clenched, but she kept her poker face.

Come on, try to look like you're enjoying it

She was dressed for the occasion. Her blonde mane had ice-green highlights, her eyes heavy-rimmed with black. Silver skulls dangled from her ears and her lips were the color of blood. Runic symbols adorned the rings that encrusted her fingers, with their nails painted black.

A black leather jacket armored with chains and steel studs was draped casually over her shoulders. Her cut-off T-shirt was black and modified by jagged razor slashes, emblazoned by a scarlet pentangle. Skin tight black leather leggings were clamped low on her hips by a belt constructed of chrome-plated bullets. Her stack-heeled ankle boots had toecaps with silver skulls on them, their red ruby eyes sparking.

Shit, these pants are killing me!

It was a typical night at the ROAD HOUSE. A small-time band playing for their friends and their local support, jam-packed in a bunch up against the stage, jumping and head banging and waving their hands in the air, while the strays and the curious milled about in the big empty spaces of the main body of the hall.

The empty spaces made the buzz-saw guitars all the more piercing. It felt like needles were being jabbed into her eardrums.

I can't take much more of this…

Then she saw the red numbers—"**666**"—on the black T-shirt worn by the girl who was walking towards her.

The girl's mouth was moving but Cat couldn't hear a word above the din.

"WHAT…?" she shouted.

The girl was in uniform too: jet black hair and big black panda eyes and black lips in a chalk white face. Black T-shirt carefully ripped, black drainpipe jeans, black sneakers. She had to stand on tip-toe to yell in Cat's ear.

"HEAVY, HUH?"

Cat bobbed her head and made that "horns" thing with the fingers of her hand.

"HEAV-VEE!"

The girl went abruptly into the ritual dance, jack-knifing at the waist and shaking her head violently up and down and from side to side, her long black hair flailing.

You'll get brain damage!

In a howl of feedback, the band concluded its set. Their supporters hooted and hollered but it wasn't cool to give encores and they just abandoned the stage and left their guitars lying there, feeding back shrilly.

Praise be!

"Hey babe…"

The drummer was ambling towards them. He was stripped to the waist and a hot gust of sweat preceded him as he approached, swabbing his armpits with a towel.

"Ya got any bread?"

Cat managed not to smile. Underneath all the posture and attitude, he was barely 18, his thin face dotted with zits.

He had narrow, nasty-looking eyes, which darted over Cat, his lips parting showing tobacco-stained teeth, sweat dripped off his hair.

"Hi man," Cat drawled. "Good set."

The drummer flashed his gums.

"Thanks."

His small eyes were locked on the peaks of Cat's breasts, poking through the thin stuff of the T-shirt. The damp towel slipped from his bony shoulder. The black-haired girl crouched down to pick it up and offer it back to him. He ignored her and she stepped back, hugging the towel to herself.

"Bread," he repeated tonelessly, still staring at Cat. "Got any?"

The girl rooted in her pants pockets. The drummer held out his hand and the girl put the money in it. The greenbacks crackled as his fist closed around them.

"I gotta score. See ya later…"

He was still looking at Cat.

"Yeah…I'll wait in…" the girl called after him.

Sheepishly, she smiled at Cat, shrugging.

"Drummers, huh?" Cat smiled back.

The girl rolled her eyes.

"Well, y'know how it is…I mean…his life is the band, y'know…"

Cat nodded.

"These gigs can't pay much."

"Just beer and gas money mostly, sure…so I do what I can…y'know…"

Cat grinned.

"Yeah, I know."

"…like…I do some modeling, y'know…and titty dancing…sometimes I go on…the game…"

Yeah, while your boyfriend spends the day in bed

"...uh...whatever it takes, y'know...t'keep ya out there makin' the scene...until ya get that break..."

Cat's ears were still ringing as she walked across the car park. The smoke in the hall made her eyes sting and the sudden impact of the cold night air had her blinking, her vision watery.

Shit!

And she was coming down. It was always the same, when the pills wore off. After the up came the down.

Stupid!

She was spaced out. Her reflexes were dulled and she couldn't focus. She knew that there was someone there, someone lurking behind her. But she couldn't turn fast enough and her body wasn't going to do what her brain was screaming at it to do.

"AH!"

A detonation at the base of her skull. A black flash behind her eyes that filled with a billion sparks that all diminished in an instant to a single white pinprick and then oblivion.

"Shit man! Ya killed 'er!"

"Naw! She's okay. Give me a hand here!"

Van doors were wrenched open. Rough hands lifted her and tossed her inside.

"Let's go!"

The doors crashed shut. The engine spluttered, gearbox grating.

"Go! Go! Go!"

Christ! I've gone blind!

Not blind, but blindfolded; a bandanna or something like that, which smelled of tobacco and stale sweat.

"Uuu...gg...g-gghh...hhh..."

There was a dull throbbing in her temples and her tongue was like sandpaper.

"MMmm-mph!"

Cat tried to sit up and couldn't. She felt a grip that pinned her down flat on her back and told her that she was spread eagled by ropes on her wrists and ankles. It was hot, baking hot, like an oven.

She could feel trickles of sweat crawling on her skin and knew that she was naked.

You really fucked up this time!

Outside, she heard the familiar sound of big fat Harleys putt-putting in the distance. The sound grew bigger as the bikes rolled up and came to a stop. She heard rough voices and heavy boot heels crunching.

A chain rattled and bolts clashed. A door creaked open on rusty hinges.
"Yew 'wake yet, bitch…?"
The boots thudded on wooden planking. Their body odor preceded them.
"It's party time!"
The blindfold was ripped away and Cat blinked, her eyeballs seared by the blast of white hot daylight from the open doorway. The door slammed shut and the white heat was replaced by the mellower glow of a single bare light bulb.

She was roped down by her wrists and ankles, spread out on the rough surface of a long trestle table. She had been stripped stark naked, the shreds of her garish costume scattered on the floorboards.

The long table took up most of the space in a crude wooden shack, the off-white paint on its warped walls in tatters, dropping off in large curly flakes onto the floor. The shack had no windows, only a rusty grille for ventilation, clogged by cobwebs.

"Party time!"
There were four of them, in their studded leathers and ragged denims crusted with faded patches, adorned by the dust of the desert roads. Bunched at the foot of the table, where Cat's feet were, they stood staring at her naked, spread eagled body, the sweat on her skin gleaming.

Cat lifted her head to look at them. The effort made subtle muscle play all over her body and the bikers' eyes sparked, lips parting to show their teeth.

"Looks like a Halloween party," she said.
One of the bikers stepped forward and put his hand on Cat's thigh. His face contorted in a vicious leer.
"Trick'r treat, baby…?"
Cat stared at him coldly.
His bent his face towards the apex of her thighs, his hand sliding upwards.
"MMMMMMmmmmm…..!" he inhaled.
His leader seized his frayed denim collar and hauled him upright.
"Cut it out!"

The others were flanking the table. Chuckling brutishly, they reached out with their large dirty hands and clamped on a breast each. Cat glared at them, stifling the exclamation of pain that leapt into her throat.

"Assholes!"

The leader stomped round to the head of the table and shoved them backwards so hard they crashed into the wooden walls and made the shack sway on its foundations.

"I said cut it out!"

The disgruntled bikers frowned, muttering into their stubble.

"Jeez, man! Whatta waste!"

"Yeah, man! Can't we have some fun wi' her first?"

The leader gave them a cold hard stare.

"Ya can have fun with what's left of her later. First she's gotta answer some questions."

The girl was barely 15. She was small and pale, deliberately pale because she stayed out of the sun so as to ensure an unhealthy pallor. Her hair had been a reddish brown, and curly, but she straightened it and dyed it black. Black like the simple, shapeless sleeveless dress that hung down to her bare feet, draped on her narrow shoulders. Her only concession to color was the heavy pentacle that dangled on a chain around her slim neck, dipped in gloss red enamel.

The Dark Angel will come to join the blood feast
The cross will be branded by the mark of the beast...

She didn't need the lyrics printed on the album sleeve that rested on her lap. She knew them by heart. Her lips moved as she chanted them under her breath, a whispered incantation. The headphones were clamped to her bobbing black head, as she sat cross-legged on a straw mat placed in front of the record player.

...the mark of the beast...

"Ya gonna talk, bitch?"

The electric prod was a stubby baton with two short prongs at its tip. Leering, the biker pressed it to her flesh.

Cat braced herself.

"Huh, bitch...?"

He hit the switch. Nothing happened.

"Aw, shit!"

The biker held the prod up to the light. The glint of its forked tip was reflected in his bloodshot eyes.

"This fuckin' thang's bust...!"

His leader shoved in and snatched it from him. Leaning over her, he wafted the twin prongs close to Cat's face.

"I think that yew's the same wise-ass bitch that turned over my bro's out there on the blacktop, and 'bin sniffin' around stickin' yer nose in where it don't belong..."

The prod moved lower and touched her again.

Nothing happened. Then there was a loud buzzing sound and the bikers' leader yelped and jumped a foot off the ground. Dropping the baton, he staggered backwards clutching his hand.

"YOW! YOW! YOW!"

Lying there bound hand and foot, Cat convulsed with stifled laughter. It made delicious movements all along the length of her naked body and the bikers stared, mesmerized.

"Bitch!"

Like a claw, his hand seized a fistful of Cat's long blonde hair. He pulled her head up harshly and looked into her eyes. She met his stare fearlessly, a mocking glint in her eyes. The leader blinked first and angry with himself turned it on his followers.

"Git on yer hogs and go back to the Roost. Load the blowtorch and the tanks on the pickup and bring 'em back here!"

The bikers grimaced.

"Shit, man! Ya gonna––?"

"Just git!"

The door crashed shut behind them. Cat heard the bikes rev up and rumble away.

"Don't worry, bitch, they won't be gone long..."

Although it was midday, the curtains were drawn and black candles flickered, dotted about the girl's bedroom. The air was heavy with the scent wafting from a bundle of smoldering joss sticks.

The only sounds were the girl's whispered chanting and the tinny noise escaping from the headphones. Then there was a tentative knock on the bedroom door and her mother's muffled voice.

"Are you up yet dear...? It's after noon...How are you feeling...? Lunch is on the table, if you feel up to it...?"

The knocking persisted for a few seconds and then ceased.

...the mark of the beast...

Suddenly, the girl was sitting bolt upright, her slight body rigid.

...the mark of the beast...

Her eyes were fixed and unblinking, unseeing. A strange light was like a glaze masking them.

The album sleeve slipped from her fingers and slid onto the mat. The numbers blazed red in the candlelight:

666

The leader stood looking down at her, at the feast of naked female flesh displayed for him.
"Yew ain't gonna be so tough, whore, when I starts on that pretty body of yours with the blowtorch!"
Cat gave him a long cold look. She didn't blink when he put his hand on her breast and tweaked the nipple between finger and thumb. She didn't make a sound or move a muscle when he pressed his face between her outspread thighs.
He straightened up and looked along the gleaming length of her body. For the first time, Cat noticed the tattoo on his brawny forearm—"**666**".
"Yeah, it would be a big shame though," he muttered. "Waste a fine piece of ass like that..."
Galvanized, he fumbled with his death's head belt buckle.
"Yeah...yeah...we got plenty of time, baby, before the boys git back..."
His 501's were down around his ankles.

I know something you don't...

She had been bound incompetently. The loop of rope around her right ankle had slipped down past her heel. The noose around her left ankle was still tight, but had slackened off where it was connected to the table.

You just keep thinking with your dick...

Beneath her outstretched body, Cat could sense that the old trestle table was creaking under the strain.
"Now yew just be good, bitch and––"
Naked from the waist down, he was climbing onto the table.
"FUCK YOU!"
Shouting, Cat made her body heave and thrash. With a splintering crash, the table collapsed at the end where her feet were.
The biker landed on his backside. Cat slid down on top of him, her shoulders jarred painfully as the ropes around her wrists twanged taut.
"YAAAH!"
She wrapped her strong thighs around him, crushing his ribcage. His eyes bulged, his face contorting and turning deep red.
"Ggghhh-aaaagg-gg-ggg-hhhh-hh-gg-hhh-hh...!"

A strangled gargle was jolted from his gaping mouth. Long strands of drool dangled from his stubbled chin.

"G-G-Gggg-ghh-ggghh-gh-gh-ghh-hhh...!"

Her face distorted with effort, Cat put the power of her entire body into her grinding thighs. She was able to slip her hands, slippery with sweat, out of the ropes, to parry the feeble blows that he aimed at her face and breasts.

"Gh..hhh...AG-HH!"

He was turning blue. There was a muffled crackling as his ribs caved in. Blood foamed on his twisted lips.

"gg...hhhhh...hh................."

His eyes rolled back in their sockets. His head lolled sideways. Grunting, Cat squeezed for a few seconds more. Then, with a great exhalation, she relaxed, her thighs parting to let the biker topple backwards to sprawl limply on the floorboards.

Asshole!

Breathing heavily, Cat rose slowly to her feet. Her long hair was a shade darker, matted and tangled, long strands glued to the sweat on her face. Her stark heavy rock make-up was streaked down her cheeks like black tears, her crimson lipstick swiped sideways. Sweat was dripping from her body, pattering on the boards.

There was a gleam in her eye, a predatory keenness and for an instant she was like a wild animal standing over its kill.

Hey! Get with it! Get the fuck out of here!

The trucker couldn't believe his eyes. When he saw it in his wing mirror he thought he was hallucinating, he thought he'd fallen asleep at the wheel and was dreaming.

"What the--?"

But there she was, pulling up alongside him, right below the window of his cab.

"Hi there!"

And she was smiling at him. A stark naked girl riding a righteous chopped hog.

"Gotta minute? I could do with some help."

In a daze, the trucker pulled his big rig over to the side of the highway, its immense bulk rolling slowly to a halt. As he climbed down from the tall cab, the girl had dismounted and was strolling towards him, smiling. She was a mess but underneath the mess she was obviously glorious, one of those supernatural unattainable pin-ups that decorated the lonely highway pit-stops, come to life.

"Uh...uh...what kin I do fer yew...?"

The trucker was an average looking, stocky man in his late 40s, with sandy-colored hair and a bushy moustache, wearing a red baseball cap, faded blue T-shirt and jeans. He stood looking up, down and sideways, trying desperately not to stare at the naked vision standing there grinning at him.

Cat nodded at the big rig looming over them.

Well, if you have the facilities", she said. "I really do need to...er..."

She looked down at her grubby self, flicked out her matted hair and laughed.

"...er... you know..."

The trucker gulped. He gave up trying and just stared. Anyway she didn't seem to care and just went on smiling and glancing at the cab of his truck hopefully.

"Uh...yeah...", the trucker pulled himself together. "Yeah, it's all there, in the back...uh...I got a WC in there...and a shower..."

The trucker had smoked three cigarettes by the time Cat re-emerged.

"Boy! That was great! I really needed that!"

He forgot to breathe. She shone like pale gold in the sunlight.

"M-my pleasure, ma'am..."

She was wearing his spare baggy blue overalls. They looked great on her.

"Thanks for these," she grinned. "I was...um...kind of in a hurry..."

The white marble corridors of power shimmered with the echoes of whispered plots and deals.

"...welcome to the State Capitol, boys and girls, if you would please stay in a group and follow your designated guide..."

The girl was unrecognizable, in the crisp green blazer and plaid skirt of her private school uniform. Gone were the panda eyes and blood red lips, replaced by a bland unremarkable plainness.

"...can you hear me at the back, dear?...Now here on the main staircase you can see portraits of all of our former Governors..."

Shifting her brown leather satchel on her slim shoulders, the girl plodded up the ornate stairway, trailing a little way behind the rest of the group. Her classmates, on their best behavior, were looking at the file of stern portraits in their gilded frames. The girl looked straight ahead.

Her teacher, a stout woman in a brown tweed two-piece, with streaks of grey in her hair, was a respectful half-step behind the official guide, a young woman in a sharp blue business suit with the State Seal on its breast pocket.

"We're so grateful," the teacher panted as she struggled to keep up with the guide's brisk stride. "That the Governor has agreed to see us."

The guide flashed her automatic smile.

"The Governor always tries to make time for his constituents."

The Governor's door was always open. He liked it that way, physically as well as metaphorically. It looked good. His greeter, a well-built young man with a blond crew cut, the Seal on the pocket of his suit, was waiting in the hallway that ran from the head of the stately staircase.

"Hi kids, the Governor is waiting for you. Go right in."

Her smile nailed on securely, the guide ushered the teacher into the office. The class followed in a tight wedge. The girl came last, a little way behind. When the teacher frowned, the girl looked straight through her.

The Governor's office was everything a Governor's office should be. The hub of power, decorated with oil paintings of State landscapes and significant moments in State history and large framed photographs of the Governor glad-handing the great and the good. He was enthroned at the same desk where the first Governor sat in 1792, behind a battery of telephones, flanked by the Stars 'n Stripes and the State flag.

"Welcome, welcome! It's grand to see you!"

Governor Wallace T. Reed was a big man, his burly frame straining the seams of his powder-blue suit. An all-American tackle in his youth, he had long since piled on the pounds, but it was solid bulk, there was no flab on him.

"Thank you for coming to visit me!"

His normal speaking voice was a hearty boom, enriched by a rural twang which he liked to exaggerate. He still had his wavy hair and was vain about it, with a habit of patting it and running his fingers through it as he spoke.

Beaming, he stood up and came out from behind his desk. The school kids, a little intimidated by his size and grandeur, stood in a bunch gazing shyly at him. The Governor shook the teacher's hand, as she stammered her gratitude.

"My pleasure ma'am, my pleasure...!"

He shook hands with some of the kids, his giant paw smothering their small hands. Then he leaned back on the tall front of his desk, thumbs hooked into the pockets of his waistcoat.

"Now then, boys and girls, what can I tell you? I'm sure you have lots of questions!"

The girl was pushing forward through the crowd, her face solemn and determined.

"Yes, young lady...?"

Her unblinking eyes were fixed on the Governor's face, as he loomed over her, his face creased by his enormous smile.

"Ask away!"

The girl was reaching into the side pocket of her leather satchel. When her hand came out it was holding her father's old war souvenir, a 9 mm Luger.

The smile froze on Governor Reed's lips. It vanished from his eyes, replaced by horror and disbelief as his brain tried to grasp what he was seeing.

"Wha——!"

The pistol looked absurdly large in the girl's small hand. She wrapped her left hand around her wrist, to bear the weight. Her unblinking stare was locked on the Governor's eyes, paralyzing him.

"Wha...?"

She fired, the gun bucking in her grip. The detonations were crushing, in the confines of the office. The tall windows rattled. Her classmates screamed, reeling.

"UGH!"

The girl fired three times. Three bright red blossoms appeared on the Governor's pale blue waistcoat.

"UG-GH-H!"

"UGG-G-GH-H!"

He was rocked three times. His eyes bugged. His jaw dropped.

"G-GG-HH-Hhh...hhh...hh..."

A ribbon of blood ran from the corner of his gaping mouth. His legs crumpled like paper and folded under him, as he descended slowly till he was sitting with his back against the desk.

"...hhh...hhhh....hh..."

The light went out of his eyes. He sat staring at the girl, his face now level with hers, a frozen mask of stark surprise.

The teacher and the guide just stood there with their mouths open. The kids were shrieking, their faces contorted by terror. Some lay flat on the floor with their arms over their heads. Some were running out the door, others ran around in circles, colliding, stumbling.

"J-Jesus!"

The blond greeter had pulled a .38 from under his jacket and was pointing it at the girl. But he couldn't do it. He couldn't shoot a kid!

"Oh....J-J-Jeee-sus...!"

The girl turned and looked at him blankly. She looked at his gun. The Luger jumped in her hand. A red dot appeared in the center of the young man's forehead. The back of his skull exploded in a pulpy pink halo. He fell down and lay on the carpet.

The guide jack-knifed, vomiting. Galvanized, the teacher shouted.

"OH NO!"

The girl was lifting the gun again.

"NO!"

The girl's lips were moving, mouthing a silent incantation. The muzzle was pressed to her temple.

CHAPTER 4

ON THE ROAD AGAIN

"Hi Cat," said Selena. "Glad to see you're wearing some clothes today." She looked Cat up and down.

"Well, kind of, anyway."

The hum of conversation in THE FOUR DEUCES bar was cut dead when Cat strolled in through the door. She left little to the imagination, in a chamois bra with Indian bead fringes and cut-off denim shorts snug on her hips, walking lightly on the rubber soles of red and white hi-tops.

The glaring blast of a hot day was blotted out as the door swung shut behind her. Blinking, the male drinkers stared as Cat sauntered past, muttered something dirty out of the corner of their mouths or whistled lowly under their breath. Hard-faced hookers, sensing competition, checked her out, their eyes stabbing daggers.

The bar was built for private assignations, low-lit in murky sepia by hanging brass lamps, divided into discreet booths walled by pinewood, upholstered with studded red leather.

"You don't look so bad yourself," Cat chuckled.

Selena's superb body was sheathed in a gold skin-tight cat suit, with diamond cut outs framing her cleavage and her navel. Gold bangles clanked around her neck and her wrists, her fingers encrusted with rings. Her fine afro was dusted with a golden glitter.

Selena rolled her eyes, made up like Cleopatra.

"Yeah well," she grimaced. "We gotta blend in."

Cat laughed.

"That's us. Just two working girls."

A shadow fell across their table. A fat shadow cast by a fat salesman sweating in a grey suit that was too tight for him.

"Hey gals, how about you an' me––?"

"We're off duty asshole."

"Fuck off."

The grey tarmac of the car park was cooking in the noonday sun. They were slipping their shades on as they walked towards Cat's car.

"...so that's about it," Cat was saying. "If you ask me, it's got something to do with that band...Six-Six-Six..."

Selena nodded.

"And that whole scene. So you do your stuff, Cat. Work your magic and get yourself noticed."

Cat laughed.

"That's what I'm best at."

Selena's car was parked next to Cat's red Olds, a silver birch Aston Martin DB5.

"Oooh, I like your style, Selena."

"I thought you only liked American muscle."

"Oh, I might make an exception in this case. This is a real––"

They heard quick footsteps behind them, hurrying to catch up.

"Hey bitch!"

There were three of them, street hookers in their garish war paint and barely legal working clothes. Out front, a strapping, well-stacked redhead in red leather trimmed with fake tiger skin; close behind, a wiry blonde in lime green and pink; bringing up the rear, a six-foot brunette in fishnets and shiny black PVC.

"Yew hold it right there!"

The redhead came close enough to smell the whiskey on her breath. She stood with her kinky-booted feet planted apart, hands on hips. Her eyes flicked over Cat, from her head to her toes.

"Well, ain't yew sumthin', blondie!"

She sneered at Selena.

"Yew's outta yore territory, bitch. This here's our turf!"

Leaning on the refined curves of the Aston, Selena gazed back at her coolly.

"Oh, is that right?"

Cat was trying hard not to smile, but the redhead saw it. Her face contorted with fury.

"Yeah, thet's right! We don't peddle no dark meat aroun' here!"

Cat was smiling broadly now, shaking her head. She took a short step forward but Selena put a hand on her arm.

"No. I need the exercise."

The redhead was spitting with rage. She lunged at Selena, her hands hooking into claws.

"I'm gonna rip yer face off, yew––!"

Selena slid gracefully off of the smooth side of the Aston. She seemed to dematerialize. One second she was there and then she wasn't and then something like a sledgehammer impacted on the redhead's solar plexus.

"OOOOOFFF!!!"

The redhead folded in the middle and dropped on her knees. She stayed there, groaning and retching loudly, clutching herself, her face pressed to the tarmac, her ass in the air.

"Yew fuckin'...!"

The tall brunette came rushing at Selena, swinging her fists, flaunting rings like knuckledusters. Her face a perfect mask, Selena waited for her. Then she feinted, dipped her shoulder and the brunette was suddenly all flailing arms and legs, flying through the air.

"YAAAAAHH-HH...!!!"

The brunette landed hard on her backside. Selena scooped her up and with only the faintest grunt of controlled effort, hoisted her up above her head.

"UH!"

Selena tossed the brunette like a rag doll, up and clean over Cat's red Olds. She disappeared behind it and didn't reappear.

"Uh-oh!" said Cat.

The blonde hooker was circling up behind Selena on tiptoe. She had an open razor in her hand.

Cat stepped out in front of her. The blonde's eyes were slits of hate.

"Get outta mah way, bitch or I'll slice yew up good!"

Cat smiled at her.

"Tut-tut..."

With a shriek of fury, the blonde slashed at Cat's face. Still smiling, Cat merely swayed out of the way.

The blonde took deep breaths, stalking Cat as she moved around sideways. She feigned at Cat's face, then stabbed at her belly. Cat didn't buy it. The fingers of her right hand clamped on the blonde's wrist. She cupped her left hand under the hooker's extended elbow and levered down hard.

"AAAAIIIEE-EEE-EEE!!!"

The muffled crack was drowned by her scream as the blonde's elbow fractured. The razor slipped from her numbed fingers and clattered on the tarmac.

Wailing, the blonde staggered away, bumped up against a parked car and fell. She rolled around, holding her arm, screeching.

"I could have handled it," Selena frowned.

"Sorry," said Cat. "I couldn't help myself."

The blonde's screams were nerve-drilling. There were faces at the bar's back door.

"Time to go," said Selena, unlocking the door of the Aston.

"Yo!" Cat replied, vaulting into the Olds.

They twisted the keys in the ignition and their motors sang a mighty duet.

"I'll be in touch," Cat shouted.

"Good luck, honey..." Selena whispered.

The office was wall-papered by psychedelic concert posters. Behind the desk, a row of gleaming gold disks hung in picture frames.

The telephone was gold-plated. It played a famous guitar riff when it rang.

"Hello...?"

Feminine fingers lifted the receiver, laden with jewels, abnormally long nails painted a metallic green. Heavy bangles jangled.

"It's me".

The figure in the chair behind the desk sat up a little straighter.

"Yes, I've been expecting your call. I––"

"You have done well".

"Thank you, I––"

"The results of the initial experiments have been satisfactory. We will soon be ready to proceed to a higher level..."

"Yeeee-hah!"

Saturday night.

"Yeeeeeeeee....hah...!"

SLIM'S BAR A-GO-GO, said the sign: TOPLESS!––GIRLS!––TOPLESS!

Under hanging saloon-style lamps that cast a brassy glow, the sprawling barn of "Slim's Bar" was packed to bursting with the usual Saturday night crowd—off-duty truckers, highway construction workers and 20th-century cowboys, crammed shoulder to shoulder around tables stacked with beer mugs and foaming jugs.

"Woooo-eee!"

A haze of cigarette smoke wreathed the orange lamps, like a veil strung across the ceiling, draped around beams hung with longhorn skulls and other phony Frontier trappings. The air was stirred tepidly by turning fans, thick with the all-male blend of tobacco, sweat and beer.

Loud music blasted from the tall wall-mounted speakers of the PA system, the predictable boozy, Bloozy bar-room bump 'n grind. There was a stage in front of the speakers and a catwalk framed by flashing multi-colored bulbs, splitting the crowded tables down the middle.

Shit! Just look at them...

Cat looked out on a sea of sweaty shiny upturned faces, all goggle-eyed and open mouthed. Whoops and hollers yelped out of the open mouths, the heat of their eyes crawled on her skin.

...bunch of no-necks and beer bellies...

65

She fixed her gaze on a point far out beyond the tops of their heads, as she left the stage and swaggered down the catwalk. She was wearing just a black leather G-string, the tiny triangle edged with glittering rhinestones.

"Ooooo...baby...!"

"OOOOOOO-WHEEEEE!"

It was hot up there and her body gleamed as she timed her long-legged hip-swaying strut to the crude beat.

God, I hate this crap!

She made her pelvis work, spreading her strong thighs. She put her hands on her breasts, exciting their coral tips.

"Yow! Mama!"

A stocky trucker in a two-tone tasselled cowboy shirt tried to heave his paunch onto the catwalk. His table companions stood and roared him on.

"Oooh baby!"

Sneering, Cat planted her foot in the middle of his chest. The trucker flung out his arms as he was launched backwards. He landed with a crash, spread eagled across the table, sending the beer mugs and his fellow drinkers flying in all directions.

A huge cheer filled the bar. They were standing up at the tables, their hands clapping up above their heads.

Cat took her lithe saunter to the end of the runway. Sinking slowly to her knees, she bent backwards until her head was touching the floor.

"WOOOO-WOOOOO-OOOO-OOOO...!"

The shouts of the crowd were waves of hot lust gusting over her. Her body arched, her belly undulating.

Assholes!

Stark amongst all the pick-ups and gaudy customized muscle cars, a white Rolls Royce stood aloof in the farthest reaches of the car park.

"WOOOOOOO-HOOOOO-OOOO.....!"

Cat was sashaying extravagantly back down the runway, making for the stage. Every eye was glued to her spectacularly swinging rear.

"...HOOOOO...OOOO...!"

There was a table in a corner, half in shadow. A hand extended into the amber half-light, making notes on a slip of blue paper with a slim gold pen. A feminine hand, with long green nails and fingers crusted with jewels.

This really is the pits!

The "dressing room" was a converted store cupboard with cobwebs in its corners and dingy white paint flaking off the walls. There was a small table and a chair and a cracked mirror framed by light bulbs, only half of which were working.

Glaring at herself in the dusty mirror, Cat ripped off the G-string and began swabbing the stale stickiness under her arms.

I deserve a fucking medal for this...

In a niche there was a rusting showerhead. When Cat turned the faucet a lukewarm trickle spluttered out.

"Oh great!"

There was a knock on the door.

"Wait a minute!"

She tugged on a long white towel bathrobe, cinching the belt around her waist. "Okay."

The door swung open and Slim Bydecker came in. "Slim" was a mound of blubber in a white suit with embroidery across the shoulders, a white Stetson and hand-tooled cowboy boots.

He looked disappointed to see Cat all wrapped up. Cat frowned at him.

"Hey, man, ever think o' givin' this dump a lick o' paint?"

Her tank town twang was perfect.

"An' the damn shower don' work right!"

Slim looked apologetic, his pink and sweaty jowls wobbled above his collar with its silver tips and his Western string tie.

"Yeah, I know baby. I've been meanin' to get to it..."

Cat snorted disdainfully.

"Better git t'it soon, man, or I ain't workin' here no more."

Slim was rooting around inside his jacket. His pudgy pink hand emerged clutching a wad of crackling banknotes.

"What's thet fer?" Cat demanded suspiciously.

Slim grinned at her with tobacco stained teeth.

"It's a bonus, baby. Yew got somethin' real special. The guys out there jest love yew."

Cat snatched the money from his fat fingers.

"Hmph! Yeah, I could smell it."

Slim's eyes were trying to see through the bathrobe.

"Girl like yew could make herself a pile of dough...I mean, we ain't got just dancin'...we got other...attractions..."

Cat crunched the dollar bills into the pocket of her robe.
"Sure," she shrugged. "I'll do most anythin' fer a buck."

The night sky was full of stars. The air was crisp and clean and Cat inhaled it deeply, luxuriously.

Hello...?

In the starlight, the white Rolls looked like it was sculpted out of pearl.

And what are you doing here?

The car's windows were tinted and looked solid black, impenetrable. When Cat took a step towards it, the Rolls came alive and purred away, out across the car park.
"Okay, let's see where you're going, Your Majesty..."
The red Olds was waiting. The top was down and Cat was poised to vault into the driver's seat when she heard heavy steps scuffing behind her.
"Tough girl, huh?"

Shit!

It was the fat trucker in his cowboy shirt. He had two pals with him. One was tall and thin, with straggly red hair showing from under a white baseball cap, clad in stonewashed denim from top to toe; the other was short, his scalp glistening through a blond crew cut, his stocky frame stuffed into a red and black lumberjack shirt and blue jeans.
They were standing in front of a white van with red letters on the side that said "Ace Building Co." The van's back doors were wide open, its bare interior gaping.
The fat trucker jerked his thumb at the open doors.
"Now why don't yew be nice, sweetcheeks, and jest climb in there so we kin have us a party...?"

Oh not now!

Way on up the sleeping small town street, the tail lights of the Rolls Royce were diminishing red pinpricks. Then they turned a corner and were gone.

Fuck!

Cat was dressed simply, in a plain grey sweatshirt and faded jeans. A bag with long tassels was slung on her shoulder. Her hand delved into it and came out holding a blue-black .357 Magnum.

"I don't think so, boys."

It was a very small town and in minutes Cat was leaving it behind and accelerating onto the desert highway.

She pipped the horn.

"Bye, boys!"

They shook their fists as she flashed by, hopping and cursing as grit and small stones stung the soles of their bare feet.

"Yew bitch...!"

Her grin was huge in the rear view mirror. Their pale capering, gesticulating forms shrunk fast behind her as she put her foot down and shot away. They were stark naked, their clothes tossed into the trunk of Cat's car, the tires of their van punctured by the combat knife that kept the gun company in Cat's shoulder bag.

"...bitch...!"

Cat followed the highway as it wound into the low hills that looked down on the town. The desert was a vast darkness all around, her headlamps casting an onrushing splash of light, advancing before her.

The engine surged urgently. She leaned forward in her seat, peering ahead, hoping to catch a glimpse of the red tail lights.

Nothing.

Damn it!

Suddenly, the muscular 442 was slowing down, rolling to a halt on the hardtop.

"What the...?"

There was an artificial glow, behind the dark, undulating horizon, a luminous pulse of light that washed out the stars in the night sky.

Cat stood up in the driver's seat. She tilted her head, listening intently, her brow knitted in puzzlement.

I can hear drums...

The screams were carried on the crisp night breezes, all the way to where Cat was hiding.

Pressed down flat to the stony ground, she parted the screen of dry scrub, lifting the compact field glasses to her eyes.

"Jesus!" she whispered.

She couldn't believe what she was seeing.

"Wha...?"

A ring of torches that glowed with a blood red fire surrounded a raised mound of earth that was artificially symmetrical in the rugged, jagged, uneven landscape. The light cast by the torches glowed on the deep ranks of upturned faces, framed by the raised cowls of long grey robes, eyes glittering like red sparks.

What kind of madness is this?

At the crest of the mound, there was a construction of heavy posts and crossbeams. From the beams dangled a row of writhing figures. Young girls, stripped stark naked.

No way! Come on! They must be making a movie...

But she couldn't see any cameras. The girls were strung up by their ankles, their hands tied behind their backs. Their bodies jerked and twisted, eyes bulging with terror, piercing shrieks ejected from their mouths.

Dropping the glasses, Cat rolled onto her side, tugging the Magnum from her waistband. Cold sweat pricked her spine, beading on her forehead.

Cursing, she shoved the gun away. It was useless. What could she do? There must be a hundred of them.

A deep murmur was swelling up from the crowd, which became rhythmic and more insistent, keeping time with the throb of a giant drum.

The screams pierced the chanting as a strange apparition rose up to the summit from the far side of the mound. Tall and wide-shouldered, it was cloaked in black that billowed to reveal a scarlet lining; and wore a long-horned black mask with slanting red-rimmed eyes.

You've got to be kidding...!

A grey-robed attendant advanced with a measured, ceremonial tread, bearing a metal tray held in both hands, its polished surface flashing in the torchlight.

The chanting grew louder, more like a guttural grunting. Focusing the binoculars, Cat identified the contents of the tray: a golden bowl encrusted with sparkling gemstones, and a curved dagger.

Merged into the chanting, the drumbeat was a physical compression, squeezing Cat's skull.

"Oh shit!"

The grey wraith was offering the tray to the horned one, who extended an arm in its billowing sleeve, gloved fingers taking the dagger. Together, the weird figures advanced slowly towards the gallows.

Seeing them coming, the girls screamed louder, their convulsive writhing became frantic.

Oh no...no...!

Twin grey-robed sentries had stood impassively, flanking the sinister structure. Now they stepped forward briskly to seize the nearest girl by her bound arms. In their iron grip her contortions were reduced to the merest twitch and quiver.

The grey wraith approached the helpless girl, who stared with pleading, horror-filled eyes, an incoherent babbling spilling from her lips. The chanting, fused with the boom of the drum, was like a roaring tide.

The grey shade extended its arms, positioning the golden bowl below the girl's head.

The horned one took a long stride forward, lifting the knife. The girl's body convulsed. Her babbling became one long wail of horror and despair.

A black-gloved hand seized the girl's hair, tugging her head back, exposing the long pale curve of her throat.

"NO-OOO-OOOO...!"

The blade flashed. The girl's shrieks were choked off abruptly. A great ecstatic groan rose from the crowd.

Cat's stomach churned. Gagging, she puffed out her cheeks. She swallowed hard, panting, hot tears forced from her eyes.

A crimson stream was splashing into the bowl. When it lapped over the rim the grey shade moved off to the side and emptied it into a large bronze cauldron mounted on a metal tripod.

The crowd was swaying forward eagerly, making the red torches sway. The hooded sentries released their victim. Her body was still twitching. Blood dripped from the point of the dagger as the horned one moved on to the next.

Cat's tears were spilling into her lap as she fumbled with the CB radio handset.

What to do? Who to call? The cops? Hell no! She'd seen police uniforms, mingling with the crowd.

The curly cord snagged on her knee and the handset slipped from her fingers, bouncing on the black rubber floor mat.

"Fuck!"

Selena's voice came up faintly from between Cat's feet.

"Hello? Cat? Do you read me?"

"Fuck! Fuck! Fuck!"

"What? Cat? Are you there?"

Bending abruptly, she banged her forehead on the dash.

"Ow! Shit!"

"Cat! What's going on?"

Rubbing the sore spot angrily, Cat grabbed the handset and sat up straight. The tear tracks were scalding on her cheeks. There was an awful taste in her mouth.

"I read you...sorry...lost it there for a second..."

"What's happening, Cat? I tried to reach you earlier but––"

Cat scrubbed her eyes with the back of her hand.

"Oh, Selena...you wouldn't believe it...!"

The road bridge was a box of shining steel girders dotted with huge rivets, a simple but effective construction that spanned the river, its fierce current rushing and tumbling over jagged rocks 100 feet below.

A car was nosing onto the bridge. Dad's blue Chevy, "borrowed" for the day, filled to bursting with teenagers, windows rolled down so the whole world could enjoy their music, Dad's easy listening ousted by some heavy duty sounds.

"...COME, COME, COME TO THE SABBATH..."

The Chevy rolled to a stop in the middle of the bridge. The doors opened and the teenagers got out.

"...COME TO THE SABBATH..."

There were five of them, three boys and two girls with pale faces and long black hair, in T-shirts and flapping bell-bottoms. The T-shirts were black; in dripping red—**666**.

"...SATAN'S THERE...!"

The teenagers climbed up onto the safety rail that fenced the span of the road bridge. They held hands.

"...COME, COME..."

Holding hands, they jumped down to where the water churned and frothed against the rocks.

CHAPTER 5

CAT-FIGHTING

FEMALE FURY!
In lurid splashes of clashing color, the posters proclaimed a fun night at the ROAD HOUSE.
TORRID VIXENS vs SAVAGE HELLCATS…
"UGH--!!!"
…BRAWLING BABES vs SEXY SLUGGERS!
"OOOO–OOG-GHH-HHH!!!"
The heat flowed down from the hanging lights like melted fat, bouncing back from the bright yellow surface of the wrestling mat.
"AGH!"
The impact made the blue ring-ropes quiver.
"G-GHAA-A-GG-Gh…!!!"
A sea of latter-day cowboy hats and baseball caps. The faces all around the ring were a whirling blur of wide eyes and open mouths that exhaled hoots and hollers and fanned a wind of stale sweat and beer.
At the hub of the cacophony, there was the harsh rasping sound of hard breathing women and the slap of sweat-wet bodies being slammed together; heaving breasts spilling out of skimpy bikini tops, grunting and groaning as they grappled for advantage.
"Wooo-eee…!"
"Go baby go!"
In their crushing embrace, cheek to cheek, their drenched red faces contorted, the combatants came crashing down onto the mat. They were tangled together, flailing legs locking and straining.
"Yeee….hah…!!!"
They rolled over and over, first one on top, then the other. In his black and white striped shirt, the "referee", a squat man with a bright pink face and thinning fair hair, was dancing around them.
An elbow drop—once, twice, three times—each time a rending groan of pain that prompted a cheer from the crowd.
The girl on top turned her opponent over into a backbreaking Boston Crab, leaning back and putting on the pressure until her victim screamed her submission.
"YEAH!!!"

Assailed by hoots of derision, the loser rolled over, clutching herself, then began crawling limply towards the ropes. Pausing to give her a parting kick in the backside, the victor strutted around the ring, flexing and posing. Her manager, a burly trucker in faded jeans and a check shirt, climbed through the ropes and pushed past the referee, wrapping his girl in a great bear hug.

The Master of Ceremonies struggled through the ropes and advanced to the middle of the ring, tugging at the long cable attached to the microphone in his hand. The big trucker put out his shovel-like hand and the Master of Ceremonies dropped a wad of banknotes into it. Beads of sweat rolled down from under the wide brim of his white Stetson and there were enormous dark patches under the arms of his embroidered cowboy shirt.

He tapped the bulbous head of the mike to make sure that it was working.

"How about thet, huh? How about thet!"

A fanfare of whistles and cheers.

"And there's plenny more where thet come from, yew betcha!"

There was a rush to the long bar at the back and a chorus of shouting that fetched girls in cowgirl costume cut to show cleavage and midriff, bearing foaming jugs of cold beer.

"Yew jest wait till yew see what's comin' next!"

There was a dark alcove off to the side of the long bar. The lip of a small table projected into the light, with a tall wine glass perched on it. A slender, bejeweled hand reached into the light and drew the glass back into the shadow.

"Are yew reddy....?"

The general rumble turned up a notch....

"AH SED ARE YEW REDDY!!!??!!"

....and became a solid shout.

"Then put yer hans t'gether fer the gal yew've bin waitin fer...!"

The shout became a kind of brutish howl as Cat stepped up and slipped through the blue ropes.

"...the one an' only...!"

She was draped in a gleaming golden cloak, with white fur trimmings.

"...the golden gal herself..."

The rising howl choked as she let the cloak fall to her feet and kicked it away.

"...the Wichita Wildcat...!"

The Master of Ceremonies almost swallowed the microphone. Bug-eyed, he stood and stared.

"..the...the..."

She was barely wearing a tiny leopard skin print bikini. She had done something with her hair to make it wild, like a golden mane, cascading down over her strong shoulders. Her bronzed body was oiled and glistening under the lights, every curve and nuance of her flawless muscle tone defined with stark clarity.

Cat moved across the ring with a long-legged, slow, arrogant swagger. The men in the hall expelled their pent-up lust in a great gasp, gusting Cat with their beer-and-cigarette breath.

Jeez! What a bunch of low-lifes!

The Master of Ceremonies was staring at her, his mouth opening and closing. When Cat moved in on him he stumbled a pace backwards.

"Uh...uh..."

Cat plucked the Stetson from his head and twirled it on her finger. There were rough guffaws from the crowd.

"Well, c'mon, honey...," Cat drawled into the mike in her best cow town twang. "I ain't got all night."

Red-faced, he snatched the hat back and jammed it on his head. Gulping, he banged the mike on the bridge of his nose, making his eyes water. A huge laugh rocked the rafters.

"Uh...uh...okay...okay...!" swallowing hard, he pulled himself together. "It's time fer the main event...the Tag Team Surprise!"

The what?

A roar and burst of applause.

"A no holds barred tag team bout 'tween four gals who've never met before...!"

Oh great!

Just what she needed, a whole three-ring circus. This wasn't her idea of undercover and she had been hoping for a quick and simple one-rounder with some hapless tank-town floozy. Now she was going to have to put on a performance.

Cat glared at the man in the hat, making him flinch. Then she hip-swayed across the ring and waited in the corner, her arms extended, resting on the top rope. Every eye in the house was glued to the gleaming, breathing sculpture of her body. She could feel it, like hot ants crawling on her skin.

Marvelous!

The surge of anticipation from the crowd was like a force grabbing the Master of Ceremonies by the throat. Scrubbing the sweat from his eyes with the back of his hand, he raised the mike again.

"And now, introducin' the Wildcat's partner fer this bout...!"

Just marvelous!

She was expecting the usual part-time porn model. Then her eyes blinked with surprise.

"The Yeller Peril in person...Miss Banzai...the Tokyo Terror...!"

Oh I don't believe it!

Aiko was strolling across the mat towards her, her dangerous kitten's face purposeful. Her slim body was sheathed in crimson silk embroidered with green fire-breathing dragons, slit all the way up the side.

Inscrutable, she stopped in front of the "Wichita Wildcat" and made a shallow bow.

"Hi, Cat," she said, out of the corner of her mouth.

The crowd was whooping and hollering. Somehow, Cat stayed in character and just stared back.

"What in the hell are you doing here?" she muttered.

The red sheath seemed to vanish. Aiko was left standing in a bikini of metallic green. Under the harsh lights her tea-colored skin gleamed, her body smooth and supple.

"Couldn't you have phoned?"

A slight smile played on Aiko's scarlet lips.

"Selena wanted us to work together on this one."

Cat rolled her eyes.

"I'm amazed she didn't come herself."

Aiko chuckled.

"Yes, she told me about your brawl in the car park. She really enjoyed herself."

They looked each other up and down.

"The 'Wichita' what?"

Cat made a face.

"Wildcat. Miss Banzai? The Tokyo Terror?"

Aiko shrugged.

"Well, it's the best I could do."

The Master of Ceremonies wrenched his eyeballs from Cat's gleaming athletic contours. He cleared his throat into the microphone.

"An' now let's hear it fer their opponents fer this evenin'…!"

The noise from the crowd was like a tide washing over the ring.

"The Cave-Girl…!"

She lunged through the ropes with her eyes glaring, teeth bared and her hair gone wild. A strapping redhead with biceps like boulders, a beefy belly and bulging thighs, clad in a chamois leather bikini with fake fur trimmings.

"WOOO-AARRGHH-HH…!"

Cave-Girl circled the canvas, making animal sounds, arms up above her head in a double-bicep flex, saluting the crowd.

The Wichita Wildcat and Miss Banzai looked at each other.

"Just your type, Cat."

"Gee, thanks."

The referee went through the motions of searching Cave-Girl's hands for rings or hidden weapons. Showing her teeth, she shoved him away. The crowd hooted, the sweaty faces of the cowboys and truckers shining with lust and anticipation. Most of them were looking at Cat.

Cave-Girl stomped towards Cat and Aiko, snarling. One hand on her hip, Cat stared back imperiously. Aiko stifled a grin, trying to look inscrutable. Nervously, the referee ushered Cave-Girl into her corner.

There was an abrupt whistle of feedback from the microphone.

"Uh…an' now…Cave-Girl's tag team partner fer tonight…!"

The tide of noise rolled in again.

"Domina…!"

Holy shit!

She stood six-foot-six in her bare feet. Her hair shone blue-black and was scraped back tight to her skull, hanging down in a long braid to the base of her spine. Her lips were glossy black. Tiny silver skulls glinted on her earlobes. Her throat was circled by a black leather collar that bristled with steel spikes. Spikes jutted from the leather bands on her wrists.

"…the Princess of Pain…!"

She wore a shiny black PVC two-piece decorated with silver studs. Her bare midriff was toned into a chiseled six-pack.

"…the Mistress of Mayhem…!"

She held a whip in her right hand, its long black coils snaking across the mat. Flicking her wrist, she made the whip crack and the hats in the front rows ducked.

From the center of the ring, Domina made the tip of the whip slither towards Cat's bare toes. Cat looked right back at her and saw a momentary flicker in her adversary's dark eyes.

Gotya!

Domina handed the whip to the referee, who took it from her gingerly. She removed the spiked collar and wristbands. Then she turned on her heel and joined Cave-Girl in their corner.

The tag teams surveyed each other across the span of the ring. Domina was sneering. Cave-Girl growled. Cat and Aiko stared back impassively.

"Aw heck," muttered Aiko. "A porn queen and a steroid junkie. We can take these two in ten seconds flat."

"Sure," Cat said out of the side of her mouth. "But we have to put on a show. We have to get noticed."

Her eyes flicking sideways, Aiko looked Cat up and down.

"Oh, no trouble there…"

The Master of Ceremonies tugged out a handkerchief and mopped the sweat from his face.

"An' now, mah friends…are yew reddy t' rumble…?"

The roar was a tidal wave that nearly bowled him over.

"Then ladies, let's git it on…!"

The Master of Ceremonies scuttled backwards out through the ropes. The referee came to the center of the ring and stood with his arms extended towards both corners and the combatants waiting there.

A discordant gong sounded, muffled by the noise of the crowd.

Domina slid elegantly onto the outside of the ropes and stood on the lip of the ring, beside the tall corner post. Cave-Girl was coming forward.

"After you," said Cat.

"No, after you."

"No, I insist, after you."

Cave-Girl came grinding her bared teeth. Her powerful thighs were straddled, her extended hands hooked like claws. Under the harsh lights, her tawny skin was shining with sweat.

Aiko was dancing on her toes. She was all light and air, elusive. When Cave-Girl grabbed for her, she wasn't there.

Spitting with frustration, Cave-Girl clawed at the air. Aiko danced in, then back, feinted, drew her opponent on, then struck, one-two, one-two, her compact fists impacting on Cave-Girl's meaty midriff.

"URGG-GG-GHH…!"
The blows were hard, but Aiko kept some in reserve.

That's it, Aiko, not too soon

Cave-Girl stopped, grunted and blinked. Then she came stomping forward again.
Aiko was slipping lithely out of the way, her smooth body arching to dodge a fist like a ham that was aiming to crack her spine. She was prancing. Her hands were a flickering blur.
"AAGG-GHH!"
Cave-Girl's head rocked back, her wild red hair flailing. She took a few steps back, wiping blood from her mouth with the back of her hand.
Aiko was dancing in a semi-circle around her, dodging this way, then that, her bare arms wafting, undulating, like two snakes poised to strike.
The crowd was enjoying this. There were shouts of "Banzai!"

Morons!

There was laughter as Cave-Girl lunged and Aiko dodged again, her face still set in that impenetrable mask. Cave-Girl bellowed with rage.
"Yew cut out all thet Jap joo-shit-soo crap, slant, an' fight right…I'm gonna…!"

Karate, actually…

Aiko pirouetted, her leg flicked out, her heel arriving dead on Cave-Girl's breastbone.
"YAH!"
Cave-Girl flew backwards across the ring and crashed into the post. She came down hard and sat at Domina's feet, looking groggy and confused.
Frowning, Domina reached down and tagged her partner on the shoulder. As Cave-Girl crawled out, she came in.
The crowd's appreciation was a warm wind of bad breath. Wrinkling her nose, Aiko skipped back to Cat's corner. They reached out and their palms slapped together.
"Your turn, sister."

In the dark alcove off to the side of the long bar, the bejeweled hand was tapping long decorated fingernails on the scuffed table top. When the wine glass was returned to the light, its rim bore the imprint of red lipstick.

Domina came out of her corner with long stalking strides. Cat was there to meet her, in the middle of the ring. The clamor of the crowd was a battering force that made the ropes sway and the canvas vibrate beneath their feet.

They got straight down to business, their sweat-wet bodies slapping together as they locked in a straining embrace, fused together in a trial of strength.

"NNNNN-NN-GG-GGHH-HHH...!"

The crowd roared them on. Backs bending, thighs quivering, they heaved against each other, beads of sweat sprinkling down onto the mat.

"GGGGHH-GGHH-HHHH...!"

Cat had rarely come across a woman who was taller than she was. Or one as strong as this. But she hardly felt the strain. The contorted fury on her face was simulated.

Okay, let's make it look good...

She let go a little and let her opponent turn her slippery body into a classic Full Nelson, her arms pinned in a grip that hooked up under her armpits and clamped on the back of her neck, her shoulders wrenched forward, hands up above her head. The crowd whooped, thrilled by the sight of Cat's gleaming physique thus displayed for them.

Pretending to struggle, Cat counted up to ten. In their corner, Aiko tried to look concerned.

Oh, come on, Cat, get it over with!

Domina was snarling in Cat's ear, her lips curling back from her sharp teeth.

"I'm going to hurt you, bitch...I'm going to--"

...nine...ten...

Cat's body shimmied and instantly she was free.

"HAH!"

And suddenly Domina was flying through the air, catapulted in a yelling arc, to hit the canvas with a loud "Oooofff!" of the air being knocked out of her.

The referee had to dive to get out of the way. The crowd was going crazy. Scooping her hair out of her face, Cat strode across the ring. Groaning, Domina rolled over and struggled onto her hands and knees.

Reaching down, Cat spread her thighs to take the weight and hoisted Domina high in the air, suspending her in an over-the-shoulder backbreaker. Domina screamed. The cowboys and truckers gasped, one great hot exhalation, transfixed by the sight of this shining, magnificent, all-conquering Amazon.

Effortlessly, Cat threw Domina down in a crushing face-down body slam.

"HA-YAH!"

Moaning, Domina tried to crawl back towards her corner. Yelling, Cave-Girl was leaning far out over the ropes, holding her hand out for the tag.

Making her lip curl contemptuously, Cat straddled her rival and sat down slowly, planting her rear on the small of her back. Reaching out, she hooked her hands under Domina's chin, yanking her body up and back in a vicious Camel Clutch.

The referee was hovering over them.

"D'ya submit…?"

Domina groaned.

"Submit?"

Gritting her teeth, Cat piled on the pressure.

"Submit?"

Domina screamed. Cave-Girl was rushing into the ring. She cocked a fist, her eyes targeting the back of Cat's neck.

"HAAA-EEEEE…!"

Aiko was a guided missile. In mid-air, she executed a spinning bicycle kick that found the point of Cave-Girl's chin.

"UH!"

Cave-Girl looked up into the lights with glassy eyes. Her legs crumbled beneath her and she swayed and then fell forward like a log, lying still.

The crowd was delirious. Cat had wrapped Domina's long black braid around her throat and was pulling hard. Domina's face went red. Her eyes bugged and her tongue stuck out.

"That's enough…!"

The referee was slapping Cat on the shoulder.

"Okay, okay. Ya won! That's enough!"

Cat let go and stood up. Domina rolled over onto her side and lay there gagging.

Standing astride her victim, hands on hips, Cat was glorious, and the crowd thundered its appreciation. The referee brought Cat and Aiko together and held up their hands in victory.

Awestruck, the Master of Ceremonies struggled through the ropes.

"Now ain't thet somethin'...? The winners...the Wichita Wildcat and Miss Banzai...!"

The "dressing room" was a concrete box with traces of dirty yellow paint on the wall. A creaking fan stirred the air tepidly. There was a kind of dressing table, with a long mirror that was pitted and grimy.
"Boy, we've hit the big time!"
The shower offered only a tepid trickle, the towels were dingy.
"Well, I needed a good work out."
They gazed upon each other's nakedness in mutual admiration.
"You don't need it," sighed Aiko. "You're perfect."
Cat smiled at her.
"You're not so bad yourself, Miss Banzai. I wish I had some of your moves."
"And you," Aiko replied. "How did you pick up all that wrestling stuff?"
Cat laughed.
"Watching TV."
There was a knock at the door and the Master of Ceremonies walked in.
"Hey, gals, I got yer––"
Naked, they stood there looking at him.
"Oh! I––! Oh...!"
He turned scarlet, backing towards the door. Ever so slowly, they raised the towels in front of them.
"Ya got our winnin's," the Wichita Wildcat drawled. "Okay. Hand it over."
She held out her hand and he slapped a roll of banknotes onto her palm.
"Thanks."
They were rubbing themselves slowly with the towels. His Adam's apple was hard to swallow.
"Uh...now yew gals come back t'see us agin...!"
They slammed the door behind him.

Although the wrestling was over, there was still a long night's drinking to be done and the car park was jam-packed with trucks and pick-ups and a collection of American Muscle.
As far as Cat was concerned, her red 442 put them all to shame.
"Ooooh, hello, baby, I missed you..."
Aiko was counting the money.
"Hey, not bad for a night's work."

"Yeah, well somehow I don't see it as a future career."

"But Wichita, you're so good at it."

Cat took a playful swipe at her and they mock-sparred for a while, dancing around till Aiko bumped up against the sleek flank of her pale jade Shelby Mustang.

"Hey, this is new," Cat said. "You didn't tell me about this."

Aiko laughed.

"That's because you'd want to test drive it."

"I do. Give me the keys."

"No way. That paintwork is expensive. You––"

A horn sounded.

"What…?" Aiko looked out over the crowded car park.

"Over there," said Cat. "You don't see many of those outside of Beverley Hills."

The horn tooted again. Headlamps blipped on and off.

"My my!"

The lights belonged to the stately snow-white Rolls Royce. The rear window rolled down and a hand emerged, beckoning them. There was a glint of jewelry in the moonlight.

They glanced at each other.

"This could be it."

"Let's go."

Navigating the lanes between the parked cars they approached the Rolls Royce. They leaned down towards the open window.

"Hello, girls," said a woman's voice. "How would you like to go to a party?"

The legend was true. Inside a Rolls Royce, you couldn't hear a thing, not the engine or the wheels on the road, or the slightest sound from the world outside.

It wasn't Cat's style. All that plush leather with its rich aroma and all that lustrous wood grain. It reminded her of her father—her father who had tried to kill her—and she didn't want to be reminded of him.

"Mmmm…"

Aiko was stroking the upholstery. Up front, silhouetted through a smoked glass partition, she saw the peak-capped head and broad shoulders of a uniformed chauffeur.

"Nice, huh?" the woman said.

"Oh," Aiko smiled ingratiatingly. "I could get used to it."

Cat pouted.

"You don't like?" the woman asked.

Cat shrugged.

"Naw, give me US Muscle and a big V-8."
The woman gave a short laugh. She kind of spat it out.
"Ah yes. The all-American girl."
"Wichita" grinned.
"Thet's me."
The woman was sat facing them, with her back to the driver. She swiveled to unclasp a polished burr walnut hatch, revealing a compact drinks cabinet.
"Can I offer you something?"
Cat looked interested for the first time.
"Whatya got?"
The woman's fingernails clicked along a row of bourbon, vodka and tequila bottles. She plucked out a little silver case and flipped back the lid.
"Oooh!" said Cat, her eyes widening.
Fat joints, ready rolled, in different colored papers.
"The pink ones are the strongest."
She pulled out a little silver tray. There were small bottles arranged neatly on it, with dainty silver caps. She lifted one of the bottles and made the pills inside it rattle.
"Or how about this? These will give the night a real buzz."
Cat recognized them. She had some just like them, in the secret place under the dash of the 442.
"Far out!"
She took the bottle and unscrewed the cap and shook three pale blue tablets onto her palm.
"How about you?"
Aiko reached for the bottle.
"Sure. Why not."
The woman watched them as they flipped the pills into their mouths. She watched them as they grinned at each other and settled back in the plush seating.
"Mmmm...yeah....!"
The woman looked at her watch. It was gold and studded with diamonds. It went with the baroque rings on her fingers and the bangles clanking on her wrists.
"We'll be there soon."
She was on the wrong side of 40, but slim and fit. Her long black hair was coiled on the top of her head, with a streak of silver in it, like a lightning flash. She wore a tight-fitting deep purple dress with a shallow U-shaped cleavage and billowing sleeves. It buttoned all the way down

the front, pearl studs down to her knees. Her boots were fashioned from grey-green snakeskin, with needle-pointed toes and high stiletto heels.

There was a hard brightness in Cat's eyes that showed that the "buzz" had kicked in. Aiko's face was tilted towards the side window, watching the darkness rushing by.

"So, who are yew anyway?" Cat asked.

The woman smiled with her mouth only.

"My name is Lana Kent."

Her voice was educated, but that was a front. Lurking behind it was the rough and tumble of the tenements. She held out her gem-encrusted hand and Cat leaned forward to shake it.

"Katie Kopinski," she drawled.

"Alias the Wichita Wildcat," the woman smiled again.

"Uh, yeah…"

"I saw you in action," Lana said. "I was impressed."

Cat rolled her eyes.

"Yeah, well…I'm lookin' fer better things, y'know…"

Lana put a hand on Cat's knee.

"Yes, you deserve better."

Cat let the hand stay there, even when it inched a little way up onto her thigh. Aiko was still staring out of the window.

"So, what d'yew do?" Cat asked.

Lana sat back again. She poured herself a shot of bourbon.

"A & R."

"Er, what?"

"Artists and Repertoire. I manage bands for King Records."

Cat put on her impressed face.

"Yeah? Wow! That's amazin'!"

She prodded Aiko in the shoulder.

"Did ya hear thet? Amazin', huh?"

"Yeah, amazing," Aiko replied, her face still pressed to the tinted glass.

"Anybody I might've heard of?" Cat asked eagerly.

There was a compartment built into the wood furnishings of the door. Lana slid something out of it. It was a '45 in a glossy picture sleeve.

"This is our latest signing."

Oh I don't believe it!

There they were, in all their pomp and menacing glory—**666**

Boy, we got lucky!

"We picked them up when they were ripe for the plucking. They've been big state-wide, but now they're ready to go national."

Cat made her eyes go very wide. She snatched the single from Lana's hand.

"Hey! No kiddin? This is one of my fave bands!"

She waved the picture sleeve under Aiko's nose.

"Oh yeah," Aiko said. "Hea-veee!"

Lana retrieved the sleeve before Cat creased it. She flicked out that short cold laugh again.

"Well, you've got a treat in store, ladies. Tonight you'll get your chance to meet them."

Somewhere on that desert highway, the Rolls whispered by another car, coming in the opposite direction.

"Come, Come...!"

It was a dirty old station wagon, hot-wired and driven away. It was occupied by standard issue teenagers, skinny boys with pimples and shaggy hair, head banging to the sounds that blared from the tinny speakers.

"...Come to the Sabbath...!"

Three skinny boys could fit comfortably onto the wide front seat. Four boys sat with their passenger in the big space at the back.

"...Satan's there...!"

Their passenger was a girl, in a tie-dyed T-shirt and scruffy jeans. She was lying on her side with her wrists and ankles lashed together, bending her body into a taut bow. A dirty rag gagged her, stuffed into her mouth. Above it, her eyes were bulging with terror.

"Hey! Cover her up again, man!"

The boys heaved the dark green tarpaulin across, covering the girl completely. She stirred beneath it, making muffled noises.

"Don't move!"

One of the boys hit her shape hard. She lay still.

"...Come...Come...!"

The station wagon rolled off the highway and onto the gritty crust of the desert. It juddered on for a while on its sub-standard suspension.

"...Come to the Sabbath...!"

It stopped. They left the lights on, making a large pool of light. The doors opened and the boys jumped out. Briskly, silently, they dragged the girl out of the back and carried her between them into the light. Struggling, she managed to spit out the gag. She began screaming.

Ignoring her outcries, the boys laid her down on the ground. Her trussed, arched body jerked and shuddered. Her wide terrified eyes were stark in the moonlight, shrill screams spilling from her mouth.

A blade flashed in the moonlight.
"Take this our offering, oh Master...!"

The white mansion was bathed in rainbows, a kaleidoscope that pulsed to the thump-thump-thump of a heavy beat.
"Wow!"
Tires crunched on the glistening gravel, as the Rolls followed the long and winding course of a manicured driveway, meandering across plush lawns that undulated on and on, past groups of trees looming dark against the purple night.
"Yike!"
A naked girl ran across their path, her body stark in the glare of the headlights. Her head flicked round to look at them as the chauffeur squeezed the brakes. She was wide-eyed and laughing. There was a brief pause before two naked men ran after her.
Lana Kent flicked a tiny switch in a panel close beside her.
"Tom, take it round the side."
The rainbows slid like oil across the polished contours of the Rolls Royce as it swung left onto a tributary branching off the main drive. There was a white wall crested with dark red tiles, punctured by an archway broad enough to accommodate the big car.
"Stop here, Tom."
They were in a walled courtyard paved with polished flagstones. The side door was tall and studded with iron. There was a big man in uniform, with a gun holstered on his hip and a shoulder patch that said "Acme Security."
The chauffeur was out and was opening the door for them. Lana Kent slid out first, Aiko followed, with Cat close behind her. The night was crisp and cool and Cat filled her lungs deeply.
Frowning, Lana looked them up and down.
"No, that won't do at all."
They were dressed casually, in baggy tracksuits. Cat's was red and Aiko's was blue, with white go-faster stripes down the arms and legs.
Cat grinned.
"Nope, we sure ain't dressed fer a party."
Lana nodded at the security guard, who flipped a brisk salute. A bunch of keys clattered.
"We can soon put that right," Lana stepped into the shaft of light that speared from the opening door. "Come with me!"

Party sounds.
The music was loud and insistent, a driving heavy rock beat. Shouts and screams and squeals of feigned alarm; breaking glass and the crash of furniture.

The party was a sprawling, disorganized affair. It careered in and out of all of the rooms in the vast mansion. It ran up the stately staircase and slid down the marble banisters. Showing no respect for ancient tapestries and antique furniture, it swung from the chandeliers and piled high in the four-poster beds.

Lush carpets squelched with Jack Daniels, Southern Comfort and Jose Cuervo. Persian rugs were mottled with squashed butts. The air was thick with sweet smells.

"Hey, fuckin' A!" said the Wichita Wildcat.

Where's the funk?

Cat liked her sounds Soulful, but Katie Kopinski got off on Rock.
"Far out!"

The pool was shaped like a huge guitar. Lit from below, the water glowed like sapphire. It was seething, crowded with bodies, men and women stripped to their underwear, and less, splashing, laughing and shouting, dive-bombing from the high board.

"Crazy!" said Miss Banzai.

There were men all around the pool, standing with a drink or a joint in their hands, sprawling in deckchairs. The older men wore silk suits or Hawaiian shirts and Bermuda shorts; the young men in leather, T-shirts and denim. They watched the half-naked and naked girls as they ran shrieking around and around the pool, their bare feet leaving wet footprints on the patio paving.

Boring...

The men all turned to stare as Cat and Aiko ventured forth onto the patio.

"OOOOOOO..."

Aiko wore a mere scrap of a black silk mini-dress that barely reached her thighs, held up by gold spaghetti straps that went with her gold sandals with bands that entwined her slim calves.

"...WEEEEEEEEEE...!"

Cat was only just contained by a skimpy suede halter-top embellished by tribal patterns and beaded fringes. Blue denim hot pants clung low on her hips. Her high-heeled boots were snakeskin.

"Oooh, cum t'Daddy...sshweet-cheeks...!"

A fat man in a florid shirt lurched towards her. A cigar stub was clamped between his grinning teeth. His piggy eyes in his pink fleshy face were glittering.

"Gimme sum a that...!"

His fat hands were reaching for her. Smiling, Cat let him come.

"Lemme see them goods...!"

He was upon her. Cat moved slightly. With a yell, the fat man somersaulted into the pool. The splash he made soaked the bystanders.

Cat received an ovation. She took a bow.

"Show-off," said Aiko.

Cat rolled her eyes.

"Let's split up and take a look around," she suggested.

"Okay," Aiko replied.

Cat wandered from room to room, down limitless corridors, up and down the stairs. She ducked the flying underwear and bottles, dodging the bodies that dashed around and banged together, the flailing arms and clutching hands. The music was a giant hammer, pounding her.

This ain't my scene

From the top of a landing, she caught a glimpse of Aiko pretending to dance with someone too stoned to notice that she was pretending, her body grooving lithely, arms wafting above her head.

Cat watched for a little while, smiling. Then she saw another door, the hundredth door, at least. She went and peered through it. She went in.

"Hm!"

Yet another guest bedroom, with embossed Regency wallpaper, rugs, oil paintings and a four-poster bed. Rarely, it was unoccupied.

Cat walked over to stand by the bed. The evening's exertions were starting to catch up with her and she was tempted to lock herself in and go to sleep.

"Hey, baby...!"

She recognized him.

"Now ain't you fine, mama!"

Mitch Brandon, a Rock God in the flesh, lead singer with triple-platinum "Valhalla." His five-foot-ten was raised to six-foot-plus by the stack heels on his silver boots. His thin legs had a second skin of glossy red leather, his crotch enlarged by a studded black codpiece. A black silk shirt cut down to his navel exposed a hairless, scrawny chest laden with a cluster of exotic medallions. Blond curls flowed down over his narrow shoulders, framing a long pale face with ice blue eyes and a mouth that was a lipless slit.

He strutted towards her, a bottle of vodka sloshing in his hand. Cat stared at him, her face a blank.

"Let's party, babe..."

The slit was curved in a nasty leer. His free hand cupped the bulging codpiece.

"I don't think so."

Cat made to sidestep him and head for the door. He clamped a sweaty palm on her bare shoulder.

"Hey", he slurred. "Dontya know who I am?"

Cat shrugged and the hand dropped from her shoulder.

"A tone deaf dickless asshole," she replied.

His eyes sparked. The slit compressed.

"Bitch...!"

He swung a punch at her midriff that was meant to make her bow to him. He waited for the pleasing impact of knuckles on female flesh.

"Uh...?"

It didn't happen. His fist was left dangling. As he stumbled, off balance, Cat slapped him. She slapped him hard, making him reel back and fall into a deep, upholstered armchair.

"UH!"

Mitch felt the warm trickle of blood at the corner of his mouth and scrubbed at it angrily. Still clutching the vodka bottle, he stood up slowly.

"So ya wanna play, huh...?"

He put two fingers in his mouth and whistled. The open door was filled by a giant of a man, straining the seams of a black suit, his shaven skull gleaming, eyes masked by dark shades. He stepped into the room and two more came in after him, just like him.

The giant triplets stood in a line, hands like shovels hanging down by their sides.

"Bitch likes t'play," Mitch spat venomously.

He swung his arm. Vodka splattered the quilt as the bottle shattered on the bedpost.

"Hold her!"

Mitch advanced, brandishing the jagged edges. The giants came lumbering up behind him.

"Hey, looks like fun..."

Aiko was leaning pertly on the doorframe.

"Can anybody join in?"

Cat grinned at her.

"Sure, take your pick."

One of the triplets turned ponderously and took a step towards Aiko.

"HAII-III!!!"

One second she was standing there relaxed and smiling and the next the giant was lying spread eagled on his back, unconscious.

"HAAA-YAH!!!"

Then she was a whirling blur of attacking hands and feet and a small side table was crushed beneath the weight of a flying giant crashing down upon it.

"Hey," Cat protested. "Leave some for me."

The sole surviving triplet was coming for Cat. He swung a casual left hook. He expected her to retreat, to be pinned up against the wall where he would crush her slowly. But Cat didn't go back. She stepped sideways and then in and the edge of her hand fell just behind his cauliflower ear.

"UGH!"

The giant stood stock still. A smile teasing her lips, Cat reached out and removed his sunglasses. Behind them, his eyes were staring blankly.

Aiko rolled her eyes.

"Oh Cat!"

Cat planted her forefinger on the giant's chest. She pushed and he rocked backwards, coming down with a crash.

The broken bottle slipped from Mitch's fingers. Cat rounded on him.

"Are you still here?"

She moved towards him. Terrified, he backed up in a rush and sat down on the bed.

"Uh…ah…hey…I was only kiddin'…I––!"

Her fist looped up from her side and connected with the point of his chin. His teeth clicked together. His eyes rolled around like glass balls and he slumped backwards across the quilt.

They stood side by side, looking at the mess.

"Are you psychic or something?" Cat demanded.

Aiko just looked inscrutable. They both laughed.

"Hey," said Cat. "I've got an idea."

She went to the bed and rolled Mitch onto his front. She unbuckled the codpiece and began tugging the red leggings down below his bony knees.

"Cat, what are you…?"

Cat was dragging one of the prostrate giants over to the foot of the bed. With a grunt, she heaved him up on top of it.

"Come on, give me a hand…"

She was tugging at the giant's belt. Laughing, Aiko ran over and began hauling on his trouser cuffs.

At the foot of the grand staircase the party was in full swing. A yelling girl in a micro-skirt was zooming down the polished marble banister while an eager photographer bobbed and weaved to get the best angle, his flashgun popping.

"Hey, man..."

Cat sidled up beside him.

"If you want some really interesting stuff, try the bedroom up top, third door on the right..."

There was a tap on Cat's shoulder. She turned and Lana Kent was smiling at them, with that smile that didn't reach her eyes.

"Having fun?"

Cat switched Katie on again.

"Yeah, rockin'!"

Aiko nodded, looking a lot higher than she really was.

Lana smiled again, with a hint of mystery. She slipped between them and put her arms around their shoulders.

"Yes, but this isn't the real party..."

Cat looked dumb.

"Huh?"

Lana turned them and was pushing them through drawn purple velvet curtains and into a long corridor that led to a small door.

"Come with me."

Suddenly, they were out in the cool fresh air, standing in a moonlit courtyard with high walls and the music and the voices and the heat and the smoke were muffled and a long way away.

There was another doorway at the far end of the courtyard, flanked by stone-faced guards in Acme Security uniforms. Lana grabbed their hands and pulled them towards it.

"Come on, I'll take you to the real party!"

They walked into another world.

"Wow!"

A sensory blast rocked them back on their heels. A wild, distorted music that ebbed and flowed on swirling currents of heady incense and familiar, illicit aromas, sustained by a hypnotic beat. Light like molten gold flowed down from the high dome of a pagan temple, its walls hung with black banners emblazoned by blood red pentagles and tapestries depicting obscene, occult rites. Exotic rugs were strewn about on the stone floor.

"Hey," said Cat out of the side of her mouth. "Looks like we've come to the boys' playroom."

Lana Kent drew them in, leading them to the temple's centerpiece.

"Oh, really!" Aiko muttered.

Cat smothered the laugh that rose in her throat.

Shallow stone steps led up to a stage shaped like a stretched oval where flames flickered in tall braziers. Guards stood beside the torches, with shaven skulls and mighty arms folded across their bare chests.

Lana Kent stepped forward. She was bowing before the occupants of five gilded thrones, perched on the summit.

"These are the women I was telling you about..."

The throne in the middle was bigger than the rest. "Snake" had room to let his lanky frame sprawl, one long, lean leg hooked over a gilt arm rest carved into a dragon's claw.

Well, well...

Bare-breasted girls with long dark hair and vacant eyes reclined with their heads resting on his thighs.

...the gang's all here

The other members of the band occupied the thrones on either side: "Cannibal", bare-chested as always, palms slapping his thighs to the demonic beat; "Tank" encased by studded black leather, blank and monolithic; "Chainsaw" in his second skin of black and silver, bending at the waist, head banging; "The Axe", never parted from his biker jacket or his skull-and-crossbones guitar, his fingers flickering inaudibly over the unplugged strings.

To each there was his handmaiden, another bare-breasted girl, with the same empty eyes. Shoving his slave girls aside, "Snake" unfolded his long legs and stood up slowly. Framed by his wild, pale mane, his piercing blue eyes sizzled when they focused on the new arrivals.

"Uh...I...er..."

A jarring note was struck by the small man with short hair and glasses, in a sensible suit and tie. Jamming a file under his arm, he walked backwards, stumbling as "Snake" glanced at him, a spark of annoyance in his eyes.

"Ah...okay...," the small man mumbled at Lana Kent. "I'll take these contracts back to..."

He seemed to fade away. Curtains closed behind him. Fingering the cluster of medallions that clanked in the plunging V of his black satin shirt, "Snake" stood gazing, god-like, down upon them.

Aiko was looking up and down and all around, still playing at being more stoned than she actually was.

Asshole!

Cat stared straight back at him. She gave him just enough of a contest to impress him, then blinked and looked away, feeding his ego.

"Snake" puffed out his wiry chest. He made a small gesture that signified approval, with a hand encrusted with silver skulls and pagan charms. Lana Kent nodded. She turned, smiling with her lips only.

"You have been chosen."

CHAPTER 6

BLACK

"Come in, Sir! Come in!"

The President was a square-jawed, stocky individual in his early 50swith thinning reddish hair and bright blue eyes set close together in a square head set on a short, thick neck. He had the look of an old College football player, the kind of guy who, in the privacy of his study, would still wear his sweatshirt with the faded letters across the chest.

He jumped up from behind his desk in the Oval Office and crossed the room quickly, going all the way to the door to greet his visitor.

"Welcome! Thank you for coming!"

He clasped his visitor's hand in both of his and pumped it vigorously.

"My pleasure, Mr. President..."

Reverend Calhoun extracted his hand, flexing his fingers to get the blood back into them.

His smile almost manic, the President indicated a shallow crescent of padded armchairs, set around a long coffee table.

"Please..."

The Reverend hesitated, a slight frown clouding his regal brow.

"I think," he stated. "That it might be best was this meeting in private."

The President bobbed his head energetically.

"Yes! Of course! Of course!"

He made a shoving movement with his hands.

"C'mon you guys!"

A phalanx of aides was piling up behind them, freshly scrubbed young men with crew cuts, in blue blazers with the Presidential Seal on the breast pocket.

"Everybody out!"

They slammed on the brakes. Then they shifted into reverse, as the Reverend raked his lofty gaze across them.

The door closed behind them. Suddenly, the President found himself all alone, in such exalted company. His collar felt very tight and he swallowed audibly.

"Uh...uh...please, Sir, take a seat, why don't you...?"

The Reverend descended elegantly into one of the upholstered armchairs. Nervously, the President wedged his burly frame into the one next to it.

"Oh!" he remembered. "I'm sorry. Can I get you some...er...refreshment...?"

Reverend Calhoun made the slightest gesture with his hand.

"No, thank you."

He plucked at the cuff of his silk shirt, making the diamonds on his gold cuff-link sparkle. His lips were compressed, that hint of a frown there again.

The President gulped.

"Uh...ah...thank you again for coming at such short notice, Reverend Calhoun. I know how busy you must be..."

The Reverend inclined his head slightly, his lips curving in the faintest of smiles.

"One could hardly refuse an invitation from the White House."

He let himself sink back into the plush embrace of the armchair.

"Now, how can I be of service, Mr. President?"

Mr. President. It reminded him. Hey, I'm the President!

He cleared his throat, squaring his shoulders.

"I've been listening to your broadcasts a lot lately, Reverend..."

Calhoun inclined his head and smiled again.

"I am most gratified, Mr. President."

"And your message comes through loud and clear."

"Indeed."

Sweat glistened on the President's brow. His fist thumped the padded arm of his chair.

"Damn it—oh I'm sorry—I mean..."

"Yes, Mr. President?"

"Well, heck...things are getting out of control!"

"So I have observed."

"The kids are going crazy, and I'm not talking about those goddamn—sorry—those darned long-haired campus radicals..."

The Reverend nodded solemnly.

"No, indeed."

"I'm talking about the high school kids."

His hands were sawing the air in exasperation.

"They're doing things...crazy things...they're burning and killing and..."

Sweat was dripping from his face. Hot blotches glowed on his cheeks. The Reverend's eyes flicked away, the corner of his mouth curling.

"It's out of control...and we don't know why. The police can't do a thing. The shrinks don't have a clue and just spout garbage and––!"

The Reverend soared abruptly from his seat.

"What is lacking," he pronounced, "is firm moral leadership."

The President heaved himself upright. His face was shining, his eyes wide and blazing with a new light.

"Yes! That's it!"

He seized the Reverend by the arms.

"And you're just the man for the job!"

Suddenly embarrassed, the President let go and stepped back.

"Uh...will you do it...?"

The Reverend glanced down at the dark damp patches on the sleeves of his white suit.

"What precisely do you have in mind, Mr. President?"

The President was pacing, circling his desk, fists clenched, the way his old football coach used to do, his battered features creased into a pugnacious scowl.

"We gotta go on the attack...!"

Reverend Calhoun nodded.

"Yes, we must launch a moral offensive."

A moral offensive. The President liked that. Surreptitiously, he picked up a pen and jotted it down.

"Yeah," he hesitated. "But how do––?"

"Leave it to me," the Reverend said, heading towards the door. "My people will contact you."

The door closed behind him. The President stood alone in the Oval Office, mopping the sweat from his face.

"Ladies and gentlemen, you may now unbuckle your seat belts..."

Take-off was the nervous time. The experienced travelers didn't look up from their magazines or break off their chat. The first-timers and the anxious flyers gripped the arms of their seats or sat silent and tight-lipped or glanced at each other, smiling wanly or making a weak joke of uncrossing their fingers. Some began talking, in a gust of relief. Children chattered.

"Our cabin staff will be passing among you with beverages and light refreshments..."

Trim stewardesses moved up and down the aisles, smiling in all directions, stooping here and there to provide individual attention.

Two teenage boys sat side by side, virtually identical in their navy blue school blazers and grey flannels. The blazers bore the pretentious crest of an exclusive military academy, with an appropriately martial Latin motto.

"Boys...?"

The steward was a plump, pink-faced young man with prematurely thinning fair hair scraped back from his forehead.

"You wanted to visit the flight deck...?"

The boys' heads turned as one to look at him, with eyes that had no light in them.

"Hi, guys! Come on in!"

The pilot was as he should be, a ruggedly good-looking man with a dash of grey at his temples. His co-pilot was a younger version. Sat off to the side and behind them, the Flight Engineer was nondescript, as befitted his more functional status.

"This is your first flight, huh?"

They all turned to smile as the steward ushered the boys onto the flight deck with its daunting array of dials and knobs and switches. The boys just nodded dumbly.

"Betya haven't seen anything like this before."

The boys nodded again.

"Exciting, huh?"

Synchronized, the boys reached inside their blazers.

"Wha––!"

The pilot went pale.

The steward fainted.

"OH MY GOD!" said the co-pilot as the Flight Engineer jumped up from his seat.

Their hands emerged, holding two unmistakable "pineapple" grenades, stolen from the school's Cadet Corps armory.

"OH CHRIST! NO!"

They pulled the pins.

Skulls.

Yuck!

Skulls were "Snake"'s thing.

I'm having a bad dream...

Skulls, sporting red ruby eyes, adorned the black wrought-iron bedposts. Clusters of skulls were welded into a giant hanging chandelier, a ghoulish green glow emanating from their eyeless sockets.

"Bow to the Master..." Lana Kent said out of the corner of her mouth, nudging Cat in the ribs, shoving Aiko a step forward, with a hand in the small of her back.

They were naked, save for scraps of silk at their loins, secured on their hips by a delicate chain of gold. They were perfumed, belled and bangled. Their skin glistened with oil.

"Bow...!"

They bowed, bending slowly at the waist.

Whatever it takes...

The bedchamber was lined with gleaming black marble, slashed by lightning flashes of glittering crystal. The bed was enormous, with black satin sheets and an enormous mirror in the ceiling above.

"Your desire, My Lord..."

Lana Kent was backing out of the chamber, slipping out through a chink in black curtains.

"H-Hey-y-y..."

"Snake" sat in the middle of the bed, his long thin legs crossed under him, his silver hair flowing down over his narrow shoulders. He was naked beneath a black silk robe with the numbers "666" splattered all over it like blood.

"H-H-Heeyy..yy..."

The folds of the robe fell open as he leaned towards them, exposing his wiry, hairless chest.

"H-Hey-y-y...laydees..."

His eyes were burning with a crazy fire, fueled by a cocktail of alcohol and chemicals. In the strange light, his eyes looked almost yellow.

He held out a twitchy hand, the knuckles encrusted with silver skulls, their gemstone eyes winking.

"C'mere...an'...an-d-d-d...d-do ya...stuff..."

Swaying, "Snake" knelt upright, pulling apart the robe.

Cat and Aiko stared at him.

"Snake" was thrusting his bony hips at them, his bloodless lips contorted in a vicious leer.

"C-C-C'mon...see whatya c-c-c-can d-do with...that...!"

Hm! Not much to work with...

"There's no way," Cat muttered "that I'm going down on that disgusting thing."

"No way." Said Aiko.

They looked at each other. Silent agreement showed in their eyes.

"Uh," said the Wichita Wildcat. "We...uh...we don't swing that way, man. We, uh, kinda like bat for the other team, like ya know what I mean...?"

Aiko giggled shrilly, still pretending to be a lot more stoned than she really was.

"We...we...," she smoothed her palm across her bare, oiled belly. "We can put on a real show for you, man..."

"Snake" blinked. The mean slit of his mouth opened and shut.

"F-F-F-Fuckin' f-f-f-f-far...out...!"

Their mouths were bold; their tongues were entangled in bubbles and breaths. They rocked each other in cradles of sweat. Hard sighs bucked out of them. Their throats emitted animal-like noises.

"F-F-F-Far...out...!"

Rhythms were established. They arched and pushed and corkscrewed and jackknifed; grunting and heavy breathing. Their bodies flowed with rivers of perspiration.

Snake sat there watching, wide-eyed, his jaw hanging slack.

"F-F-F-F...!"

Low moans and short gasps of breath. Loud liquid sounds. They swam in a sea of lubricity.

"Snake"'s hand was flexing between his thighs. His ragged grunts underpinned the flood of sound.

Mouths moved, tongues moved, hands moved. They writhed dizzily, clutching at each other desperately in their strained ecstasy.

Eyes burned through the dark slit in the curtains. Lana Kent was watching. She clutched at herself with hands that were out of control. Clenching her teeth, she strangled the scream that rose in her throat.

"AH! UGH-G-GH...G-G-UGGHH-H...AAAAG-G-GG-HHH...!"

"Snake"'s face contorted, his eyes bugged out, his body jerking.

Their breathing was coming in great wrenching gasps and raw groans and then they bucked and shuddered, screaming.

"Oh...m-my...."

"...G-G-God...!"

They rolled over and sprawled on their backs, side by side in a cloud of heat rising from them.

"Snake" lolled in a deep armchair, groaning.

"Congratulations..."

Her face flushed and glinting with perspiration, Lana Kent stood over them as they lay there, panting.

"...you've joined the band...!"

"Live from the Oval Office...the President of the United States...!"

His bull neck bulged, constricted by the tight shirt collar. He hated wearing a suit and tie.

"My fellow Americans..."

The President looked nervous. In the glare of the TV lights, beads of perspiration penetrated the shield of make-up on his face, glistening on his forehead. He clasped his hands together on the desk in front of him, to stop them fidgeting.

"...My fellow Americans..."

He cleared his throat, his eyes blinking at the cue cards, behind the lenses of the new spectacles that he was embarrassed to wear.

"I am speaking tonight to the parents of the nation..."

He coughed and took a sip of water. Off to one side, a senior aide winced.

"Jeez," he whispered. "All the coaching we give him and he's getting worse."

A younger colleague shrugged.

"Heck," he replied. "That's what they like about him. It's the human touch."

His senior looked doubtful.

"He made too many tackles without his helmet, that's what they're saying."

The President took a deep breath and squared his broad shoulders. The aides looked happier.

"That's more like it..."

"Yeah, that's what we want, some of that sincere emotion..."

He took off his glasses and looked deep into the camera lens.

"I am speaking to you as a parent myself, sharing your concerns for your children, for our children..."

His fist thumped the desk top, making the inkwells rattle.

"The children are our future! The future of the nation is at stake!"

He had the look of a man struggling to contain his emotions. The aides were loving it.

His elbows on the desk, he was leaning forward, into every living room in the country.

"We've all seen the headlines, we've seen it on our TV screens. We've sat and watched helplessly as all over the country our children have gone out of control."

His big hands were reaching out to them.

"As parents we live in fear that our own children will be next."

The aides were nodding approval. One gave him the thumbs up.

"The time has come to take a moral stand. The country cries out for moral leadership..."

In his booth, the TV director hunched closer to the control panel.

"Ready...on my cue..."

The President was galvanized, suffused by a new fervor.

"We have a man who can give us that leadership. A man known to you all for his high moral qualities...!"

"Ready...ready..."

"My fellow Americans, I give you the Reverend Thaddeus P. Calhoun!"

"And go!"

The TV director slumped back in his chair with relief. OK signs all round.

On television screens in every state of the Union the President's pugnacious features dissolved and were replaced by the Reverend's aristocratic profile. Standing at the center of his plush oak-paneled study, he turned smoothly to face the cameras.

"Good evening..."

He was resplendent in his trademark cream-colored suit, jeweled cufflinks winking, and the heavy gold watch chain strung across his waistcoat.

"I am here tonight to address the mothers and fathers of this great nation..."

In their living rooms, side by side on their sofas or in their armchairs they sat up straight, eyes glued to the screen, craving reassurance from the man who radiated certainty.

"The past decade has seen this land convulsed by social unrest and civil strife. Our streets and campuses have become a battle ground. Public order is under threat from the forces of anarchy."

...kill...

"And now our children are consumed by this evil that stalks our streets and creeps into our homes..."

...kill...kill...

"...inciting them to commit acts of wanton destruction and violence..."

...kill...

"...a malign influence that seduces them, the so-called 'counter-culture' with its siren song of 'Sex and Drugs and Rock and Roll'..."

...kill...

The apartment was carefully selected, for its exclusive zip code, for its views of the verdant oasis of the Park.

Everything in the apartment was carefully selected: the incomprehensible—but modern—art; the uncomfortable—but modern—furniture; all in the most modern and minimalist taste.

The young mother was trim and chic, from her faultless coiffure to her painted toenails, as she turned away from the TV set and padded barefoot across the polished floorboards.

Her baby lay gurgling in its cot, looking up at her. She lifted it out and, cradling it in the crook of her arm, went to the glass doors that opened onto her spacious balcony.

She slid aside a tall panel of glass. Her bare feet silent on the tiles, she crossed to the rail.

The Park looked beautiful in the morning light. She smiled at the baby in her arms. And then the balcony was empty.

The farmland undulated all the way to the horizon in a vivid patchwork of fallow fields and rich dark earth that had been furrowed by the plow.

The barn glowed in the evening sun, freshly painted white with a red roof.

The farmer, a tall lean man with nut brown hair, switched off the TV and took his young son to the barn, wading through the long grass; a sturdy boy dressed like his father, in a plaid work shirt and faded blue overalls. Brushed by a warm breeze, the grass gleamed like waves of bronze, tinted by the setting sun.

In the barn were stacks of aromatic straw bales, heaped high to the wooden roof beams. There were tools and bits and pieces of machinery. There were boy's toys, and the remains of an old fort built out of wood.

The father found lengths of rope, coiled on hooks on the wall of the barn. His son watched as he fashioned a noose.

The kitchen was like all the other kitchens in the leafy suburb, with its identical garages and freshly mowed front lawns, its crazy paved garden patios and barbecues and swimming pools.

The family that sat around the kitchen table was much the same as all the other families in the leafy suburb. The kids were tucking in to their cereal, competing for the small gift toy in the box, one eye on the TV.

Their mother was pouring the coffee.

"Good morning, dear. Breakfast is——"

But this morning, Dad wasn't wearing his jacket and struggling with his tie. The morning paper wasn't tucked under his arm. He wasn't asking his wife if she had seen his briefcase.

He was unkempt, unshaven. He was still in his bathrobe. He was holding the Colt Woodsman, the one that he took to the pistol club on Sundays.

He fired until the clip was empty.

"YEEEEE…"

She was his pride and joy.

"…HAH!"

A cowboy's modern thoroughbred.

"Woooo-eee!"

Headlights blazing, they were making a dust cloud that glowed silver in the moonlight, weaving from side to side, across the white line that divided the blacktop.

"Woo-woo-woo!"

A classic; a 1950 GMC Longbed pickup, with its big bull nose and massive grille and bumper like a battering ram of glittering chrome. Waxed and polished till it gleamed like glass, its whitewall tires immaculate, it was re-sprayed metallic purple, with tongues of yellow flame racing back along the hood.

"Hey, man…grab me another brew…"

One hand on the wheel, the driver sucked the bottle dry and tossed it out of the window with a flick of his wrist, into the streaking blur of the desert blowing by.

"Sure thang."

His passenger simply stuck his hand out of the tall cab and waved it to attract attention.

"Comin' raht up…"

They were brothers, Jake and Lyle, 20th-century cowboys, young guns, lean and mean, dressed to kill in their snow-white Stetsons with the silver bands, embroidered Country 'n Western shirts and tight blue jeans tucked into fancy boots.

The good ol' boys rode in the back of the pickup, just a roarin' and a rarin' t'go, ready for a Saturday night on the town. Laughing, they jostled to get at the crate and its rattling bottles, competing to be the one to lean out dangerously and slap a full bottle into Lyle's waiting palm.

"There ya go!"

There were five of them, in their Frontier finery, laughing and backslapping and boasting about the conquests they were going to make that night, hanging onto their hats as the pickup surged onward, propelled by its tuned-up engine.

Lyle passed the brew on to his brother. One hand on the wheel, Jake wrenched off the bottle cap with a chrome-plated opener mounted on the dash. Lyle caught the cap in his cupped hands before it dropped onto the pristine plush carpeting and flicked it out of the window.

"Hey!" he said, pointing.

"I see it," said Jake.

Eyes glowed on the road, a coyote with its pointed snout, looking right at them, frozen in the onrushing glare of the headlights.

"Go git 'im, man!"

Lyle grabbed his brother's arm. Jake shrugged him off.

"Naw, don' want 'is guts all over mah whitewalls…"

He turned the wheel and the pickup swerved. In the back the good ol' boys hooted and hollered, rocked and rolled from side to side. One pulled out a nickel-plated pistol and banged away at the mesmerized coyote as the twin pin lights of its eyes receded behind them.

Lyle stuck his head out of the cab.

"Hey, Cletus, yew cut thet out now! Yew gonna shoot a hole in the truck!"

"Thet boy cain't hit the side of a barn from the inside anyway," Jake muttered.

He was frowning, leaning forward in his custom black leather bucket seat to squint out into the darkness beyond the advancing bright splash of his headlights.

"What's the matter?" Lyle asked, taking the bottle from him and lifting it to his lips.

His brother shook his head.

"Dunno. I think we shoulda made a turnin' back there…"

He grabbed the bottle back before Lyle drained it.

"…dang coyote and thet Cletus fuckin' about lak thet…I think we done gone missed it."

Lyle looked doubtful.

"Naw, man, I think we's okay, I think the turnin's a way ahead yet."

"HHH…AAAAAAAAAHH…HHH…HH…!"

Whirling searchlights raked the heaving mass that surged in waves up to the lip of the stage.

"…HHH…AAAAAAAA…HHHH…HH…!"

Oil slides dappled the walls with flashing blood red runes and spinning pentangles.

"…AAAAAAAAA…HHH…HH…HHH…!"

The band was riffing, sending out mighty surges of sound that burst like the wind from the twin towers of speakers. The sound rolled the crowd all the way back and then they rolled forward again in a great tide, arms aloft, hands shaping the "horns" sign with their fingers.

His long black hair flaying the air in a spray of sweat, "Cannibal" pounded the skins, muscle flexing like corded steel across his bare torso.

A hulk in studded black leather, "Tank" hunched over the fret board of his bass, his body rocking back and forth to the pulverizing beat, his long dark fringe swinging like a curtain across his slab-like features.

"Chainsaw", a silver wraith, pranced perilously along the cliff edge of the stage, leaping and capering, leaning out towards the arms and hands like a sea of snakes reaching out to him, as he wrenched the slashing chords from his buzz saw guitar.

Followed by an ice blue spotlight, "The Axe", an angel of death in his biker's regalia, wielded his death's head guitar like a weapon. Strutting, posing, his left hand scuttled like a white spider over the frets with their runic inlay, his right producing flurries of shredded metal, the notes like red hot shrapnel.

"YAAAAAAAA...AAAA...AAAAAHHH...HHH...!"

A great howl pierced with needling shrieks; a chorus of exultation.

Wreathed by tendrils of glowing red smoke, the "Throne of Skulls" advanced ponderously into the light. A giant, single skull that gleamed like marble, with blazing red lanterns in the vast eye sockets, and a gilded throne carved out of its gaping maw.

"HHHH...HHAAAAA...AAAHH...HHH...!"

"Snake" reclined upon the throne, his long legs folded beneath him. His white mane caped his narrow shoulders, his body sheathed in a black cat suit spangled with silver stars, cut in a deep scoop to bare his wiry hairless chest. His bright blue eyes stared out above the heaving mass that came in waves towards him, unseeing, on some higher plane.

A searing spotlight lanced towards the wings, heralding some new arrival. "Cannibal" morphed the beat into something processional. And suddenly the others stopped playing and there was only the pounding of the drums.

Cat strode onto the stage. The crowd went crazy.

The drums were primitive, primal, tribal.

She was an Amazon warrior goddess, a barbarian. Her long hair was a golden mane, wild and untamed, hanging down to veil her bare breasts. Clad only in a leather loincloth trimmed with fur, her tawny flesh gleamed with oil.

To the beat of the drums, she crossed the stage with a long, slow, stalking stride, leading with her pelvis. In her right hand she carried a mighty broadsword. A heavy chain dangled from her left, trailing out of sight, into the wings.

Head down, "Tank" plucked a slow, exotic pulse. Dancing backwards before her, "Chainsaw" ripped out jagged chords.

"AAAAAAAAAA…AAAAA…HHHH…HHH…!"

The crowd were roaring. Knee deep in a glowing mist of dry ice, "The Axe" picked out a shrill, entwining counterpoint.

"HHHH…AAAAAAHHH…HHH…HH…!"

Aiko emerged on the end of the chain, secured to a metal collar fitted loosely round her neck. She was nearly naked, her modesty preserved by mere scraps of silk.

Leaning back, Aiko tugged on the swinging chain, grasping it with both hands, bound together at the wrists. Glaring, Cat hauled hard, the gleaming oil in the hard spotlight highlighting her flexing muscle tone.

Aiko stumbled forward, as Cat dragged her towards the throne. With a hand on her shoulder Cat made her captive kneel. Standing proud before him, the Amazon saluted "Snake" with a flourish of her sword.

"Snake" unfolded his long legs and rose from his seat. He brandished a microphone shaped like a scepter carved with skulls.

"AAAAAAAA….AAAAHH…HHHH…HHH…!"

Legs astride, he stood over the kneeling slave girl. Seizing a fistful of her long black hair, he forced her bowed head back so she looked up at him. He lifted the microphone to his lips.

"Aw, shee-ut!" said Jake. "Thet ain't right!"

Lyle squirmed in his seat, looking confused.

There was a banging on the roof of the cab.

"Hey, boys, we gonna git movin' sometime?"

The pickup was stationary, on the white line in the middle of the road. The engine idled in neutral.

"C'mon yew guys, there's beer an' pussy a-waitin'!"

Brow furrowed, Jake heaved open the door and stepped out of the cab. The desert was chill at night and he reached back in for his short denim jacket, draping it over his shoulders.

"Well…?"

He glared at his brother.

"Whadda we do now, Lyle?"

Lyle jumped out to join him. The good ol' boys all stood up to see over the high roof of the cab.

"Any suggeshuns…?"

Ahead of them, the blacktop split in two, into twin forks that disappeared into the night.

Lyle took off his hat and scratched his head. He looked up at the sky awash with stars. He looked all around at the desert receding into the surrounding darkness, a darkness full of rustles and clicks and the mournful sound of a coyote howling at the bright disk of the Moon.

"Uh...uh..."

Cursing, Jake rooted in his pockets.

"Aw, fuck it! C'mon, heads or tails?"

The small changing room rang with laughter.

"Oh Jeee-zus...!"

"Oh...Oh...Oh my...!"

They were bent double with laughter, clutching the towels to their naked bodies.

"...oh...oh...oh shit..."

Cat dabbed tears from her eyes. Aiko clapped her hand to her chest, gasping for breath.

"F-F-Fuck!" Cat panted. "I don't know how I kept a straight face!"

They heard approaching footsteps in the corridor, a muffled voice.

"Hey, get with it, ladies, it's time to par-tay!"

They looked at each other.

"Better keep the act up," muttered Cat.

"Damn right," Aiko agreed. "No way in hell are those freaks getting their paws on me."

They dropped the towels and wrapped their arms around each other, pressing their lips together.

As the door opened, they were moaning softly.

"Shit!" exclaimed "Chainsaw", wrapped in a black silk robe. "Are you bitches on heat 24 hours a day?"

He stood in the doorway looking at them, as they grinned at him, their arms around each other. His eyes roved all over their naked bodies.

"What a waste," he sighed. "But hey, it's a real turn on."

He jerked his thumb back over his shoulder.

"Now move yer asses. The gear is loaded and we got booze and a whole lotta candy waitin' on the bus."

Jake slammed on the brakes.

"Fuck it! We're lost!"

Tires smoking, the big pickup slid sideways, screeching to a halt. Jolted out of his seat, Lyle grabbed onto his hat as it levitated from his head. Yelling, the good ol' boys tumbled in a heap.

Jake made a fist and thumped his brother on the shoulder.

"Why dontya admit it, Lyle? We's lost!"

Lyle rubbed himself ruefully.

"Okay, okay," he muttered. "We's lost."

The doors banged open and they climbed down out of the cab. The good ol' boys were picking themselves up and dusting themselves down, standing up in the back, passing their hats around until they all had the right one.

Shivering, Jake buttoned up his jacket.

"Shit, it's cold!"

Shoving his hands into his pockets, he walked out a few paces in front of the truck and stood looking all around.

"Jeez! Where the hell are we?"

Lyle shrugged.

"Beats me. It ain't like nowhere I ever seen before."

Some of the good ol' boys had vaulted the tailgate and were down on the ground, stretching their legs. The rest remained standing in the back. Cletus was swigging noisily from a beer bottle.

"Aw, cut that out, Cletus!" Jake shouted. "Any of yew boys got any idea where we are?"

Head shaking all round. In his shirtsleeves, Lyle shivered and wrapped his arms around himself.

"Brrr! Shit! When did it get so cold, man?"

Jake frowned, rubbing his chin.

"Somethin' sure is wrong about this..."

They all stopped and looked and listened. The sky was black and starless and the Moon was a pale phantom. The darkness had crept to the very edge of the highway, like a black blank wall, impenetrable. And the darkness was silent, no rustle or scamper or slither, nothing.

Even the blacktop looked different. Disused and dusty, cracked, its surface crumbling.

Someone cleared his throat nervously.

"Heck, boys, I don' lak this. Let's us back up and git outta——"

Lyle grabbed Jake's sleeve.

"What's thet up there?"

A faint shape in the abnormal gloom. It looked familiar.

Lyle was delving into the cab. He came out with a heavy flashlight in his hand. The beam lanced through the darkness and struck its target.

"Jesus!"

Tacked high on a leaning pole, a rusting metal shield, the green paint faded and flaking.

"...666..."

"What?"

"666, that's what it says, man. 666."

There was a tense silence.

"Uh..."

"Jeez...666..."

"...Route 666..."

Angry, Jake rounded on them.

"Aw shit! What's the matter with ya?"

Cletus giggled, a high nervous sound. He threw the beer bottle away and pulled the silver pistol from his waistband.

"Yeah!"

He fired twice, three rounds, rapid, at the target still fixed by the beam of Lyle's flashlight.

"Yeah! Yeah! Yeah!"

The bullets impacted with a dull clang. Holed, the metal shield was wrenched sideways and then hung down, held by a single rivet. The pole vibrated.

Laughing shrilly, others pulled pistols and laid down a barrage, firing till the shield dropped to the ground. Grinning, Lyle held the flashlight steady for them, till Jake snatched it from his hand.

"Cut it out, ya dumb bastards! Will ya cut––!"

They all felt it before they heard it. A deep vibration that made the asphalt tremble beneath their feet.

"What––?"

The sound was a physical thing that they felt in their chests. A sound they recognized with mounting excitement, as they all turned and looked behind them with keen anticipation.

"Somethin's comin'."

"Oh yeah."

Then they saw it.

"Holy shit! Willya take a look at thet!"

It was black, all black. Except for the pale ghostlike "Boss 429" stenciled on its flanks and the tiny red white and blue banner behind the pony badge on the grille.

"Oh my––!"

It gleamed like black glass. It was relentlessly black, inside and out. The tinted windows were so dark they looked black. The tires were all black, with no maker's name.

It was a beast, with the big air scoop on the hood, bulked up by the slats that masked the rear window, and the rakish airfoil on the back.

"Wooo-eee!"

Rumbling, it slowed to a roll and then came smoothly to a stop. There it stood, its deep rumble tickling the soles of their feet, a sound that seemed to come from the bowels of the earth.

"Hey!" Lyle blurted. "D'yew see what it says on them plates?"

Jake levelled the flashlight and directed it at the black Mustang.

"Huh...?"

The powerful beam seemed to wither and fade away.

"What the f––?"

Cursing, Jake stomped towards the dark car, brandishing the flashlight at it. But the closer he got, the faster the beam died, till the bulb itself flickered and died.

"Hey, ya sonofabitch! What the hell do yew––?"

The Boss Mustang's lights blazed into life. The engine revved, its mighty torque rocking it from side to side.

The lights were a searing green fire. Jake reeled backwards, shielding his eyes.

"Aw sheee-utt...!"

Jake was on fire. Green flames consumed him. He staggered and collapsed. Screaming, he rolled on the ground.

"Yaaaaa-aaagghh-hhh...!

"Aaaaaggg-gghh-gghhh...!"

One by one, the good ol' boys went up like candles, running around in circles, shrieking like rabbits, falling and rolling around kicking.

The pickup was glowing green. It was melting, like molten green glass. Then it blew up, in a bubbling eruption of green fire.

"YAAAAAHH!"

Lyle was blown off his feet. Scrambling upright, he turned and ran.

It let him run and run, until he was like a toy in the distance. Then, with a bestial roar the black Mustang sprang from zero to 60 in seconds. A beast of prey, it launched itself upon him, rolled over him and left him mangled and scarcely recognizable as something that had once been a man.

It kept on going, till its black became a part of the darkness.

CHAPTER 7

TRUCKIN'

Big wheels turning.
CRUNCH!
"Gotya!"
"Yeeeeee-hah!"
Impaled by the headlights, the jack rabbit didn't stand a chance. Its wide eyes, twin reflectors, were sucked up by the onrushing bulk of a towering monster.
"Grease spot!"
Night's shroud was descending on the desert. A purple dusk was slowly darkling, the remains of the day clinging palely to the sweep of a jagged horizon. The first stars pierced the black dome of the sky.
"That's three to me, man...."
The tour bus was a gleaming silver leviathan. It was a luxury pad on wheels, with all the mod cons. Stairs led up to the top deck, where you could sit and look down on the world from a great height. Down below, there was a well-appointed galley, with modern wood and chrome trimmings. At the back, by way of a carpeted corridor that passed between curtained-off sleeping berths, a tiled bathroom and a shower.
"...and one to you...."
A black and scarlet "**666**" T-shirt taut across his narrow chest, "Snake" was doing the driving, the tendons twisting on his forearms as he put all his strength into manhandling the big wheel. "The Axe" was leaning over him, sheathed in skin-tight black, the cigarette that dangled on his lower lip dribbling ash onto "Snake"'s shoulder.
"Aw, c'mon, man....," he whined. "My turn...."
He grabbed at the wheel and the mighty bus swerved sluggishly. Hovering nearby, the official driver, a slim young man in a pale blue cap, shirt and trousers, flinched and frowned anxiously.
"Aw, c'mon! Gimme...!"

"Get used to it, ladies. You've hit the big time."
The top deck was appointed plushly, like a playboy's lounge; padded leather armchairs and a sofa, a big screen TV, even a pool table and a polished cocktail bar.

Lana Kent strolled, ankle-deep, across the snow-white carpet, in something red and slinky, slit up to her hip, her dark hair piled in coils on top of her head.

"You're on a ride to the top."

"Yo! To the top!"

Sat cross-legged in one of the armchairs, "Cannibal" thrust up a hand in the twin-horned salute. He was stripped down to a pair of frayed blue jeans and sucked noisily on a beer bottle as a slender girl in an open shirt and nothing else leaned over him, her long hair hanging down over her face, and slowly massaged his bare broad chest.

"All the way!" mumbled "Tank".

He was stretched out on the long sofa which wasn't long enough for him, his feet propped up on the padded armrest. His giant body matted with hair, he wore only black underpants and his massive Frankenstein boots.

"All...the...way...."

He yawned and drifted off again. A fat joint slipped from his fingers and smoldered on the carpet. Without breaking stride, Lana Kent stooped elegantly and retrieved it.

"Hey...."

Draped in a silver cape, "Chainsaw" reached out and plucked the joint from Lana's fingers. He took a deep hit on it before passing it on to one of the naked girls who sat at his feet, a blonde and a brunette, gazing up at him with dull, adoring eyes. In a world of his own, he went on flicking chords from his unplugged guitar, the sound tinny and distant.

There was a muffled whoop from down below and the bus swerved again.

"Number four!"

Frowning, Lana swayed, reaching out for the chromed edge of the cocktail bar.

"Can I get you anything?" asked Aiko/Miss Banzai.

Trim in a pale green mini-dress cinched in at the waist by a belt of silver links, she was standing behind the bar, busy concocting something in a tall glass, her bare feet luxuriating in the deep soft carpet.

"No thanks," Lana Kent regained her composure, angry with herself.

Aiko shrugged.

"How about you?"

"Sure!"

Perched on a bar stool, Cat/the Wichita Wildcat/Katie Kopinski grabbed the glass and took a gulp.

"Wow!" she gasped. "Woooeee! That's got a kick alright!"

Gaudy bangles clanking on her wrists, she looked the part, in a brief leopard-print halter-top that scarcely contained her, tight pink pants low down on her hips and pale blue sneakers with stars all over them.

Cat grinned right back as Lana's eyes rolled all over her.

Trailer trash... Lana burned. *But oh God what a body!*

Cat drained the tall glass and set it down with a bang, smacking her lips.

"Gimme 'nother!"

Aiko obliged and Cat raised the glass in salute to Lana, who jerked her eyes up from her cleavage.

"Hey...K–K–Katie...," "Tank" was stirring. "C–C'mon over...here... an' p–p–please me...."

Cat grimaced and gave him the finger.

"Aw, why dontya jest please yerself!"

Aiko laughed. "Tank" went back to sleep. "Chainsaw" went on strumming his unamplified chords. The girl yelped and giggled as "Cannibal" reached back and pulled her head down into his lap.

Cat made her body move on the bar stool and saw Lana's eyes widen.

Hmmm...interesting...looks like I got a spell on you lady...

She grinned again.

"So, tell us," she drawled. "How'd we do?"

Lana swallowed hard.

"You two were great. You put on a good show."

"Thanks," said Aiko. "What's our next gig?"

Lana replied without looking at her. She had eyes only for Cat.

"It's a big step up. From the bars and halls. The Rockford Bluffs County High School football stadium. It seats five thousand."

Cat made her eyes go large.

"Wow! I ain't never performed fer a crowd that big."

Lana smiled at her.

"Oh, you'll be just fine."

Like a pale ghost, an illuminated sign flashed by, in the rush of darkness. In phony Frontier script, it proclaimed: THE TRADING POST—WE GOT EVERYTHING YOU NEED—STOP ON BY

"Hey!" said Cat/Katie. "I betya they got beer. We could always use more beer."

Shoulder to shoulder, they strode briskly across the illuminated forecourt, a wide space of flattened dirt, overhung by strands of multi-colored bulbs, stretched between wooden poles.

"Have you got it?" Cat asked.

All around, the desert was a fathomless darkness. The sky was full of stars.

"Yes, it's in the bag."

Aiko patted the leather bag, slung across her, decorated by colored beads. She had draped a tasseled shawl across her slim shoulders. Cat was wearing a faded short blue denim jacket, embroidered with flowers.

"Okay, but let's be careful."

The "Trading Post" was a long low slung adobe box, scarred and peeling, with tall weeds growing from its flat roof. A musty glow glimmered through the chinks in its flaking wooden shutters.

Loungers sprawled on benches on a porch of warped planks, beneath a long wooden awning supported on posts that leaned sideways and swayed slightly when someone stood to ease the kinks out of his spine, a leathery old man in a straw hat, check shirt and faded dungarees.

"Whooo-eee!"

"Now ain't yew sumthin', sweet thang!"

There was an ancient hitching post and two gleaming, customized Ford pick-ups parked nearby, side by side. Four modern-day cowboys stood around, bottles in hand, getting a few beers in before heading off for a night on the town. They wore their best hats with the fancy silver bands, two-tone shirts embellished by fancy stitching and fringes, blue jeans as tight as they could be, tucked into polished, hand-tooled boots.

"OOOO-weee!"

A chorus of shrill wolf whistling blew in their direction as Katie and Miss Banzai strolled across the forecourt.

"Hey, baby, c'mon over here!"

"C'mon, why don'tya, we'll show yew a good time!"

Aiko rolled her eyes.

"Gentlemen prefer blondes," she said out of the side of her mouth.

Katie Kopinski gave them a big grin as she hip swayed on by.

"Sorry, boys," she jerked a thumb towards the waiting tour bus. "But I got places t'be."

The cowboys groaned, and made grand imploring gestures.

"Aw, don't be like thet, baby...!"

"C'mon now, baby, and––!"

Light spilled onto the shadowed porch as the door banged open. A bulky figure emerged, as broad as he was tall, his big belly threatening to pop the buttons of the red plaid shirt that flapped around his knees. He had a massive head and no neck, his hair cropped down to short greasy stubble. His eyes were framed by scar tissue and his nose had been broken many times. He exuded violence.

"How many times do I gotta tell yew redskins t'stay the hell away from here?"

His hands were massive, with enlarged and scarred knuckles. In both, he had a fistful of shirt collar, belonging to two slender, dark-skinned teenagers, one dangling, the other dragged, feet scrabbling on the planking.

"If I see yew aroun' here agin," he rasped harshly. "I'm gonna break yer goddam spines!"

He let go and the boys rolled in the dirt. Aiko sensed Cat tense beside her and reached out to touch her arm.

"No," she whispered. "Now's not the time."

The cowboys were guffawing and saluted the proprietor by raising their beer bottles up high. Glaring, the big man stomped back onto the porch and disappeared inside.

Katie Kopinski just stretched out her long legs and stepped over the boys as they sat there gasping on the ground. Miss Banzai marched ahead with her nose in the air. The wolf whistles followed them all the way to the door.

There was even a telephone in the bus.

"Tell me…"

Lana Kent was watching, veiled by the tinted glass of a top window. Her eyes were fixed upon the sway of Katie's hips.

"I think I may have something special for you."

Kicking the door open, Cat came out first, hefting a tower of clanking beer crates. Aiko followed, a large brown paper bag under each arm, stuffed with candy bars and all kinds of treats.

Progressing smoothly down off the porch and out onto the forecourt Cat peered around the side of the crates, to see where she was going.

"Just keep going straight," Aiko grinned. "You're doing fine."

"Gee thanks," Cat muttered. "Don't strain yourself, will you?"

They heard a gunshot; the sound of shattering glass.

"Now jest yew hold still, Geronimo, dontya move now…."

Cat put the crates down.

"Oh shit," said Aiko.

The two boys stood side by side in the middle of the forecourt, their dark eyes wide in their round brown faces. One had bits of glass in his long black hair, matted and sticky. His plain white shirt was stained and his scuffed sneakers stood in a puddle of beer and broken bottle.

"Don' even breathe, Tonto, I gotta 10-spot ridin' on this…"

The boy's companion stood quite still, with his arms down by his side. Still capped, a full beer bottle was perched on the top of his head. His eyes held a kind of dull resignation, as if he was accustomed to being treated like this.

"Go on, Richie, do it…!"

"Go fer it!"

Blue steel gleamed as the cowboy slowly lifted a long-barreled revolver. The click of it cocking carried clearly across the illuminated forecourt.

Cat sucked in her breath sharply. She turned and looked at Aiko, her eyes pleading.

Aiko's eyes were burning. Setting down the paper bags, she nodded.

Cat let her breath out slowly. She reached behind her, beneath the short jacket. Quickly and precisely, she drew the compact automatic, a nickel-plated Walther PPK. In a single fluid motion, she took aim and fired.

"YOW!"

Dropping his gun, the cowboy jumped two feet off the ground. He fell back against the flank of his pickup and slid down, rolling around, clutching his shattered hand.

His pals just stood and stared down at him, as he thrashed about screaming. Cat strolled towards them, the pistol traversing from one to the other. Wide-eyed, they thrust their hands up high.

"Hey, baby, yew cool it now…!"

"Heck, we was just funnin'!"

The door grated open on its rusty hinges. Heavy feet made the porch planks creak.

"What the fuck is it now?"

The imposing bulk of the proprietor was advancing, with surprising speed for such a big man. He glared at the two boys.

"Yew damn redskins still here? I told ya––!"

He saw the stricken cowboy, curled up in the dirt whimpering, cradling his mangled fingers. He stared in amazement at his friends, with their arms up in the air. He looked at the gun in Cat's hand, his battered lips twisting.

"So yew likes t'play with guns, huh gurlie…?"

His piggy eyes were like black pebbles, glittering viciously.

"Jeez, Verne!" one of the cowboys whined. "We was jest havin' sum fun, thet's all…!"

The big man glared at him.

"Keep a tight ass, Red, I'll handle this."

Glowering, he held out a vast, shovel-like paw.

"Now, yew hand me over thet pretty little pop-gun, slut, 'afore I gives ya a spankin'."

Her face a cold mask, Cat tossed the pistol to Aiko. She caught it deftly and had the cowboys covered before they could blink.

Cat looked Verne up and down, her eyes frosting with contempt.

"Take your best shot, tough guy."

The big man's mouth contorted into a mirthless grin.

"Go git 'er, Verne!"

He came forward, his great arms swinging.

"I'm gonna hurt yew, sweetcheeks, I'm gonna hurt yew bad...!"

Cat just stood and waited for him.

"Bust 'er up good, Verne!"

He grabbed for her. She wasn't there.

"YAAAHH!"

She dipped her shoulder and dematerialized and Verne's great bulk was suddenly featherlight and flying through the air.

"OOOOOFFF!"

He landed hard, raising dust, the wind jolted out of him.

"Uuu...uuhh....hhh..."

Panting, he rolled over and struggled to his hands and knees.

"I'm over here."

She was standing tall, her long hair shining like pale gold, garlanded by the strands of bright bulbs. She was blinding, and he blinked and rubbed his eyes.

"No, over here."

And then she was behind him, as he lurched to his feet and stood there swaying, gasping for breath.

And then she was right in front of him, smiling.

"B-B-B-Bitch...!"

He lunged, his fist propelled like a battering ram. He expected to feel her face crumble and see it crushed into a bloody pulp.

"YAAAAAHHH....!"

Still smiling, she simply swayed out of the way. Bellowing, he swung again and again, his arms wind milling.

"...AAAAAA...HHHH...!"

Cat slipped and swayed and danced around him. Exhausted, Verne stood hunched over, with his broad shoulders heaving, his panting breath rasping hoarsely.

Cat slapped him, hard, rocking his head sideways and making sweat spray.

"Is that all you've got, tough guy?"

She slapped him again.

"Come on, tough guy!"

Spitting curses, he lurched towards her.

The edge of her hand whispered across his windpipe.

"AHHKK-KK-K-KK...!"

His eyes bulged. His face went beet red and then purpled. He sank slowly to his knees, gagging, drool spilling from his twisted lips, both hands clutching at his throat.

Cat stood over him. Her fist traveled a short distance and impacted just behind his ear.

"UH!"

Verne's eyes rolled up till only the whites showed. He toppled forward and fell on his face. His leg twitched once, twice, a long breath sighed out of him and he was still.

"All done?" asked Aiko.

The cowboys stood frozen, their eyes wide and amazed, darting from Cat to the gun in Aiko's hand.

"Yes thanks. I enjoyed that."

"Maybe too much," Aiko suggested.

"Maybe."

She prodded Verne with her toe. He stirred and groaned, blowing bubbles. Retrieving the Walther, she took a step towards the cowboys, who backed up hastily, bumping into the pick-ups. One nearly fell over their wounded companion, who shrieked, rolling around.

"Now, yew boys jest pick up yer buddy there," she remembered to talk like Katie. "An' git!"

They stared at her blankly. She flourished the gun.

"Go on, git!"

Car doors slammed, engines revved, tires squealed, crunching on the gritty surface. Tail lights diminished and were gone.

Cat slipped the Walther back into its hiding place. She smiled.

"Aw...."

The two boys were still standing in the middle of the forecourt. One still had the beer bottle on top of his head.

The loungers had all jumped off of the bench on the porch and were standing there with their jaws dropped and eyes wide and amazed. Gliding past the prostrate Verne, Cat sauntered over and plucked away the bottle, tossing it over her shoulder.

She picked bits of glass from the other boy's sticky hair.

"Time to go home, guys," she murmured.

The boys gazed at her with their enormous dark eyes. Their eyes were wary, confused, not knowing whether they could trust themselves to trust her. Then they turned abruptly and ran away, vanished into the surrounding darkness, their padded footfalls sounding softly.

Aiko appeared at Cat's side, the paper bags tucked under her arms.

"You will be spoken of around the campfires," she chuckled.

Cat frowned. She watched the place where the boys had disappeared, her eyes welling.

"Those people have had a raw deal, for a hundred years now. Nothing's changed."

Aiko sobered. She touched Cat's shoulder.

"Let's go."

"Far out!" "Snake" told "The Axe", as he eased out of the seat and returned it to the relieved driver. "That bitch got skills!"

Up top, "Chainsaw" was lost in his chords. "Tank" was mumbling in his drugged sleep and, eyes glazed, "Cannibal" was mesmerized by the head bobbing rhythmically in his lap.

"Oooh, baby...that's sooo good....yeah...."

Lana Kent turned away from the window, her hand over the mouthpiece.

"Yes indeed", she said lowly. "Very special."

The bus had a spacious luggage compartment low down along its side. Cat thumbed the latches and lifted the hatch. She lifted the beer crates in and shoved them deep inside.

"Hold it."

Aiko's slim hand flickered like a magician's. There was a tiny silver box balanced on her palm. She reached in and, magnetic, it glued itself to the metal.

"How's that?"

"That's fine, you can't see it."

"Let's hope it has the range. Who knows where this crazy trip is going to take us."

The big screen glowed green, spanning the entire wall; an electronic grid, a web of roads and highways, the whorls and swirls of contours, cryptic codes and strange hieroglyphs.

On one glowing green artery, a bright red dot winked into life, moving slowly.

Smiling, Selena sat back in her tall leather chair. Long glitter-gold fingernails played a drum roll on the desk top.

"Right on, sistas," she drawled. "Now do yo' thang!"

The "Trading Post" was burning. Tall flames cast writhing shadows; the spit and sizzle, the crack of glass fractured by the heat. The roof buckled in a tower of sparks, fizzing in the night sky.

The door crashed open and for a moment the bulk of the burly proprietor was framed against the red fire raging inside.

"YAAAAA....AAA....HHH....HH...!"

He was wearing a cape of fire. Arms flung out sideways, he lurched off the wooden porch and staggered forwards on splayed legs.

"....AAAAA....HHHH...!"

Muzzle flashes in the dark, stabs of flame, beyond the bubbling lake of light cast by the fire.

"AH!"

He was rocked back on his heels.

"AH!"

"AH!"

He stood stock still, his contorted features frozen. Then his legs buckled and he thudded to his knees.

The muzzle flashes spat again, one-two-three.

"UUUU...HHH.....!"

His arms sagged limply to his sides. Wrapped in flames, he toppled forward on his face.

In the shadows, darker shadows flitted silently. Something flew out of the darkness. It came out the sky, down from the stars. A streak of firelight, it impaled the ground and remained there, quivering; a painted lance, decorated by eagle's feathers.

"Ooooohhh...I'm....sooo-ooo-oo....high....!"

Moonlight turned the winding side roads into ribbons of silver.

"M-me t—t-too...man...I'm flyin'....!"

Tinkling giggles. Unsteady feet scuffling in the grit that blurred the edge of the asphalt.

"...'scuse me...!"

Two boys and two girls. Teenagers, with round brown faces and dark eyes and blue-black hair hanging down past their shoulders.

"....while I kiss the sky...!"

They were dressed in defiance of their elders. The girls clanking with beads and bangles, with bare bold midriffs, the boys in tie-dyed T-shirts and two-tone flares, encrusted with patches proclaiming the slogans of the counter-culture.

Swaying and laughing, they were passing a fat joint around.

"Hey, don't drop––!"

Suddenly, they stopped, looking all around. One of the girls shivered, wrapping her arms around herself.

"It's c-cold...."

And dark. Suddenly it was dark. The world either side of the road was a blank black wall. The moon and the stars had disappeared.

It became colder.

"What's goin' on...what's hap––?"

"Hey! What's that?"

Ahead of them, the road rose in a shallow hump, against the faintest glow of the skyline. A shape rolled slowly to the crest, a blunt, brutal silhouette.

"Hey...!"

As the girls hung back nervously, the boys began to walk up the slope.

"Hey...?"

A low idling rumble, a deep dark vibration that made the soles of their feet tingle and filled their whole bodies.

It was black, black all over; as they approached it they couldn't see through its black glass.

"Hey...?"

Headlamps blazed into life. An eerie green with a searing white core.

The girls shrieked. The boys howled as they were consumed by green fire, as their faces dissolved and their flesh melted from the bone.

Screaming, the girls turned and ran, wild-eyed, running down the road. With a roar, the simmering beast ignited and the black shape surged forward.

Gasping, stumbling, the girls veered sideways off the road, and for an instant were swallowed by the darkness. But the green beams transfixed them, snared them. There was no escape. Helpless, they fell to their knees, sobbing.

Yike!

Cat swayed, as a great warm wind rocked her back on her high heels.

"Holy––!" exclaimed Aiko, astounded.

Swirling searchlights played over the crowd that filled the football field and overflowed up onto the terraces. Baying, it surged forward and back like a great tide, a sea of hands waving and making the twin-horns sign, of bright, upturned young faces, with wide eyes and shouting mouths.

There were figures clambering nimbly up the swaying goalposts, clinging there precariously. In vain, an anxious voice issued from the PA system, urging them to desist. It was swallowed by a rhythmic chant, to the crashing beat of clapping hands:

"Six-Six-Six !--Six-Six-Six!»

The stage was a shallow semi-circle, projecting into the rippling tide of waving hands and excited faces. It was sunk in semi-darkness, red pin lights picking out the towering stacks of amplifiers.

"SIX-SIX-SIX!--SIX-SIX-SIX!»

Suddenly, an eruption of thunder, a primeval drumbeat and in the sizzling white cone of a spotlight there was "Cannibal", his naked torso gleaming, hair flying, his face contorted manically, pounding the skins, the drumsticks like clubs in his hands.

Stage left, there was the mighty frame of "Tank", bathed in a blood red light, hunched over his bass, pumping out his subterranean, bone crushing sound. The kids whooped, delighted, as they felt their ribs bend and their chests compress.

And then it was like the tops of their skulls were being sliced off, by the slashing chords that "Chainsaw" was ripping from the strings, as he materialized in a glare of eerie green. And there, standing on top of his stack of amps, his left hand a blur on the fret board, "The Axe", impaling the crowd with notes like volleys of lightning bolts—still playing as he leapt from the summit, still playing as he landed lightly and rolled, still playing as he slid on his knees to the edge of the stage, as he sprang to his feet and struck a pose.

"YAAAAAAAA...AAAAAAAAA–HHHH...HHHHHH...!"

A long runway extended from the stage, projecting into the crowd. It lit up, a shaft of silver. Then, all along the rim of the stage, there was a mighty detonation and tall fountains of sizzling sparks.

"....AAAAAAAAAAA....AAAAHHHH....HHHHHHHHHH....!"

"Snake" was striding out through the curtain of fire. He wore a golden cape, a tall top hat adorned by flashing mirrors. He strutted along the illuminated runway, gazing out imperiously across the sea of adoring faces, the surging tide of hands reaching out to him. The noise was a physical thing, battering and churning.

Jesus!

Cat/Katie was close behind him, high stepping like a model on a catwalk. She was displayed in a skimpy concoction of studded black leather, with a spiked collar and knee-high boots like black glass with perilous heels.

The noise was a hot wind, scalding her skin. Her ears were suffering.

This is insane!

As the band riffed on, "Snake" reached the end of the runway. In his right hand, he held the mike. In his left there was a long leash of tiny chain links. The leash was attached to a velvet collar and in the collar was Aiko/Miss Banzai, in the revealing costume of a fantasy slave girl.

Aiko glanced at Cat and raised an eyebrow. Cat rolled her eyes. Behind them, the wall of sound segued into a familiar opening riff. The crowd howled in recognition, making them flinch and take a step backwards.

"Snake" raised the microphone to his thin lips. Aiko pretended to struggle on the end of the chain, "Snake" tugged and she fell to her knees. Cat strode forward and stood over her. She had a long bullwhip in her hand. She flourished it, made it slither across Aiko's body. Aiko made a show of cringing and cowering at "Snake"'s feet. Looking up, she winked at Cat.

Oh stop that! You'll make me laugh!

A boy in the crowd somehow squeezed between two giant security men. Before they could stop him he was scrambling up onto the runway and hurling himself fervently at his hero.

Panic flared in "Snake"'s eyes, the lyrics stuttered as he stepped back and almost fell over Aiko.

Sorry man...

Elegantly, Cat extended a long leg and planted her high heel in the center of the boy's chest. She thrust effortlessly and he was hurled off the runway. He was held up on the upraised hands and carried backwards, spread eagled. Then he vanished, his gaping face sucked downwards.

Relieved, Cat saw him pop up again, gasping for air. One of the security men decided to make an example of him and was advancing, shoving the kids out of his way, his big fists clenched.

Oh no you don't!

With a flick of her wrist, Cat made the whip curl up and out and coil itself around the security man's fat neck. He staggered and fell and the kids all danced, cheering.

Forgetting herself, Cat took a bow. "Snake" glared at her. Puffing out his narrow chest, he ordered her gone with a commanding gesture.

Okay, okay...

Cat/Katie bowed again, deeply, and to him this time. He tossed her the leash and she led Miss Banzai away, back down the runway towards the stage.

Asshole!

This was a private ceremony, deep and dark and underground.
"Take this our offering...."
The temple was a sunken bowl of glistening granite, descending in concentric terraces. Lit by a pulsing amber torchlight, it was ringed by a wall of tall archways, their fathomless depths lost in shadow. Within each archway stood a strange figure, cloaked and cowled in grey, hands folded in front, resting on the jeweled pommel of a long sword, point down on the flagstones.
"....oh Master...!"

"This way, ladies...."
The changing rooms were down a long yellow-lit corridor, underneath the stadium. Lana Kent was brisk and impatient.
"Come on! Come on!"
She wrenched the door open. It exhaled a warm breath of beer and sweat and marijuana, a gust of male voices raised in triumph.
Breathless, their pretty painted faces bright with anticipation, the eager groupies piled inside. Lana slammed the door behind them, muffling the welcoming hoot and holler, the raunchy guffaws and giggles.
"Sluts....!"

In the well of the bowl stood a mighty slab of black marble, veined by pale crystal.
"Oooo...ooohhh..."
"....N-N-nooo....oooo...!"
The girls lay stretched out side by side, bound by the wrists and ankles. Their writhing bodies gleamed, coppery, in the torchlight.
"To you this offering...."
Their eyes were wide and wild with terror, glaring through the veil of their tangled dark hair, as they tossed their heads from side to side, straining frantically against their bonds.
"....oh Master...!"
A strange figure loomed into their field of vision; tall and broad-shouldered, draped in black that swirled with each slow measured stride

to reveal a scarlet lining. A black mask gazed down upon them, with slanting eyes outlined in red, crowned by curved horns.

"N-N-N-n-nooooo...oooo...!"

In its gloved hand, the apparition raised a knife, slowly and deliberately, its curved blade shining. The knife quivered above them, poised to strike.

"....p-p-pleeeeze....!"

Flashing, the blade descended.

Lana Kent moved on down the corridor, to another door, and knocked.

"Come in."

Miss Banzai sat on a long bench, wrapped in an embroidered robe, restoring herself with the aid of a hand mirror.

"Great show, girls", said Lana as she entered. "Did you enjoy——?"

Katie Kopinski stepped out of the shower, naked and dripping, drying her long hair with a towel.

"Oh yeah!" she drawled. "We sure knocked 'em dead!"

She rubbed the towel slowly all over her body. Forgetting to breathe, Lana stood and stared.

Enjoying the show...?

Katie held out her hand and, dumbly, Lana handed her a blue towel bathrobe.

"Uh...yes...," she blurted. "It was a great gig...."

Katie grinned at her, cinching up the robe at her waist.

"Yep, the band was cookin' alright."

I'm going to wear earplugs next time!

Swiveling round on the bench, Miss Banzai frowned.

"Why do I always have to be the slave?"

Katie laughed, turning her back. Lana's eyes rolled across her strong shoulders.

"Well, my dear, somehow I can't picture your friend as a submissive."

Aiko went "Hmph!" Katie laughed again.

"Hey?" she asked. "Anybody seen my undies?"

She was grinning right at Lana.

"Oh yeah, there they are."

Katie pointed. Lana saw the wisp of Katie's tiger-print G-string, draped over the open door of a metal locker, the matching brassiere fallen to the tiled floor.

"Hand them t'me, will ya?"

Those mocking eyes seemed to bore right through her. Lana went rigid, her face turning to stone.

"Get them yourself!"

The door crashed shut behind her.

"This way, Sir...."

"We're all ready for you...."

They bowed and scraped before him, retreating as he made his stately progress down the carpeted corridors.

"You'll be on air in just 10 minutes...."

The Reverend was in his pomp, in one of his trademark cream-colored suits. His host was more used to turning up casually to work, in a Hawaiian shirt and ragged blue jeans. But today he was stuffed into the brown suit he'd last worn to a wedding five years ago. It didn't fit him anymore and he gave up trying to button the jacket, as Reverend Calhoun stepped imperiously into the modest radio studio.

The radio jock was sweating as he jumped up from his seat and stepped forward to greet his guest. He was a short, squat man and had to tilt his head back and look way up to meet that steely gaze. The hand he offered was moist and the Reverend gripped it briefly before letting it drop.

"S-So g-glad to have you here, Rev...er...Sir, I'm Don Weston...p-please take a seat....!"

Don Weston blushed as the Reverend tugged the silk handkerchief from his breast pocket and wiped his palm with it. Stumbling, he ushered his guest to a chair and a microphone.

"If you w-would....Sir...."

The red light went on –– **ON AIR**

Don Weston was adjusting the bulky headphones clamped to his ears.

"Good morning to all of you in this great state of ours and to all our neighbors, welcome one and all to the Breakfast Hour here on Radio KWUT....!"

Reverend Calhoun sat impassively. He glanced sideways at a water jug set down before him and someone tiptoed forward quickly and filled the glass for him.

"....it is my great pleasure...and immense privilege...to introduce to you this morning a very special guest...someone known to you all for his integrity and moral leadership....Reverend Thaddeus P. Calhoun!"

With a quick thumbs-up, he gave the Reverend his cue. The oration lasted half an hour, unscripted, his voice resonant and compelling, urging a nation that was on the road to hell to make a stand against a rising tide of chaos and dissention.

He ended with a rousing battle cry.

"....this is a call to arms, my friends....TO ARMS!"

A rosy dawn made the desert pink. It was going to be another beautiful day.

....TO ARMS...!

Two trucks made up a small convoy, rolling swiftly down the road in a halo of dust that glowed pinkly, towards the pale disk of the rising sun.

....TO ARMS...!

The trucks were twins, heavy-duty Army issue, olive drab and canvas-topped, with freshly stenciled serial numbers and insignia and in large yellow letters: NATIONAL GUARD.

....TO ARMS...!

It wasn't a town, not even a village, just a few wooden and adobe boxes in a cluster going up a shallow slope tufted with scrub, a few animals in a pen fenced by teetering rails, some chickens scratching around.

A tattered curtain that made a door twitched aside and a small naked brown child wandered out, with an upturned basin of blue-black hair that hung down to its eyebrows. He took a pee, amusing himself by making a pattern in the dirt. Then he began stalking the chickens, which scuttled away in short measures each time he approached.

A young man emerged, blinking and yawning, stripped to the waist, with dark hair that flowed to his shoulders. He stretched and scratched himself. A cigarette was dangling from his lower lip and he was patting the pockets of his faded denims, searching for his lighter.

"Hey, leave them chickens alone...."

Pouting, the child sat down on the ground and began scratching with a stick.

"Your momma's gonna spank you if––"

There was a rattle of rifle fire.

"UH!"

Arms out flung, the young man was hurled backwards, crashing to the ground. He lay motionless, the cigarette still fixed between his lips.

….TO ARMS…!

Another volley and a splintering of glass, a woman's scream inside. Suddenly, there were figures moving on the ragged ridge above the houses, coming down the slope.

….TO ARMS….!

A man burst out into the daylight, working the lever of a Winchester carbine, a blue plaid shirt flapping around his bare knees. There was a short burst of automatic fire and the blue became red and ragged. The man was slammed back against the wall of the shack, sliding down to the ground.

….TO ARMS…!

After that, they came out with their hands in the air; seven men and five women, three with small children clinging to their skirts, their dark eyes huge in their frightened faces. The Guardsmen formed a shallow crescent in front of them, booted and helmeted, in full combat gear.
 Gesturing with the barrels of their rifles, the Guardsmen herded the women and children to one side. The men were prodded and shoved till they stood in a line with their backs to a cracked adobe wall.
 The women began to wail and sob. Some fell to their knees. Confused, but seeing their mothers crying, the children began to sob also.
 "No!" one of the men took a step forward. "You can't do this!"
 The officer, a baby-faced lieutenant, raised his .45 and shot the man through the forehead. His men began firing and went on firing until their magazines were empty.

….TO ARMS…!

Howling, the women clawed at the corpses. The children stood where they were, sobbing.
 The lieutenant turned on his heel and began marching up the slope, making for the ridge. There was no sound, no word of command. The Guardsmen's faces were set in stone, their eyes dull and unblinking.

"Can you speak?"
"Yes, I'm alone, I…."
"I monitored the police radio."

"The experiment was a success. A great success."

The trucks veered off the road and drove deep into the desert. They scraped to an abrupt halt, parking side by side.

The young lieutenant vaulted out over the tailgate, down to the ground. Walking slowly round to the front, he opened the door of the cab. The driver sat rigid, staring straight ahead. The lieutenant shot him.

He strolled across to the other truck and shot the second driver. Then he shot himself.

Under the canvas awnings of the trucks, the Guardsmen sat motionless, staring across at each other with their dull dead eyes. They plucked grenades from their belts. They pulled the pins.

"Our power is growing…"
"Yes!"
"We will soon achieve our goal…the Day of Doom is nigh!"

CHAPTER 8

HIJACK

"Heeeyyy...yyy... m-m-man...looka th' p-pretty lights...!"

Leaning over him, the young driver reeled backwards as "Snake" stood on the brakes.

"...f-f-f-far...out...!"

The bright yellow beams of the headlights flayed back and forth across the glistening blacktop as the big bus rocked and rolled and slithered to a stop, slewing sideways across the road.

"What the––!"

Seated in a plush armchair, Lana Kent was jolted backwards, her wine propelled out of its glass, soaking her cleavage.

"Yike!"

Aiko was spun off her bar stool. Arms flailing, Cat lost her balance and sat down hard, cushioned by the deep carpet.

"Shit!"

"Jeez!"

"Chainsaw"'s search for the lost chord ended on a discordant note as the guitar was jarred from his hands and landed at his feet. "The Axe" staggered and played a bum note. His face contorted in fury. He never played a bum note!

"What the f––!"

A half-naked girl slid off "Cannibal"'s lap. "Tank" rolled heavily off the sofa, stirred and then went back to sleep, mumbling into the carpet.

"Whooo!"

Slammed forward then back in the driver's seat, "Snake" whooped and slapped his palms hard on the steering wheel.

"Whooo...eeee....!"

Pale-faced and gulping for air, the driver put a hand on his shoulder.

"Uh, maybe I'd better take over."

"Snake"'s eyes were hard and bright and a little bit crazy. Blinking, he put his face close to the glass and peered out at the lights.

"Yeah, m-man...," he giggled. "Maybe you'd b-b-better..."

The lights were red, white and blue and formed a flashing chain across the highway, mounted on police cars, parked to make a barricade. There was a cluster of lights behind them, more cars, and men standing around them, bristling with gun barrels.

Cursing, Lana Kent glared from a high window.

"Uh-oh!" said Cat. "It's the Heat."

She was shoved out of the way, by Lana moving briskly around the lushly appointed lounge. She plucked a fat joint from "Chainsaw"'s lips, scooped up some purple pills from the bar top, some little plastic bags.

"Here," she dropped it all into Aiko's cupped hands. "Flush this down the can!"

Aiko crossed the lounge swiftly and vanished through an archway screened by a beaded curtain. They heard the toilet flushing.

"Now you all just keep your mouths shut!"

She leaned over a chromed rail to shout down the curving, carpeted stairs.

"Snake, get the hell up here!"

He ascended, still giggling, his eyes getting crazier by the second.

"Hey, g-guys...wha's happnin'...?"

Snarling, Lana grabbed Cat by the arm.

"Katie, sit on him!"

Grinning broadly, Cat marched "Snake" to a vacant armchair, shoved him down into it and wrapped herself around him, entwining him with her arms and legs, her embrace muffling his protests.

Aiko came back into the lounge. She stooped to look out of the window.

"Here they come."

They heard the doors of the bus hiss open and voices interrogating the driver. There were three of them, coming up the stairs; two big patrolmen, cradling pump-action riot guns, preceded by their sergeant, a burly bull-necked man with the battle-scarred face of a former boxer.

"What's the problem, officer?" Lana Kent stepped forward, all smiles.

The sergeant had his hand on the butt of his holstered pistol. He stared straight past her as he led his men into the lounge. He stopped and stood in the middle of the room, hands on hips, surveying the scene with blatant contempt.

He looked at the occupants of the lounge, one at a time. He looked at them hard and one by one they dropped their eyes and gazed at the floor. Lana cleared her throat nervously. She nodded towards the windows, alive with the lightshow on the road.

"Er...surely this can't all be for our benefit...?"

The sergeant hooked his thumbs into his belt, puffing out his barrel chest.

"Yew picked up any strangers on the road?"

They all shook their heads vigorously. "Tank" sat up ponderously, rubbing his eyes.

"Uh...what...?"

The sergeant stood looking down at him. He looked all around. He was sniffing the air. His eyes glowed with suspicion and opportunity.

His men read his thoughts.

"Hey Sarge..."

"...y'know, we oughta turn this here fancy palace over..."

Lana's shoulders sagged. The sergeant was nodding.

"Yew betcha," he replied.

His men were stepping forward, hefting the shotguns. Lana retreated, her mouth opening and closing.

"Aw, c'mon Sarge..."

Cat/Katie flowed to her feet. As the cops advanced she sashayed towards them, grinning broadly, her hips slow-rolling. She was wearing a skimpy tanned leather bra with beaded fringes and faded blue jeans way down on her hips.

"Yew don' wanna be wastin' yer time on us," she jerked a thumb at the chain of lights strung across the highway. "Yew got bigger fish t' fry..."

Approaching the sergeant, she made her pelvis arch provocatively towards him. She leered at him saucily.

"C'mon, Big Guy..."

He stared. At the fabulous breasts, ready to tumble out of those scanty cups, at those naked hips, offered to him.

"...it'll be worth it..."

She was back in 15 minutes, stomping up the stairs. Her hair was tossed and she was scrubbing her lips with the back of her hand.

"Jeez!"

She bent back, flexing her spine.

"The ground sure is hard. I ain't done it like thet fer a long time!"

They all stared at her, astonished. Snatching a whiskey bottle from the floor between "Cannibal"'s feet, she twisted the cap off and took a big swig. Sloshing it around in her mouth, she tilted her head back and gargled loudly, then bent across the bar top and spat into a small wash basin.

She glanced out of the window. There was a gap forming in the chain of lights.

"I think we can go now."

The black mountain was a hulking phantom, a darker shadow looming, blotting out a starless sky. Its rugged slopes were silent, lifeless.

Nothing moved, nothing breathed, no breeze to freshen the dry sterility.

Then there was movement, something emerging from the mountain top; and a sound, a faint mechanical humming.

Gleaming dully, a metal stalk was extending, telescoping upwards, higher and higher. It was topped by a tall, furled leaf-like spike which began to bend back till it projected sideways at 45 degrees. Then it began to open like a fan, expanding, multiplying itself in long steel petals, in a circle, till it was joined as a great dish, a shallow bowl tilted up towards the sky.

"I...c-can't...g-g-go any...!"
In the darkness, someone stumbled and fell.
"You g-gotta...leave...me...!"
Feet scrabbled for purchase on a shifting slope, pebbles rolled and skittered, a sliding carpet underfoot.
"Hold on!"
A ragged horizon was picked out by a shifting glow and there were headlamps and flashlight beams criss-crossing.
"I'm comin'!"
Getting closer, the sound of engines revving, urgent voices, dogs barking.
"We can make it, man! Keep goin'!"

The humming intensified and became a shrill vibration. The metal petals quivered as the dish began to rotate slowly.

The bus had a shower, a glass box with barely enough room to turn around in but nevertheless a shower.

Your body is a weapon, Cat told herself. *Just like any other*.

She soaped and scrubbed herself briskly, and re-entered the lounge wrapped in a short white towel robe that showed off her long strong legs. She was glowing, golden and all talk ceased as they turned to stare at her.

"Fuckin' A, baby!" said "Chainsaw", fan faring her with a flurry of dramatic chords, rasping from a small practice amp.

"Yo...!"

Half asleep, "Tank" tipped her the twin-horned salute. "The Axe" dipped in a courtly bow.

"Snake" jumped up out of the armchair and practically stood to attention. His mouth opened and shut but all he could say was "wow!"

Heey...yyy...Momma!"

"Cannibal" heaved himself to his feet and his girl, who was totally naked now, was tumbled onto the carpet again.

"That was some show...a real turn on...!"

Cat took a step back out of the range of his body odor.

Yeah well turn yourself off man

Aiko was shaking her head and smiling. Perched on the bar top, she bent close and put her lips to Cat's ear.

"I can't wait to read about this in the report," she whispered.

Cat made a face.

"I think we'll just edit this out", she muttered, and then louder: "Pour me a cold one, willya!"

Grinning, Aiko swung her slim legs up and over and dropped down nimbly behind the counter. Beer gurgled into a glass.

The metal dish was turning, faster and faster...

Tucked to the side of the road, the bus slumbered, some where they lay, some fallen into their bunks.

All except Lana Kent, who was on the telephone.

"Speak..."

"I was right about her. She is the one. The Master will be delighted."

...as the humming intensified and became a shrill whistle that threatened to split the sky.

Soft lighting and hushed tones muted the Control Tower's martial purpose. Bathed in a gentle green glow, men hunched over their screens and twinkling control panels, watching closely and listening intently to the muffled radio chatter that came in bursts through their bulky headsets.

"Flight zero-two-seven, you are cleared for take-off..."

Panoramic windows gave a 360-degree view. Outside, in the darkness, the runways were picked out by their borders of bright beacons, narrowing to a distant vanishing point. On the fringe of a vast darkness beyond, floodlit hangars clustered in pools of light, hives of activity as maintenance went on through the night.

"Roger that. We are ready for take-off."

A tall man with a lot of silver braid on his cap was standing at the window, his hawk-like profile etched by the green glow. A subordinate hovered in attendance, glancing nervously at a clipboard.

"We're ready to go, General."

The tall man held out his hand and took charge of the clipboard. He glanced at it briefly.

"Are you sure this is going to work, Colonel? The last time they couldn't even find the goddamn target."

The Colonel cleared his throat.

"Uh, yes sir, General. The bugs have all been ironed out now."

He gestured towards a group of men, seated at a distance from the others, at a console shoe-horned at an awkward angle into an available space. These men were civilians, in their shirt sleeves, the light from their green screens reflected eerily in the thick lenses of their spectacles, perspiration gleaming on their drawn and nervous faces.

"We can guide them blindfold right onto the target...we––"

"And what's the target this time? Something real I hope, not just some bull's eye painted in the sand."

"Er, yes sir. We've replicated an enemy missile launch command center, General. Genuine concrete bunkers and even dummy missiles and launchers. Just like the real thing, sir."

"Good. Because I'll be wanting to go and see the damage for myself tomorrow."

"Yes sir! I think you'll be pleased, sir. There will be no interference this time."

"I'd damn well better be! This time I want our boys to be hearing my commands in those cockpits, not some goddamn local rock and roll radio station!"

Oh yes, you are special!

Lana Kent hesitated, as she made her way down the narrow corridor that ran between the stacks of well-upholstered sleeping berths.

But you don't know it yet

Cat always slept naked. As Lana passed by, she twisted, murmuring, smiling in her sleep. A thin blanket slipped from her bare shoulder, and there was the revelation of a glorious breast, its coral tip aroused by some subconscious excitement.

Entranced, Lana put out her hand, like a child. She wanted to touch it. Then she frowned and withdrew her hand abruptly and put it to her mouth, biting down on the knuckles, stifling the groan that rose in her throat.

No! I am not worthy. You are meant for higher things!

Heavy metal thunder.
"King Bee to Swarm...vector nine-oh-five..."
"Roger King Bee..."
A lean lizard bobbed up, alert, its senses jangling. With a flick of its tail it slipped into a crack. The jack-rabbit's long ears twitched. It vanished down its hole. A stalking bobcat froze, then cowered, as the sky seemed to come roaring down to crush it.
"...nine-oh-five..."
They flew low, rising and dipping to follow the undulations of the desert. Boulder and scrub were streaked by speed, a rush of silver in the moonlight.
"Swarm to King Bee... estimate 12 minutes to target..."
Fleeting phantoms, flickering by in the blink of the eye, like darts hurled across the star spangled sky. Three silver F-100 Super Sabers in a tight arrowhead, their swept back wings bristling with ordinance.
"This is King Bee...confirmed...12 minutes to target..."
In the control tower the civilians shifted nervously in their seats. They could feel the General's hot breath on the back of their necks.
"Uh, it's looking good, General..."
The chief scientist had tugged off his glasses and was scrubbing the lenses with a handkerchief.
"In five minutes we'll be switching them over to automatic guidance."
The General grunted skeptically.
"It had better work this time. Last time we tested this newfangled gizmo of yours, two out of three failed to find the target and the one that did dropped its bombs a mile wide."
The chief scientist's face was shining with sweat, a sickly green in the light from his screens. He mopped his brow, and then fumbled to replace his spectacles, almost dropping them.
"Oh, it'll work this time, General, I assure you..."

The spinning dish became a blur. Its shrill song achieved a pitch that was barely audible. Sand and grit was bouncing on the ground, which vibrated like a drum skin. Small stones rolled and tumbled. A jagged boulder quivered and shifted and then split down the middle with a resounding crack.

"Look!"
"What's that?"

The tour bus was dark and silent, parked for the night on the fringe where the asphalt blurred into the desert sand.

"I don't believe it..."

"This is our chance!"

The General saw the chief scientist's shoulders tense, his brow furrow. "What? What is it?"

They were dragged from their bunks and herded into the lounge.

"Wha...?" mumbled "Tank", stirring on the sofa.

"What the f--!" yelled "Cannibal", rubbing his eyes. The naked girl sat up blinking in the light, then screamed when she saw the guns, throwing her arms around herself.

"Now don't anybody panic and no one will get hurt!"

There were four of them, all in black, their features concealed by black ski masks. The speaker was taller and broader in the shoulder, his gloved hands grasping an old lever-action Winchester. His companions were uniformly short and stocky; one stood at his leader's side, aiming a stubby M-1 carbine from the hip; the other brought up the rear, laboring to support a wounded comrade, a slighter figure that shivered, moaning lowly.

"We don't want to hurt anyone but we'll do what we have to!"

Their captives wore what they had been sleeping in. Her back pressed to the bar counter, Lana Kent held together the plunging neckline of a pink silk negligee. "Snake"'s modesty was preserved only by tiny black leather briefs. "Chainsaw" was enveloped by an oversized Dallas Cowboys football shirt, hanging down to his knees. "The Axe" always slept in the black T-shirt, with the bloody "666"; and surprisingly uncool Y-fronts.

"Okay, okay, we get the message...!"

Cat had wrapped the thin blanket around herself. Prodded by the muzzle of the carbine, she stumbled as it tangled in her toes. Fetching in embroidered silk pajamas, Aiko reached out to steady her.

"Thanks!"

A groan came from the young driver, as he swayed and sagged against the bar. He was clutching the back of his head, blood seeping through his fingers. Cat and Aiko caught and supported him, as he sank slowly to the floor.

Cat shot an accusing glance at the leader.

"You didn't have to do that."

His eyes were hard and bright, through the slits in the black mask. Cat stared back, till he dropped his eyes. Then she bent to cradle the driver's bloody head, while Aiko pressed a folded bar towel to his wound.

"Heey...m-man..."

Lana's eyes went wide with panic as "Snake" lurched forward, a cocktail of chemicals scrambling his brain. She tried to grab his arm but he shrugged past her on rubber legs, gesturing haphazardly.

"...it's cool, m-m-man..."

Struggling to focus, he clapped an unsteady hand on the tall man's shoulder.

"...like...we're with you, m-man..."

And brandished a clenched fist under his nose.

"...f-f-fight the P-Power...man...!"

Cursing, the tall man speared "Snake" in the chest hard with the muzzle of the Winchester. With a yell, arms flailing, "Snake" backpedaled rapidly and performed a backward somersault over the sofa and the supine and groggy "Tank". They saw him disappear and heard him land heavily and all that they heard from him after that was the occasional moan.

The chief scientist was sweating and his glasses were fogging up.

"I don't believe it!"

Frantically, he hunched over the console, twiddling knobs and flicking switches, his anxious features garish in the glow of the screens.

"This can't be happening!"

The others were staring, wide-eyed, at the gun in the tall man's hands. Aiko nodded and Cat rose slowly to her feet.

"You have a wounded man there. Let me see."

The fury faded from the tall man's eyes. He hesitated for a moment, and then stood aside.

Lana Kent's eyebrows arched with surprise.

You've changed your tune. What's happened to Katie Kopinski?

They laid the slim figure on the carpet. Tucking in her blanket to secure it, Cat advanced swiftly, dropping to her knees. Cutting short the tall man's protest, she pulled off the black ski mask.

"He can't breathe, damn it!"

She sat up straight.

"Oh hell, he's just a boy!"

It was one of the boys from the fracas at the trading post, with his round brown face and long blue-black hair. Recognition flared in his pain-filled eyes and he reached up to her with a trembling hand, his smooth features contorting.

"...A-angel...," he gasped. "...our a-a-avenging...angel...!"

Cat held his hand and pressed it to her cheek. She squeezed his hand tight, and looked deep into his eyes and watched the light go out of them.

"...angel..."

The tall man was looking hard at her, in a way that said "I know of you". Cat glared at him, angry, her eyes welling. She let the boy's limp hand down gently. There was blood on her face.

"You let children do the dying for you!"

The eyes behind the mask were hard and unyielding.

"Boys become men in times of oppression."

Cat stood and stared at him.

"And you can live with that?"

She saw the hardness in his eyes dissolve into sadness and the broad shoulders droop a little. Her eyes overflowed and she hung her head to hide her tears.

There was a taut silence. A sudden sound was Lana Kent knocking over an empty beer bottle with a nervous jerk of her arm. She cleared her throat harshly.

"What are you g-going to d-d-do...with...us...?"

His eyes steeled again. He took a deep breath, squaring his shoulders.

"We're taking this bus," he stated. "And you're all coming with us."

Lana opened her mouth and then shut it. "Cannibal" stood up and then sat down again. "Chainsaw"'s "Heeyy...!" trailed away when the gun barrels jerked in his direction.

Cat was wiping her eyes, angrily, roughly, with the back of her hand. She stepped up to the tall man.

"I'll drive," she said.

The suburbs slept; snug beneath the blue blanket of the night. Here and there, a teenage bedroom glowed dimly, lit by a flashlight hidden under the covers, illuminating Dad's dog-eared copy of "Playboy"; teenage girls giggled in the darkness, conspiring; Mom lay awake staring at the ceiling, unsatisfied, while her husband snuffled and snored beside her.

"Will somebody tell me just what the hell is happening!"

Out over the desert, the steel arrowhead dipped its wings and banked, changing course.

The scientists were all clustered at a single console, leaning anxiously over their chief's shoulder. Beads of sweat dripping from his forehead, his hands were fluttering helplessly.

"I don't understand it," he wailed. "We're transmitting loud and clear, but they're just ignoring it."

He tweaked a knob or two, and then he limply fell back into his chair.

"It's as if something's controlling them!"

The streets were silent and secure, broken only by the raucous squabbling of a pair of rival tomcats, the scuffing soft soles and excited whispers of some boys out on a dare.

"What do you mean controlling them?"

The General's voice boomed like thunder and the scientists recoiled, their frightened faces contorting.

"I-I-I'm s-s-orry...S-Sir...I c-can't explain it..."

In their cockpits, lit by the soft glow of the instruments, the pilots' movements were concise and automatic, made all the more robotic by their domed helmets and the blankness of their visors. The voice in their earphones had been drowned by a kind of rhythmic static.

"Well unscramble it, damn you, and get them back!"

The silver F-100s were locked on now, heading straight and true. On the onrushing horizon, strands of streetlights twinkled.

Satisfied, the housewife rolled off the groaning man who wasn't her husband and sprawled, limbs splayed, panting. Her naked body gleamed with sweat in the silver moonlight that flooded through the open curtains. Her husband's picture grinned at her blandly by the bedside and she flicked it onto the floor with the back of her hand. He was no doubt making hay with some bimbo he picked up at yet another sales conference; revenge tasted sweet, and she started laughing.

The chattering static in their headphones became a pulse, an impulse. They thumbed off the safety catches and lights blinked red. Arming switches "ON".

Out in the street, the boys stopped running and tilted their faces up to the night sky. They looked at each other, puzzled.

"I...I...it's hopeless, General...oh God!"

Cat eased on the brakes. The big bus rolled to a stop, smooth and steady.

"What now?" she asked.

She was dressed as the driver, in his pale blue overalls with the name "Steve" embroidered on the breast pocket, her long hair tucked up into his red baseball cap, her eyes masked by his tinted Ray-Bans.

Hunched over her shoulder, the tall leader tightened his grip on the Winchester.

Up top, the others sat on the floor in a bunch, their hands on their heads, watched over by the hooded men, the muzzles of the carbines twitching nervously.

"Well…?"

Up ahead, another roadblock, nose to tail across the highway, lights flashing, buzzing with urgent radio chatter.

The tall man worked the lever of the Winchester.

"Smash through it!"

Cat gazed at him coolly.

"That's your plan, is it?"

A single figure detached itself from the throng milling behind the barricade and stepped forward out into the open; a big man in a tall cowboy hat, holding a megaphone.

"We know yer in there. Ya don't stand a chance. Put down yer guns and c'mon out with yer hands up!"

Cat rolled her eyes.

"That might be a better plan."

The eyes in the mask were blazing.

"We're not going to die in a white man's jail."

The big man raised the megaphone again.

"Ya got 30 seconds an' then we start shootin'!"

Impulsively, Cat jerked sideways. She leaned out the driver's window and wrenched off the baseball cap, shaking out her long blonde hair.

"Hey! Cool it, you guys! They have hostages!"

A single shot and then a rattle of distant rifle fire. Cat said "Yike!" as a bullet pinged past her ear and ducked back inside.

"Jeez!" she gasped. "These guys mean business!"

The tall man slammed his fist down on the bulky dashboard, more like the flight deck of a jet airliner.

"They'll kill everyone; they'll kill all of you to get us, if they have to, and then say that we did it."

Cat nodded grimly.

"That figures."

She squared her shoulders, wrapping her fist round the handbrake.

"Shall we…?"

His eyes mellowed for an instant, appraising her.

"No," he said. "I'll drive."

It was a feeling, a sensation, coming out of the sky, something approaching, something unseen and undefined.

The boys turned this way and that, looking up and all around them.

"Open fire!"

The silver leviathan roared into life, its battery of headlamps blazing. Tires smoking, it hurled its great bulk forward.

"H-h-hee...yyyy...!"

On the top deck, they were tumbling, rolling on the carpet in a tangle of flailing limbs and startled faces. The masked men were smashing windows with the butts of their carbines.

"Let 'em have it!"

Back and forth, all along the barricade, bright muzzle flashes. The tall man ducked as low as he could, his chin almost touching the steering wheel. Cat threw herself down behind the mighty dashboard.

"Pour it on, boys!"

Bellowing, haloed by a cloud of exhaust that glowed in the moonlight, the bus swerved momentarily, twisted by a surge of power, tilted perilously, then righted and hurtled onward, devouring the distance to the barricade.

The naked housewife sat up suddenly, frowning.

"What's that? Did you hear that?"

Half asleep, the man who wasn't her husband grumbled into the pillow.

"Huh...? Wha...? Hear what...?"

Clumsily, he reached up and dragged her down on top of him. Squirming, she burst out laughing.

They were firing from the top windows but the rocking of the bus made their bullets fly wild.

"Aw...Jeez...!"

Glass shattered. Ragged rents appeared in the real wood veneer of the wall paneling. As shards and splinters rained down on them, the hostages pressed themselves down as flat as they could, crawling behind the furniture, scuttling on their hands and knees for the shelter of the bar counter.

There was a rasp of machine-gun fire, like the sound of canvas tearing. A line of bullet holes was stitched across the panoramic windshield, a web of cracks radiating from them.

"Oh shit!"

The windshield seemed to hang for an instant and then disintegrated, dissolving downwards like a curtain of water, covering them in a million mosaic fragments of glittering glass.

"Fuck this!"

Furious, Cat was raking the bits of glass out of her hair.

These bastards are trying to kill me!

A movie reel of stark images flashed by her angry eyes. The times she'd been hassled by the Heat. The times she'd seen them harass and beat on people because of the length of their hair or the color of their skin.

They want to kill me!

She saw the face of the dead boy.

"Motherfuckers...!"

The tall man had leaned the Winchester on the dash beside him. Startled, he saw Cat jump up and grab it, lift it to her shoulder and open fire, working the lever and firing, her long hair billowing, tossed by an onrushing wind as they roared on to the barricade.

A thin whistle, growing and growing till it became a hideous shriek that split the sky.

"Wha––?"

Rolling thunder overhead, the sky coming down to crush them.

"Run!"

"Let's get out of––!"

The boys stopped running. They stood and stared. They pointed.

"Hey, what's that?"

Tumbling over and over in slow motion, long pale grey cylinders came rolling down out of the night sky. They struck the ground and for a split second looked like they were going to bounce intact right down the middle of the lamp-lit street. Then they ignited, in a great boiling bubbling tidal wave of oily black and orange flame.

"YAAA-AAAA-AA...!"

Engulfed, the boys were incinerated in an instant. Green front lawns became charred and brown. Trees and bushes were transformed into twisted black skeletons. The uniform house fronts bulged and blew outwards, as the roofs peeled off and blew away like dead leaves.

"Look out!"

A roaring monster, the bus bore down on the roadblock and crashed through it, smashing the parked patrol cars aside like feeble tin toys, flipped nose over tail and sent spinning to the dusty fringes of the desert.

Wide-eyed, throwing away their rifles, the cops scattered, diving to safety. One wasn't so lucky and the mighty leviathan hardly noticed as it rolled over him, turning him into a grease spot on the asphalt.

A pathetic, haphazard volley followed it, chasing the receding red tail lights.

"Aw, goddamn it…!"

Thunder made the windows rattle.

The housewife and her lover had an atom of consciousness in which to register the end of their lives.

The core of the explosion first crushed them and then sucked them inside out. The walls buckled inwards and the roof descended, then the entire structure blew outwards, shredded like confetti, stirred by a whirlwind.

The General stood rigid, his features taut and pale. The chief scientist was rocking in his chair, hiding his face in his hands.

"Oh my God oh my God oh my God…!"

Hurtling down the dark highway, the bus was impaled by a shaft of light.

"Fuck!"

Above the boom of the engine they heard the clatter of whirling blades.

"The Pigs have a chopper!"

They had guns too and bullets were coming through the roof. On the top deck everyone yelled and made a dash for the far corners.

"Stop the bus," Cat said calmly.

Levering another round into the breach, she knelt behind the dash. The tall man hunkered down beside her.

"Let me," he suggested.

Cat grinned at him, patting the battered rifle stock.

"I've won trophies for this. You just watch me."

The 'copter was descending, circling the bus slowly, keeping it within the radius of the beam. A megaphone was squawking but they couldn't make out what it was saying.

"Come on…come on…"

She waited till it swung round in front, then she straightened up, lifted the rifle to her shoulder and fired.

"Bull's-eye!"

The beam withered and died. Cat fired again, and again, with obvious effect because the chopper appeared to recoil, leaping upwards and turning its tail before climbing away to a safe distance, its lights shrinking.

Cat handed back the rifle.

"Now's your chance. Get away in the dark while you can."

They stood up, facing each other. He hesitated, then slowly reached up and pulled off the black ski mask.

Oh my!

It was a fierce face, a warrior's face, with eyes that burned with a dark fire, above high chiseled cheekbones. His long black hair tumbled down to his broad shoulders, glossy like the feathers of a bird of prey.

Oh man, you're beautiful!

Suddenly, they were smiling. He reached out and brushed her cheek with his fingertips.

"You're a creature of dreams," he murmured. "A legend."

Cat laughed softly.

"Well, you know, I do okay, but I wouldn't go that far."

Then she was serious.

"Go now. Go!"

They climbed the stairs to the top deck.

"Hey, yew guys okay?"

One by one, they rose from behind the furniture and the cocktail bar and came warily out of the corners.

"It's okay, fellers, yew kin c'mon out now."

Lana Kent was smoothing out creases and fussing with her hair, trying to restore her dignity. She gave Cat a long hard look.

So, Katie's back

On the sofa, "Tank" sat bolt upright, rubbing his eyes.

"Hey...whassup...?"

And all of a sudden everyone was laughing, a raw jangling sound with a hard edge to it.

Embarrassed, "Snake" sucked it up and got his bravado back. He was fingering the bullet holes in the wood paneling.

"Cool....!"

One of the masked men was leaning heavily on his comrade, clutching his shoulder, blood oozing through his fingers. Concerned, the tall man moved towards him.

"Just a flesh wound," said Aiko. "Nothing to worry about".

Her eyes were bright with excitement. She was holding an M-1 carbine.

"So you joined in?" asked Cat.

"It was us or them," Aiko laughed. "You too?"

"Aw shucks," Cat laughed. "I couldn't resist."

They paused in the moonlight, where the highway blended into the desert.

"I'll see you again," said Cat.

"I'll see you in my dreams," he replied.

For a moment, she thought he was going to kiss her. She saw the impulse in his dark eyes.

"Take care," she whispered.

And then he was gone, taking his companions with him, and the limp body of the boy, slung across his shoulders. She hung her head for a moment and when she looked up again they had vanished and the desert was vast and cold and empty.

"Oh my God oh my God oh my God...!"

Regrouped in their tight arrowhead formation, the silver Super Sabers began to climb. For an instant, they were silhouetted against a full Moon.

Then they dipped their wings into a dive. In perfect formation, screaming down and down, straight into the ground, obliterated in a giant fireball.

"Pour me one, will you?"

Aiko was gulping down a large Scotch. Cat slumped onto a bar stool beside her.

"Oh hell, just give me the bottle!"

She tilted her head back, swallowing.

"Phew!" she gasped. "I needed that!"

She frowned at the bloodstains on the plush white carpet.

"Those people are having a bad time of it."

"They've been having a bad time of it for the past hundred years."

Aiko saw anger and the light of battle in Cat's eyes. She shook her head sadly.

"They don't stand a chance you know."

"But they'll go down fighting!"

The band was dashing up and down the stairs, whooping and hollering, counting the bullet holes.

"Hey!" yelled "Snake". "We gotta get some pictures of this for the record cover!"

Looking pale and drawn, Lana sprawled in a deep armchair. She nodded dumbly. She was looking at Cat.

Aiko's brow clouded.

"Speaking of covers," she muttered. "I think ours might be blown."

Cat took another pull on the bottle.

"My fault," she replied. "I never could stay in character."

Aiko smiled.

"No, not when you see an injustice done and a wrong to be righted."

Chuckling, she squeezed Cat's shoulder.

"All that's missing is the cape and the big S on your chest."

Cat glanced at Lana, who stared back at her.

"Well, okay. Good. Maybe it'll make things happen."

Forcing a big grin, she hoisted the whiskey bottle and saluted Lana. Lana opened her mouth but then "Chainsaw" came running up the stairs, showing her a lead bullet that he'd dug out of the woodwork, shouting he was going to have it made into a pendant.

"Some bad shit is going down and this bunch is part of it."

The flags and the Presidential Seal were hung with black ribbons.

"My fellow citizens…"

The President wore a black suit and a black tie. He looked like he hadn't slept for a week.

"This is a tragic time for all of us…"

The front pages had black borders. The headlines screamed it:

EIGHTY-NINE DEAD IN BENSON SPRINGS!

"…and in this time when our faith will be sorely tested…"

Sitting tall and solemn, Reverend Thaddeus P. Calhoun shared the stage with him, shining like a ray of hope in his cream-colored suit.

"…I have asked the Reverend Calhoun to lead the nation in mourning…"

Selena got up from her huge carved desk. She paced the floor like a tigress trapped in a cage.

There was a small silver remote in her hand. She pressed a button. On the vast screen above her desk a single state was highlighted within the map of the USA. She enlarged it till it filled the screen and then illuminated the intricate web of roads and highways.

Selena keyed in a code and a winking red light appeared, inching along a bright artery.

"Come on...come on, sistahs, do yo' stuff!"

CHAPTER 9

BAD MOON RISING

"Welcome...!"

The silver Aston Martin DB5 glided down Main Street and rolled elegantly to a stop in front of the converted old church.

"Hey big man!"

The car door swung open and Selena stepped out. She flowed out lithely, in a supple black leather cat suit that looked like it was painted on her awesome curves, striding out in shiny high-heeled boots.

A small convoy pulled in behind the Aston. Two Jeeps, painted blue, with pale canvas tops. Each seated four, in the shade beneath the canvas; slim young women with serious faces, clad in crisp blue jumpsuits and forage caps, with short carbines cradled on their laps.

"I see you came prepared," said John Warburton.

Selena nodded, her smile fading.

"It pays to these days, it's a bad scene."

She patted the bulky automatic, holstered on her hip. John frowned.

"That's what I'm hearing," he replied. "But I just can't get a handle on it."

Selena smiled again and hooked her arm in his.

"Well, that's what I'm here for, man, so let's get down!"

Scented by a blend of exotic oils, fragrant veils of steam caressed Selena's dark skin, as she eased and undulated her body into the hot water.

"Oooh, baby, I needed that!"

She sighed, laying back and luxuriating, with the water up to her chin.

"That was a long and dusty road!"

Her descent made ripples that fanned out and lapped up against John's barrel chest. Smiling, he sat up, propped against the side of the broad basin, his arms spread out along its marble rim. They were alone; the Chinese girls had gone away, giggling; Selena's bodyguards were outside the door.

Selena raised herself up a little, till her spectacular breasts were bobbing on the surface, with their tips like dark chocolate. Rolling his eyes, John Warburton made a sound deep down in his chest.

"You're still magnificent!" he gasped.

His eyes misted over, remembering.

"It's been a long time."

Chuckling, Selena extended a long leg underwater and teased him with her toes.

"Later, big man..."

He squirmed suddenly, making waves, his laughter booming. With a shimmy of her strong shoulders, Selena slid across and was beside him, cradled in the crook of his brawny arm.

"Hey Mama...."

"Hey Big Daddy...."

Then they sobered and sat a while in silence.

"So, how much to we know?" asked John Warburton.

"Not much," Selena replied. "Not much more than what you read in the papers."

John Warburton frowned.

"Have you heard from my crazy niece?"

Selena shook her head.

"Not a word. All I got is her light flashing on the map, moving on down the road.

"Uncle John's brow unfurrowed, a twinkle glowing in his eyes.

"Well, one thing's for sure," he chuckled. "Where she is, is where it's happening."

Selena grinned.

"And if not," she replied. "She'll sure as hell make it happen."

John laughed.

"Cat Warburton—the human hand grenade!"

Suddenly, his face was serious and sad. Selena dipped her head and kissed his damp shoulder.

"Don't worry, Daddy. She'll be fine."

He nodded gravely.

"Whatever it is," he stated. "It's going to be big, real big."

"Are we ready for it?"

"I hope so...I sure hope so..."

Their faces floated like ghostly masks of amber, glowing in the firelight. Confined by the surrounding darkness, their voices were low and conspiring.

"We must attack!" said a voice, a young man's voice.

"Yes attack!" he had a chorus. "Attack! Attack Attack!"

"Hit 'em hard! So the whites know they can't mess with us!"

The chorus of young men's voices swelled with passion and grew in ambition. Brandished like the spears of old, rifle barrels flashed in the firelight.

"We gotta fight for what's ours!"

"Take back what's ours!"
"Take back what they stole from us!"
"Take back the land!"

A hand extended and plucked a stick from the edge of the campfire. Its glowing tip ignited a hand-rolled cigarette.

"The land..."

The firelight shone on a fierce face, a warrior's face, the face of a leader.

"We can't take back concrete and steel. We can't conquer skyscrapers and factories and highways and bridges. We can't defeat tanks and jet planes."

Angry, one young man jumped to his feet.

"Hell, the Cong are making a damn fine job of it over there in 'Nam!"

The warrior shook his head slowly.

"North Vietnam is a strong and united nation. Our people are weak and scattered. We are poor and disenchanted. We have had our fire extinguished first by the white man's religion and now the white man's drugs and alcohol."

He smiled wryly.

"And the Cong get weapons from Russia and China. All we get is warm words from history professors and long-hairs with posters of Sitting Bull on their bedroom walls."

He stood and put his hand on the young man's shoulder.

"All we can do is make a stand and remind them who we are and who we once were, let them know that we're still here and that we demand respect and fair treatment."

The young man's eyes still blazed with the light of battle.

"But––!"

"There is a greater evil out there..."

It was an ancient voice. An old man's voice from another age. Coming from the dancing shadows beyond the fringes of the firelight. Instantly, a fresh chorus of youthful disapproval fell silent and they all listened respectfully.

"Out there, in the desert, on the road. A great evil that seeks to devour the world..."

Light the Fire!

Blood red, the words blazed from the laminated sleeve. Above the sneering, leering faces of the band, posturing with their guitars held like weapons. Their backdrop was the side of the bus, etched with strands of bullet holes.

The kids came home clutching the latest '45 like a religious icon. The record player was an altar that they knelt before. The bedroom door was slammed shut, an inner sanctum.

"Far out...!"

They always discussed the sleeve first. The girls debated their favorites, "Snake"'s ice blue eyes competing with "Cannibal"'s bare chest. The boys groaned and sighed out loud, over an exotic girl, belled and bangled, in the filmy skimpies of a harem slave, straddled by a stunning blonde in studded black leather, flourishing a bullwhip.

Their fingers traced the lines of bullet holes, as they mouthed "Oh wow...cool...!" in hushed tones. They recited the legend, preserved in newspaper clippings tacked to their walls, beside the posters and ticket stubs.

The disk was laid upon the turntable like an offering on an altar. The hiss of the grooves engaging provoked a shiver of anticipation. Sat cross-legged in a semi-circle, they leaned forward eagerly.

"Yeah...!"

"Oh, man...!"

An instant classic, a riff of jagged chords reached out and grabbed them and their eyes went wide with delight, all glancing at each other with confirmation: this was gonna be good!

"Wooo!"

Rolling thunder, the drums kicked in, the bass pumping, a dark compelling pulse, the heartbeat of a monster. Their heads began to nod to the beat, long hair swirling around their faces.

A fanfare from the lead guitar, a shrapnel burst of notes like shards of steel. And then "Snake"'s voice, raw and shrill, flaying them.

"...*Light the fire...*

...blood for the Devil's pyre...!"

But no schools burnt that night. Watchmen did their rounds in plodding monotony. Parents relaxed and the suburbs slept soundly.

"The convening is called to order...!"

It was a board meeting, in a boardroom with a boardroom table and boardroom chairs.

"Order!"

Except the boardroom was a cavern carved out of black rock. The table was a monumental slab made of the same sinister stone, incised with jagged runes fanning out from a large pentangle set at its epicenter. The chairs were gothic thrones, carved elaborately from dark wood.

The scene was lit by a spectral glow tinged ghoulish green, cast by twisted candles set in tall iron-wrought candelabra that were clusters of screaming skulls.

A tense murmur was hushed by a command from the head of the table. There stood a true throne, taller and more spectacular than the rest, its carvings richly gilded. The figure that occupied the throne was robed and hooded in black, edged with scarlet. His pointed hood, masking him entirely except for the slanted red-rimmed eyeholes which pierced it, was taller than the blunter hoods of the men around the table, whose robes were uniformly grey and humbler.

The voice that resonated from the black mask was disguised, its tone rendered supernatural.

"We grow stronger every day..."

They all sat up straighter.

"We began with children and now we can control men..."

Eyes glowed within the eyeholes; the hoods seemed to grow taller.

"But the Master demands more sacrifice. The Master's power feeds upon the souls that we deliver to him. A child's soul is a petty morsel. We have no further use for children...!"

At the far end of the table, hanging above it, there was an empty frame, a broad oval fashioned from bronze, with strange hieroglyphs running along its rim. The black-robed figure gestured with a hand sheathed in a black gauntlet, its fingers flashing with blood-red gemstones. At once, the empty frame began to fill with a glowing green mist, which slowly became colorless and solidified into a moving image.

"We have no further use for these, their pied pipers..."

The movement was the massive tour bus, rolling down the dusty highway. Then the picture did a dissolve into the interior of the bus and found the members of **666**, chilling out and indulging, living the life.

"They have served their purpose."

The roving lens paused on Lana Kent, looking on with her usual distant disapproval.

"They have all served their purpose."

The all-seeing eye stopped when it discovered Cat/Katie, in a skimpy red halter top and frayed denim shorts low down on her hips. It seemed to rest purposefully on her, zooming in slowly in to close-up on her face.

There was a sharp intake of breath from the figure in black.

"All except..."

Then the gemstones flashed as the black-gloved hand slammed down on the table.

"Yes! More sacrifice! The Master's strength must be maintained until the Great Plan can be fulfilled!"

Rising from his chair, he rounded on the men sat before him, who all flinched, scalded by the fire in his eyes.

"More sacrifice!"

"We're lost", the driver admitted to himself.

Applying the brakes, he brought the big bus to a smooth slow rolling stop.

"Ummnn…nnn…wha…?"

The gentle jolt was enough to wake Cat from a shallow sleep.

"Now what?" muttered Aiko, from the bunk above.

Cat swung her long legs up and out and stood rubbing her eyes, her toes deep in the thick pile that carpeted the aisle that divided the curtained sleeping compartments. She heard voices and approaching movement in the semi-darkness and swiftly concealed her nakedness with a long white towel robe.

She was just in time. The lights came on, making her wince and blink, and then the others were shoving past her in the narrow space, making for the front of the bus, yawning and complaining gruffly.

The doors hissed open. The passengers disembarked, into the chill of the night.

"Brrrr!"

Clad in a thin silken nightshirt that barely reached her knees, Aiko shivered, wrapping her arms around herself.

"What the––!"

"Chainsaw"'s black satin robe billowed around his bony ankles as he swiveled this way and that, looking all around him, falling open to expose his scrawny chest, his modesty preserved by leopard skin briefs.

"Where the…?"

"Cannibal"'s eyes rolled up and down and around, as he tried to focus, his arms flung across the shoulders of his handmaidens, as they strained to support him, their faces pale and worried.

A tinny jangle was "The Axe" riffing on his unplugged guitar, his eyes glazed over, somewhere else. He even slept with it; he played it in his sleep. Meandering, he blundered into "Tank", who stood dumbly, bare-chested, oblivious to the sharp bite of the night, scratching an itch in his armpit.

"Hey!" "Snake" giggled. "They named the highway after us!"

His black robe trailed behind him, the satin slithering on the tarmac. It snagged his feet as he stumbled forward, pointing.

"F-f-far out...!"

The night sky was a starless void that merged into the surrounding darkness. The road was made of dull lead, sucked into a black hole. Beyond the blurred fringes of the blacktop was a gloomy grey wasteland; a dead land in which the silence was crushing and absolute, where nothing stirred or made a sound.

"Whooo...!"

"Snake" was hanging off the signpost, spinning around it, his weight making it shift and tilt. He grabbed it with both hands and shook it, reaching up and tugging.

"Hey! Gimme a hand, man...!"

The highway sign, grey in the half-light, swung askew on the leaning, jolting post. Its enamel was flaking and pitted with rust. But the numbers stood out boldly: **666**.

"I want this for the record cover!"

Laughing, "Cannibal" dismissed his handmaidens with a resounding stereo slap on their backsides. The girls squealed and peeled away as he jogged forward, shoulder charging the post like a pro tackle.

Yeah!"

The signpost toppled, ripping up clods of dirt. With a whoop, "Cannibal" fell flat on his back. "Snake" reeled, clutching his trophy.

"Gotya!"

With a flourish, "The Axe" played a tinkling fanfare. "Tank" grunted and applauded sluggishly.

Cat's brow furrowed in a puzzled frown. Aiko was standing off to one side, away from the others. When Cat glanced at her, her eyes were oddly blank and unresponsive.

What's going on...?

Sheathed in a fancy nightgown with flamboyant ruffles at the throat and the cuffs, Lana Kent had edged up close behind Aiko. As Cat watched, she thought she saw Lana's lips moving, murmuring some mysterious incantation in Aiko's ear. Almost imperceptibly at first, she saw Lana retreating, drawing Aiko back with her, away from the bus, towards the curtain of darkness.

"Hey bitches!"

Sat with his legs splayed out on the ground, "Cannibal" held out his arms.

"C'mon, bitches...!"

Obediently, his girls came running.

"Help me up!"

They stopped abruptly. Wide eyed, they were staring beyond him.

"Hey, what the...?"

What the---!

Eyes, twin orbs of blazing green, were glaring at them from the curtain of darkness, floating where the void swallowed the highway.

The green light intensified, a searing white at its core.

"Aaaiiieeee...!"

Their hair aflame, the girls were twin candles. And then the green fire wrapped around and consumed them. Arms out flung and flailing wildly, they reeled, staggered a few paces and toppled, curled up, shriveling till they were something black and twisted with nothing left for the few remaining licks of fire to feed on.

"Hey....!"

"The Axe"'s guitar suddenly burst into flame, spraying green sparks as the strings melted.

"Cool!"

He was a fireball, a blinding detonation, and was gone, vaporized.

"Uh...whadda way t'go, man..." "Tank" mumbled.

He was on fire, but he scarcely seemed to notice. He just stood there, a pillar of fire, till he was reduced to a blackened husk which crumbled into a pile of ashes.

"Yaaaaa...aaaahhh....!"

"Chainsaw"'s robe was a cape of green fire, a tail of flame trailing behind him as, like a human comet, he ran wildly into the surrounding darkness. He vanished as the void engulfed him. There was one last muffled scream and then a dull reverberation and a single dimmed pulse of green light, swiftly smothered by the blackness.

"Yikes!"

Alarmed, Cat jumped back, her back slamming into the side of the bus, as "Snake" came running past her, his eyes and mouth gaping, shrieking in terror. A strand of glowing green fireballs pursued him, looping out slowly then merging into a long and slender lance of flame.

"AAAA–AAGGHH–HH!"

The spear of green fire transceted him, between the shoulder blades. He ran on a few paces and then stood stock still, striking one final pose before the fire withered him to a charred and blackened twist.

With a yelp, Cat spun around, detaching herself from the bus, jolted by a sudden shock. Eyes wide, she stumbled backwards.

The bus was green, green hot. There was a cacophony of tormented metal as it began to twist and buckle, its mighty bulk crushed like a tin toy.

Glass shattered as the windows blew outwards in a spray of vicious shrapnel. With a yell, Cat dived off the tarmac and onto the grey sand. The fragments whizzed all around her, twinkling against the blackness, as she tried to press her body deep into the dirt, clamping her arms over her head.

"Hey......"

As if he had been overlooked, "Cannibal" still sat in the middle of the road, staring at the grotesque remains of the two girls. A spike of glass arced towards him, in slow motion, turning over and over like the blade of a knife. Its flight ended abruptly, as it impaled the drummer's forehead.

".....bummer...."

His eyes rolled up in their sockets. His head lolled forward, his chin on his chest.

The storm of glass ceased. Cat waited, then rolled over and sat up.

Aiko!

But Aiko wasn't there. She was nowhere to be seen. Only Lana Kent, miraculously untouched, one hand clutching the fancy ruffles at her throat, her eyes reflecting the green fire that consumed the mangled wreckage of the bus and made wildly shifting patterns on the blacktop.

Lana was amazed, exultant. Her arms stretched out in adoration, she walked swiftly towards the glaring green eyes that floated in the veils of darkness.

"No!"

Suddenly she was halted, as if gripped by a giant hand, squeezing the breath from her. Her eyes bulged with horror.

"No, Master!"

She was choking. Blood burst from her gaping mouth, black in the strange light. Her body was bending, breaking. Her screams were strangled.

OH MY GOD...!

The invisible fist seemed to lift Lana up and then cast her aside. Her limp body rolled raggedly across the tarmac, limbs splaying loosely at un-natural angles, a broken doll.

Dazed, Cat lurched to her feet. Her face was streaked with dirt and sweat, glistening in the green glow. She swayed dizzily as the green eyes swelled in size and ferocity until they were twin moons and it hurt her to look at them.

She reeled backwards, flinging up her hand to shield her eyes. The void came rushing up behind her. It was a giant wave that rose up and fell upon her, stifling her screams, a cold black terror that was sucking her down and down and down, drowning her.

CHAPTER 10

THE DISCIPLES

"Mmm...mm...uuunn...nnn...hhh...!"

Surfacing, Cat woke in a bed that was only slightly smaller than a football field.

"Oooooo..."

Her body jackknifed, and she sat bolt upright. Wincing, she screwed her eyes tight shut as a sharp pain slashed across behind them, her temples throbbing.

"...ooo...hhh...!"

A wave of nausea washed over her, a clenched fist twisting her guts violently. She sat very still for a while. Slowly, the storm abated. All was calm. She opened her eyes and glanced around warily.

Yipes!

The bed sheets were a sea of black satin. The bed stood like an altar, at the hub of an expansive circular chamber, more a temple than a bed chamber. A monumental four-poster, its towering canopy was draped in black, black tassels glittering with twists of silver. The floor was paved with slabs of black marble. The curving span of the high walls was hung with heavy tapestries, woven with black and scarlet and silver, a grotesque panorama of the horrors of hell. Grinning demons capered and cavorted in a ghastly revelry, inflicting hideous torments on the flesh of the damned, a writhing mass of flailing limbs and twisted faces, contorted with agony and despair.

The tapestries were punctuated by tall black iron candelabra, fashioned into scaly snakes and grinning skulls, a cold pale light radiating from their eyeless sockets.

Wide-eyed, Cat gulped audibly.

What a crazy pad!

She shivered and it was then that she realized that she was stark naked. The black satin covers hissed, slithering down her thighs, as she pulled them back and swung her long legs sideways. Perched on the edge of the mighty bed, her toes barely brushed the floor. The touch of the cold marble was an icy shock that made her flinch and shiver again.

She wrapped her arms around herself, rubbing vigorously. And then relief warmed her, as she saw what she was looking for, folded neatly on the end of the bed.

Unfurled, it was a hooded robe of purple velvet, lined with scarlet silk. A red rope cinched it in at the waist, as she wrapped the long folds around her, all the way down to her ankles. She let the hood hang down behind her.

"Ha!"

There were slippers too, of the same plush purple velvet, a perfect fit, snug and cozy on her feet.

"That's better!"

Fully restored, Cat took stock of her surroundings. She saw a door, like a church door, dark wood and ironbound. Her slippered feet padding softly on the stone floor, she crossed quickly and pressed her ear to it.

She heard nothing. Tentatively, she twisted the heavy iron ring of its handle. Expecting it to be locked, she was surprised when the door swung open. She expected to be betrayed by a rusty creaking, but it opened smoothly and soundlessly on oiled hinges.

Cat stepped into a long gleaming stone corridor, stark and bare, bathed in the same cold colorless light, shining in the eyes of iron skulls mounted at intervals along the walls.

She looked both ways; saw only the stone passage receding to a distant vanishing point.

Now what...?

Then she heard it, or felt it, a faint pulse, far away.

"Okay......"

She walked on and the pulse became audible, the insistent throbbing of muffled drums. As she quickened her pace, striding out now, there was another sound, underpinning the drums; a deep dark drone, the ebb and flow of chanting voices.

The LAST CHANCE was just that, your last chance to fill your tank and be watered and fed, before the highway vanished into the melting heat haze of the baking desert.

No one knew how it had got there, a solitary railway carriage converted into a fully functioning diner, with panoramic windows and steps leading up to the entrance at the front end and down from the exit at the back. Long ago, someone had painted it red and gold, but it was faded and dusty now. Behind it, scattered about, were the grey skeletal remains of a long gone ghost town, dry bones pocked with the eyeless sockets of empty window frames—like the rail car, a mute monument to failed ambition.

"Keep smiling...."

Sat in plywood booths all along one wall, the handful of diners belonged to the battered pick-ups parked outside. Twentieth-century cowboys in faded denim and baggy work shirts, darting sidelong glances from under the broad brims of their hats and the bills of their baseball caps, talking low out of the corner of their mouths.

Perched on the swivel stools that ran along the counter, the girls put on a show, laughing and making the stools turn back and forth.

"....we need that ride..."

Hippie chicks, a blonde and a brunette, with beaded headbands, fringed halter tops and their tight bell-bottomed jeans low on their hips, encrusted with threadbare patches proclaiming peace and love and the joys of turning on. The cowboys eyed them with conflicting lust and contempt. No one smiled back.

The blonde pouted, rolling her eyes.

"Jeez, dig the straights!"

The brunette shrugged.

"Let's go wait outside. Maybe someone will come along."

Cat had walked for miles. Or so it seemed. Down a maze of eerily lit stone passages, watched by the glowing eyes of the iron skulls; chasing that distant dull drone of chanting voices.

"Oo-oo...hhh...."

Everything was spinning round. Her head was pounding with a sharp pulsing pain.

Oh my God! I'm blind!

Aiko scrubbed her eyes frantically. Fuzzy blobs of light took shape.

"Oooo...ooo...hh...!"

Gradually, the room came into focus. A bare stone cell bathed in a pale cold light, shining from above.

She was naked.

Oh shit!

She saw a door and sprang up and stepped towards it. A wave of nausea turned her legs to rubber. Something seized her by the ankle and she fell painfully to her knees.

OW...!

On the other side of the door, Cat stopped for a moment, her brow furrowing. Puzzled, she cocked her head, listening hard. Then she shrugged and moved on.

Aiko discovered that she was manacled by the ankle, secured by a heavy chain that ran from a ringbolt on the wall.
Furious, she hauled violently on the chain. The effort made her sweat, chilling her. She dropped the chain and heaved a heavy sigh.

Oh Cat, where are you?

Cat arrived at an ornate archway of writhing snakes and grinning gargoyles, framing mighty ironbound doors.
The sound came from behind those doors. When she placed her palms flat on them she could feel the vibration. Boldly, she pushed and the doors swung inwards.
"Welcome...!"
She entered a chamber of horrors, bathed in that stark lifeless light. From a high vaulted ceiling, ropes and chains and iron hooks dangled. There were machines, fitted with straps and winches and barbed with spikes. Hot coals glowed in squat braziers; the walls were hung with tools and implements designed to crush and mutilate.
"Come and join us, my dear..."
A high table dominated the scene, draped in a black cloth decorated by silver pentangles.
"We have been waiting for you."
Lining the high table, facing outward towards her, figures concealed by grey robes and masked by pointed hoods.

This must be the boardroom...

Center stage, enthroned, was one robed in black and scarlet, the point of his hood taller than the rest.

...and that must be the Chairman of the Board...

She barely stopped herself from bursting out laughing. There was an empty chair beside the black-robed leader. His gloved hand gestured.
"Come, sit beside me."

Composing herself, Cat decided that a deep bow was in order and then stepped forward. As she settled into her carved throne, the gloved hand rested lightly on her forearm.

"We have been watching you," his voice was deep and dark. "And you have proved to be exceptional. We have deemed you worthy..."

The eyes behind the red-rimmed slits in the black hood were glowing. All of the hoods and the eyes behind them were turned towards her. Cat couldn't think of anything to say, so she merely nodded. Her eyes darted nervously about the stone chamber and its ghastly furnishings.

The gloved hand commanded again. At one end of the table, there hung a large bronze gong. Its somber tones rolled out of the open doorway and on and on, fading into the distance.

"NNN-n-n-nooo-ooooo....!"

There was a scuffling of bare feet on stone. Cat's blood froze.

"P-P-p-pleee-eeee-eezze....!"

Struggling figures filled the doorway, barging into the chamber; two muscular men in studded black leather. Held between them, twisting and writhing, was a slender dark-skinned girl, her long blue-black hair flailing as she fought to escape.

She caught sight of Cat, shining like a beacon. Her dark eyes were wide and imploring.

"Help m-m-me...!"

With every ounce of her strength, Cat kept herself rooted to her chair. From ice to fire, she was boiling now. But her face was a frozen mask.

She almost flinched as the gloved hand touched her arm again.

"And you have arrived at an auspicious moment, my dear..."

Screaming, the girl was being dragged towards a long, raised slab of stone, with ropes and ringbolts at its corners.

"It is time once more to partake of the blood..."

And then Cat saw that all along the table, before each chair and its robed occupant, and her chair also, was a goblet carved of black stone, etched with ancient runes.

Oh no! You have got to be joking!

They were spread eagling the dark girl, tying her down.
"You will drink of the blood and be one of us!"

In these parts the cruisers were blue and white.
"Aw shit!"
"It's the Pigs!"
Standing on the dusty, blurred fringe of the blacktop, the hippie chicks

frowned and tried to be invisible.

Not a chance. They were the first thing the patrolmen saw. The cruiser rolled up beside them.

"Hey, girlie…"

They opened the doors and got out slowly, slotting the batons into the loops on their belts. They looked the girls over. The girls didn't look back at them.

"Where ya from?"

They were two of a kind, lean and tanned in their pale blue uniforms and broad-brimmed hats, their eyes hidden by dark lenses.

"Where ya headin'?"

Eyes fixed on the ground, the girls mumbled.

"Huh, what? I can't hear yew…"

The driver leaned back against the flank of the car, folding his arms across his chest. His partner stepped up close to the blonde, and she winced as his stale tobacco breath fanned her face.

Some of the LAST CHANCE's customers had come outside to watch the show. Leering, one of them guffawed and called out.

"Hey, Lem, why doncha search 'em!"

That prompted a chorus of coarse cackling.

"Yeah, Lem, strip search 'em!"

The girls blushed hot pink. The brunette looked worried. The cop saw it.

"Okay, sweetcheeks, whadda we got here?"

He plucked a bag from her shoulder, decorated with beads and fringes. His hand dived in and rooted about. The girls glanced at each other, alarmed.

The cop's face lit up, triumphant. His hand emerged, clutching a small plastic bag.

"Well, whaddya know!"

The girls hung their heads. The driver stood up straight and opened the rear door.

"Ladies, yew's comin' for a ride…"

The screaming had stopped. The girl wasn't struggling anymore.

"You fools!"

The black-robed figure had risen from his throne, a towering spectacle of rage.

"You stupid fools!"

His leather clad henchmen wrenched their hands from the girl's body and jumped back hastily. Heads bobbing, they were bowing and scraping contritely, terrified.

"You've choked her! You've killed her, you clumsy oafs!"

Cat said rigidly, her fingers clutching the arms of the chair till their tips went white. Her face was a staring mask. Behind it, she was in turmoil.

There was nothing you could have done! Nothing!

Looming above her, the leader was pointing dramatically at the doorway.
"Be gone! I shall determine your punishment later!"
Still bobbing and bowing, they exited, babbling shrill apologies. The doors slammed behind them.
The leader descended slowly into his throne. His hand wafted dismissively.
"Have that taken away. Dispose of it."
He shifted in Cat's direction and she forced herself to turn her head and look back at him.
"The girl is no use to us dead." He explained. "We must have living blood. Blood that flows from living flesh."
She wanted to throw up. She merely nodded. She saw his broad shoulders relax. He seemed appeased by her obvious compliance. He rose again and held his hand out to her.
"Come. There is much for you to learn."

"Hey! Where are you taking us?"
They had been driving for nearly an hour. The desert was different now. It was grey and the shrubs and stunted trees were black and withered and there were no birds wheeling in a blank sky.
"The nearest town is back that way. Where are we going?"
Beyond the grille that enclosed the rear of the car, the heads in the front seats stayed focused straight ahead. The driver was muttering lowly into the handset plucked from the dash.
"...Yessir, they're perfect...yessir...just what the Master wants..."
The girls were frightened, their eyes wide and bright.
"Who are you talking to? What do you mean...?"
The girls recoiled, as the driver's partner turned suddenly, his face twisted with anger.
"Now yew jest shut it, girlie, or I'll come back there and––!"
There was a bang and the cruiser lurched as the left front tire burst. The driver yelled, dropping the handset, as the wheel was jerked from his hand.
Suddenly and violently, the big car veered sideways. It seemed to twist and then flipped off the highway, rolling over and over in a cloud of grey dust and debris, the engine grinding, metal rending.

"Please, my dear, you may enter".

He stood aside and let her pass; to return to the black bed chamber, with its grotesque décor.

"Here we can be alone."

Knowing what was expected of her, Cat crossed the room and stood facing him, at the foot of the giant bed. The mask she wore was obedient, expectant.

Still hooded and cloaked, he let the door swing shut and approached her with a slow, measured tread, the hem of his robes swishing softly on the black marble floor.

He stopped, his eyes like burning coals. Cat stared back at him, for just long enough, and then let her eyes fall meekly.

There was a long pause.

"Show yourself to me."

Okay, if that's how you want it…

Keeping her head bowed, she pulled the knot apart and let the red rope coil like a snake at her feet. The folds of the purple robe parted, exuding the warmth of her and a glow of golden flesh.

He sucked in his breath sharply.

"Quickly…!"

So, underneath that fancy costume you're just a man after all…

Cat lifted her face and smiled at him and glimpsed the tremor that transfixed him. Reaching up, she slipped the robe off her shoulders. It cascaded to the floor.

"UUUUHH…HHHH….GGGGHH…HHH……!"

Smoke seeped from the crumpled wreckage. There was a sound of escaping liquid splashing on the ground, the tang of gasoline clogging the hot air.

The driver was dead, his body wedged against the buckled dashboard, head lolling at an unnatural angle. Groaning, blood dripping from his face, his partner was crawling slowly towards the wreck on his hands and knees.

"L-l-let's g-get out of here…!"

Miraculously, the girls had survived with only scratches and bruises. They stood a little way off, gasping, leaning on each other, eyes wide in their smudged and dirty faces.

The patrolman heard them. Grunting with pain, he rolled onto his side, clawing at the flap of his holster.

With a yelp of panic, the girls turned and ran, back down the highway, stumbling and falling, picking themselves up and running again. The patrolman cursed as the pistol slipped from his fingers, slick with blood.

Scrabbling in the dirt, he began scrambling towards the overturned cruiser. Licks of flame were flickering in the smoke. He sagged against the battered wreck grabbing at the handset dangling from the driver's window. A voice was crackling urgently from it.

"Come in Car 42! What's happening? Come in...!"

Scrubbing the blood from his eyes with the back of his hand, he depressed the red call button. He had to spit blood before he could speak.

"Th-th-this is C-c-car f-f-f-f-f....t-hey g-g-got away...tell the––!"

A tongue of flame lapped at a thin stream flowing from the cracked gas tank. There was a dull detonation as the car and the dead driver and the man sitting on the ground were engulfed in a billowing fireball.

She was naked, magnificently naked. She posed proudly for him, standing tall, a living breathing golden statue.

"Superb!"

Gasping, he remembered to breathe again.

"You shall be a worthy consort!"

Yeah right, if that's what you want to call it...

Backing up, she sprawled on the bed, her limbs splayed extravagantly. The robed figure lurched towards her, ripping at the sash that held the robes together at his waist.

Er, are you going to keep that hood on?

A bell was chiming.

"Damn!"

The leader jerked to a halt, spun around and strode swiftly across the room. Spitting curses, he wrenched the receiver from its hook on the wall.

"Yes, what is it?"

The earpiece hummed indistinctly.

"What? Escaped! How?"

She saw his shoulders rise and then descend slowly. Replacing the receiver, he turned back towards her.

"I regret that our pleasures will have to wait, my dear. I have business to attend to."

"What the––!"
The young men saw the fireball rise up into the sky, a writhing bubble of bright orange flame.
They came running, rifles in their hands.
"Stop!"
The ground beneath their feet was grey. The color was gone from the sky.
"The Forbidden Lands!"
They stopped and retreated, until the sky was blue again.

The girls screamed and ran faster, lungs bursting, as the fireball rose and seemed to chase them, rolling over and over above them.
"AAAA-I-I-I-EEEEEEEE…!"
And as they ran, the sand turned from grey to gold and the pale sky became blue again.

"There! Their tracks go that way!"
The charred ruin of the police cruiser was still smoldering, its bold livery obliterated, now bubbled and black.
"No you fools…!"
Cat stared at the twisted black thing that lay splayed beside the wreck, shaped like a man but shrunk by the fire to the size of a child.
"…that way!"
Sucking in a deep breath she wrenched her eyes away. A hand rested lightly on her shoulder and it was all she could do to keep herself from flinching.
The voice was hard, brisk and businesslike.
"Will you join the hunt, Miss?"

The girls were stumbling, gasping, sagging to their knees on the hot asphalt. Above them, the sun was a bright and brassy, banging like a gong, battering them.

"Miss…?"
The big pickup was brawny and bull-nosed, painted in shifting tones of grey and sand, to blend in with the desert. Its martial image was matched by the men who rode it, clad in tan battle dress and black berets, semi-automatic carbines in their hands.

Wearing a similar costume, Cat stood stiffly, almost at attention, at the front, looking out across the roof of the cab. There were armed men on the ground, waiting.

"The High One thought that you might enjoy the thrill of the chase."

The officer was young and bland with pale eyes and a smooth face. The insignia on the cloth epaulettes of his battle dress jacket were red pentangles.

Cat forced a grin.

"Yeah...sure...let's go!"

He smiled back, briefly, with his thin lips, though his eyes were blank. He barked an order. Bolts and short chains rattled and then the heavy tailgate crashed down. Men were jumping onto the sand.

The candles were black. The vapors that writhed from them were glowing yellow then green and then yellow again.

"I am certain of it, Master..."

His black robes spread across the dark flagstones, the cloaked figure knelt between the twisted, grotesque candelabra, his head bowing till the tip of his hood almost touched the floor.

"...she is the one. She is worthy of you, Master!"

Shading her eyes, Cat looked out across the baking, barren landscape.

Aiko, where are you?

CHAPTER 11

MEDICINE MAN

"Fan out...!"
They left the camouflaged pickup on the crest of a low ridge, parked slantways, nose down, tail in the air.
"...and keep yer eyes peeled!"

I have to make a break for it

They didn't let Cat have a gun. There were four of them, plus the driver, who remained in his cab, waiting for a signal on his walkie-talkie. They had guns, vicious M-1 carbines and holstered pistols at their belts.

I need a plan...

They looked like robots in their identical uniforms and headgear, advancing at a slow, mechanical pace, line abreast, spaced out at a shallow angle, about 50 feet apart. They hefted the carbines hip high, cocked and ready, their active eyes masked by blank, mirror-lens shades.

Shit...!

Keeping her face front, her eyes darted left and right. The desert was flat and unrelenting. There was no shade, no shelter, nowhere to run, nowhere to hide. If those girls were out there, they didn't stand much of a chance.
The men came to a synchronized halt at an urgent crackle from their leader's walkie-talkie. He unclipped it from his belt and spoke into the mouthpiece.
"No sir...nothing yet...not a sign...."
The response galvanized him, stiffening his backbone. Replacing the handset, he rounded on his men.
"C'mon! Let's move!"

"Pick up the pace there!"
They were striding out now. The desert floor was cruel to walk on, a gritty crust that gave underneath. A slight dip in the ground was hiding the distant truck from them. If she was going to do something, she needed to do it soon.

Well, I guess the old ones are the best...

It was a sham, her labored gait and her strained panting. Pure performance, when she scuffed to a sudden stop, scrubbing the sweat from her face with her sleeve. The men kept moving, their leader calling out without looking back.

"You gotta keep up, Miss! Or d'ya want me to call the truck to come and getya?"

Sucking in a deep lungful of the hot dry air, Cat shook her head vigorously.

"No, no...I'm fine...I'm okay..."

Leaning into the wall of heat that blasted off the sand, she set off with a rubber-legged stumble. Then suddenly, she shouted.

"Ow! Ah! Ow!"

Her left leg crumpled abruptly and she sat down on the ground.

"Oooo....ooohhh...!"

The squad leader barked a command and the men halted with the precision of a well-drilled chorus line, maintaining their formation.

"Ooooo...hhh...ow...ow........!"

Cat sat on the ground, rubbing her ankle. The leader was marching towards her, in a stiff manner that betrayed his annoyance.

"What is it?"

She was flexing her ankle gingerly, her face contorting with a twinge of simulated pain.

"I...I think I've twisted it..."

Exhaling an angry gust of breath, the leader shouldered his carbine and unclipped the walkie-talkie.

"I'll call the truck to collect you."

Cat flapped her hands, waving him away.

"No, no, it's alright," she insisted. "It'll be fine, I can walk it off, I'm sure..."

The leader hesitated, staring down at her. Cat could see her twin reflections in the mirror lenses. She forced a brave grin.

"I don't want to miss it. I want to be in on the kill!"

The leader grunted. With a flick of the wrist, he signaled to his men: two to me, now!

This is it...

They came jogging at the double, side by side, in perfect step.

"Help her to her feet."

Slinging the carbines on their shoulders, they stooped, reaching down to her.

"HA-YA!"

Cat released the coiled spring inside her. She exploded upright, on her feet. Her arm extended, the heel of her hand impacting on the point of the first man's chin. His head jerked back, his neck snapping. Eyes like glass balls, he crumpled.

"HAH!"

One movement flowing into another, Cat rotated, her long leg whipping up and around, a heavy boot heel crashing into the side of the second man's head. She heard the crunch of his skull collapsing, like an eggshell. He fell without a sound.

The man had a heavy combat knife sheathed on his hip, opposite the pistol holster. As he sagged, Cat plucked it free, its blade dulled by a non-reflective coating.

The squad leader was tugging the carbine from his shoulder. Her arm like a whip, Cat threw the knife with a fast underarm motion. Suddenly, he was dropping the gun, clawing at the heavy hilt that projected from his throat, just below the Adam's apple. Blood bursting from his mouth, he fell backwards and sprawled on the ground, legs kicking.

Shit!

A bullet pinged close by, flicking her hair. The two survivors were running at her, firing from the hip. With a yell, Cat was diving and rolling. Scooping up a fallen carbine, she was firing as she rolled, as bullets made spurts of dust around her, grit peppering her face.

Silence; a startling stillness after the flurry of noise and violence. A pale veil of dust drifted across the jagged ground, glowing in the sun.

"Woo...!"

Sitting up, Cat blinked the sweat from her eyes and smeared her palm across her face, wiping away the flecks and fragments glued to her skin. The tang of cordite pricked her nostrils and was a bitter taste in her mouth.

Hefting the carbine in her lap, she looked around warily. The sprawled bodies were still and lifeless.

That was a close one!

There was the sound of an engine approaching. In a halo of glowing dust, the pickup was rocking and rolling towards her, jolting on the rough ground.

"Oh shit!"

In a spray of dirt and small stones, the truck slammed to a grating stop. The cab door flew open and the driver was jumping out and clambering into the back.

"Shit!"

There was a big .30-cal. on a swivel mount. The driver was wrenching back the cocking lever.

She saw the merest fold in the earth. Cat pressed herself into it. She heard the rattle of the machine gun. The bullets hissed inches above her and carved a furrow in the dirt close behind.

Pinging off a shot that made the driver pause and duck, Cat rolled sideways, bumping up against the first man's corpse. Propping him up on his side, she took shelter. There was another short burst and the limp body juddered, ripped apart.

Another burst and Cat flinched, grimacing, as she was spattered in blood and shreds of flesh.

"Fuck this!"

Shouting, she jumped to her feet and was running towards the truck, weaving and zig-zagging. The .30-cal. chattered and flowers of dust blossomed around her dancing feet. Lead ricocheted, whining thinly into the distance.

The tail of the ammo belt fed through and the big gun fell silent. Wide-eyed, the driver was scrabbling at the flap of his holster.

"Motherfucker!"

Cat lifted the carbine to her shoulder. She fired once. Drilled through the forehead, the driver was knocked backwards over the tailgate and disappeared from sight.

The cold fury seeped out of her slowly. For a few moments she was utterly drained. Then her fire re-ignited.

She looked the truck over. It was intact, the engine idling. With her hand for a visor, Cat scanned the broiling expanses of the desert, its horizons melting in the heat haze.

Where are you girls?

The gears grated. Cat swore as the pickup skittered on the loose skin of grit that carpeted the barren desert. The truck jerked sideways with a jolt that made her teeth rattle, twisting the wheel from her grasp.

"Fuck!"

She jammed on the brakes and slotted the gear stick in neutral.

"Fuck! Fuck! Fuck!"

The heat inside the cab was crushing. Cat banged the door open and jumped out. Buttons popped as she ripped off the baggy olive drab shirt, a limp rag that she tossed away angrily. A sleeveless undershirt was glued to her and she had a struggle peeling it off. Her plain white bra was purely functional, designed for action.

The sun was directly above her and came crashing down, scalding her bare shoulders.

"Idiot!"

Scooping up the crumpled undershirt, she swiftly fashioned it into an Arab-like head-dress that draped her neck and shoulders, and then dashed back into the cab of the truck, slamming the door with a bang.

Let's go!

When the truck was moving, the warm breeze that was sucked like syrup through the rolled-down windows cooled the sweat on her bare skin; her face, the fettered mounds of her breasts, her bare midriff. It wasn't much, but it was an improvement.

There was a creased map on the dash, but it told her nothing.

Come on girls! You can't have got far!

Bouncing on the seat beside her, a walkie-talkie buzzed and a distorted voice crackled thinly.

"Seven-seven to all squads...we found 'em...!"

Her eyes flashed fire as she reached out to shift gear and accelerate. Then she remembered something.

"Aw, c'mon, dummy! Think!"

For a second time she brought the truck to a slithering, scraping halt. Jumping out of the cab, she vaulted up and over the side, into the back, and was wrenching open the clasps of the metal boxes.

"C'mon...c'mon...c'mon....!"

The gleaming brass snake of the ammo belt draped her strong shoulders, as she deftly opened the oiled breach of the .30-cal.

The girls were screaming. They stumbled and fell to their knees, arms outstretched in supplication.

"P-p-please...!"

Raising a ring of dust like the loop of a noose, the camouflaged pickup was circling them. The men in it were laughing.

"N-n-n-noo-ooo...!"

The truck slid to a stop. As the pall of dust enveloped them, the girls crawled blindly on their hands and knees, choking. When the dust cleared, two men stood over them, with leering grins that cracked the masks of dirt on their faces. They brandished heavy manacles that clanked and rattled, as the girls cowered at their feet, moaning with terror.

No way, ya dumb muthas!

Wide-eyed, the girls watched as the men began to dance. A dance like crazy puppets, held up by some invisible force that made them jerk and judder. Ragged, shredded puppets, with pieces falling off them.

Screaming, the girls curled into balls, covering their faces, as a bloody rain pattered down around them.

And now the men in the back of the pickup were toppling like toys and falling out onto the sand. Their truck rocked, dinged and donged, pocked by neat holes that stitched it back and across, back and across, as if by magic. The glass of the cab exploded, as the driver slumped over the wheel.

"Hey! Let's go!"

Cat released the grip of the .30-cal., letting the barrel tilt up to the sky. She was every inch the desert warrior, in her billowing, improvised head-dress.

"Move!"

They were lost. They drove and drove as the dusk first crept and then rushed up behind them and the night descended suddenly.

"What the––?"

And the desert changed. Where were the stars? The sky was a fathomless void. The earth had the grey dullness of lead, the black blank horizons pressing in closely.

There was room in the cab for the three of them, shoulder to shoulder. The girls rode in numb silence, while Cat cursed herself and everything. She stopped the truck and they all got out.

"Okay, let's try again..."

She dug the rugged military compass from the deep pocket of her GI pants. Once again, the needle just spun round and round aimlessly.

"Shit."

She listened. The silence was absolute. Nothing.

"This is weird. I just don't get it."

The girls screamed.

Eyes. Great glaring sizzling orbs floating in the blackness, blazing with green fire.

Run!

She was frozen. She was freezing. Her blood, her bones. Her heart was a dagger of ice piercing her core.
The girls screamed again. They were living candles, pillars of green fire. They were withering, crumbling as the flesh fell from their charred bones in twisted flakes.

RUN...!!!

Not knowing how she got there, Cat was hurling herself into the cab of the truck. Groping for the controls, she was jolted sideways as the truck rocked violently.
"Oh--!"
All around, the grey sand was seething and billowing like the waves of an angry ocean. The tires were melting and the truck began to sink.
As the cab submerged, Cat tried to force the door open but it was jammed shut. Somehow, she writhed and twisted and squeezed herself through the open window and with a jerk and painful contortion fell into the back of the truck, jarring her shoulder.
"Ugg-gghhh!"
The tide was rising, battering the truck from side to side. Cat scrambled to her feet, only to fall back down again.
"AH!"
The grey waves were smashing against the tailgate. The metal was corroding. The spray was scalding and Cat scrambled backwards, covering her eyes.

Jeez! What a crazy way to die!

And at that moment, the cold terror dissipated and a great warmth enveloped her. The warmth was a slowly whirling cone of mellow golden light.
"Ooo...oohhh...hhhh..."
There was a face in the light, a floating mask. An old face, as old as time. It tilted down towards her and smiled. The cold and the aches and pains went away; the fear was banished. She was like a little girl, cradled

by the warm light and as she fell asleep she knew that she was safe and everything would be alright.

Free Town slept a troubled sleep. This night, their simple, honest dreams were dark and disturbed.

As dark as an oily mist that flowed slowly down Main Street, a sluggish black river, lapping at the edges of the boardwalks. Twisting tendrils coiled like snakes, and like snakes' tongues seemed to taste the night air, seeking out the window frames, locating the doorways.

Serpents of black vapor came in through the keyholes, slithered up and over the sills of windows left ajar to admit the cool night air. Once inside, the coils merged and became a creeping dark carpet and then a smothering blanket that enveloped the beds and their dream-tossed occupants.

Cat lay close to a fire, surrounded by darkness. She was jolted into wakefulness, as if from a bad dream.

"Mmmmm...!"

She sat up stiffly, her mind dull and confused. She was wrapped in a blanket the colors of the earth and sky with strange patterns that contained a wealth of ancient meaning.

The fire was very pale and gave little heat. Cat shivered and drew the blanket tighter around her hunched shoulders. She sensed that it was somehow protecting her.

The Old Man's face was floating above the fire. It seemed to pass through the flickering tongues of transparent flame and his hands were reaching out to her, bearing a simple clay cup.

"Drink..."

His lips did not move but she heard him.

"Drink of this..."

It was a voice that came from another time and in dumb obedience she reached out and took the cup from the disembodied hands that extended through the flames, hands gnarled and desiccated with age.

"...and you shall see all..."

The cup was full to the brim with a thick, dark liquid, crowned by a film of paler froth. As Cat lifted it slowly to her lips, its bitter odor assailed her, making her flinch and hesitate.

"Drink...!"

The eyes in the old face were stern and unrelenting. And suddenly, Cat's mind was emptied of all confusion and complication. All was clear and calm and certain.

She raised the cup again and drank. It had a bitter, biting taste, but she drained it to the last drop.

"Uuuu…uuuhh…hhh…"

A warm numbness was spreading from her core, slowly at first, and then accelerating till it reached the tips of her fingers and her toes. The empty cup slipped from her grasp.

She sighed, smiling, her eyelids fluttering. Her lips moved, murmuring. She felt weightless, as if she were floating.

The flames intensified. They writhed and crackled and swelled with many colors, dancing rainbows. The licking, flickering tongues of fire became a spray of flowers, and fluttering butterflies.

Laughing, Cat tried to catch the bobbing, weaving, darting butterflies. And then she cried out loud, ecstatic, as a great fountain of bright sparks soared up and up and up, filling the black sky like stars.

"OOOOHHH…HHHH….!"

The dawn was blood red and streaked with fire, the sky a shimmering warning flag.

All over Free Town, doors were slamming open, revealing empty rooms and empty beds, cold blankets tossed aside.

Alarm bells rang in the old church steeple. Blinking the sleep out of his eyes, John Warburton ran out onto Main Street, an M-16 like a twig in his huge hands. Gripping their rifles tightly, young men were flocking to him, with taut pale faces and wide and anxious eyes.

"What's happening…?"

"What's going on…?"

Cat was flying, as free as a bird, a warm wind washing her face, her long hair floating behind her.

The world unfolded below her. She could see the whole world, rolling by below, from pole to pole.

"Oh God!"

It was a panorama of pure horror, on a scale so vast it overwhelmed her shocked senses.

"No!"

She saw a world laid waste. Entire cities were shattered and crumbling. Smoke and flames gnawed at the wreckage. And beyond the cities, a charred wasteland, new deserts of ash where the steaming lakes and rivers boiled, bubbles bursting to vent sulfurous gases.

Cat flew on, faster and faster, caught up in a shrieking whirlwind. Through ragged rents in leaden cloud, she glimpsed the vast oceans like black tar, smothered by banks of dirty yellow fog. She saw the burnt-out hulk of a great cruise liner, drifting aimlessly and a Navy aircraft carrier wrapped in green fire.

Over land again, a land mottled black and brown and poisonous yellow. The highways were cluttered with abandoned cars and trucks strewn around like discarded toys. A military convoy, tanks with melted tracks and turrets, trucks consumed by that same green fire, bodies tumbled out and reduced to something black and twisted.

A military airbase was blotted out by an enormous black stain. With a stab of cold terror, she saw what was once Free Town, now jagged mounds of ash and rubble, divided by the cracked and fractured grid of its derelict streets.

"NO!"

Screaming, she recognized her own city by the Bay, crushed beneath a vast tower of black smoke veined by jagged flashes of green lightning.

Extending far into the ravaged landscape, through veils of smoke and yellow vapor, Cat saw the drab grey columns of humanity. A subjugated people, heads bowed, cowed by utter hopelessness.

They were marshaled from above. The sky was filled with wheeling, soaring black dragons, rent apart by their hoarse, metallic cries, as they swooped and plunged, exhaling gusts of green fire.

John Warburton's brain was scrambled, his thoughts in jangling fragments. Images from a night of nightmares were flashing by like a rapid-fire slideshow.

"The girls..."

"The girls––!"

"THEY'VE ALL GONE!"

The dragons had seen her. Jaws gaping and spewing green flame, they banked steeply, coming for her.

Like a child, Cat screwed her eyes tight shut.

Make them go away! Make them go away!

CHAPTER 12

AN EVIL IN THE LAND

The Stadium was a bowl of fire. It was a vast cauldron seething with light. Light that bubbled and boiled to the beat of a thousand drums, scalded by trumpets.

The fanfare peaked on a shrill cascade soaring into a night sky that glowed a deep red. Perched on tall towers, searing floodlights swiveled to impale the crest of a monumental rostrum, its looming battlements carved from glistening white marble.

A great gust of breath, a gasp, a huge exhalation of pent-up excitement. A solitary figure was pinpointed by the lights. The crowd rocked back, then surged forward, a tide of writhing arms raised in salutation and supplication.

On giant screens towering above the rim of the great bowl, the Reverend Thaddeus P. Calhoun was an impassive mask, enormous, a stark light exaggerating the chiseled hollows of his handsome features.

Baying, chanting, imploring, the crowd cried out to him; then shrank into silence as he raised his hands slowly.

He began to speak. His voice was booming. Deep and dark with foreboding, his voice rolled around the great arena. He spoke of sin and retribution, of the grim reckoning to come.

His voice was a mighty wind that stirred waves of fear washing over the crowd in long, visible ripples that rode on moans and groans of terror.

In the glow, his white suit made him a being of supernatural light. Hands sawing the air, his voice tolling like the bell of doom, the Reverend conducted his symphony of horrors.

"Mmmmmm...."

Cat woke gently from a perfect dreamless sleep.

"...mmmmm..."

She was naked, beneath a blanket of lustrous, deliciously soothing dark fur. Above her, the roof of the tepee was a cone of mellow amber, aglow with warming firelight.

"Ooooo...hhh..."

She felt wonderful, rested and restored. And then it all came back to her and suddenly she shivered.

There was someone outside; the soft scrape of a footfall.
"Who's there?"
The flap drew back. The warrior looked in on her, his long black hair falling across his face.
Cat sat up, the fur wrapped around her.
"Come in."
The faded jeans were tight on him. He wore a scuffed pale buckskin shirt with ragged fringes; unbuttoned, and Cat was ensnared by a glimpse of his muscled torso.
There was a short carbine in his hand, and he tilted the barrel back to rest on his shoulder, as he stood gazing down on her.
"I was just coming off guard duty. Sorry I woke you."
Her mind went back to the besieged tour bus and his dramatic entry.

God! Ain't you the brown-eyed handsome man!

"That's okay, I'd woken up anyway."
She smiled up at him and his thoughts tumbled over. Her hair was like glowing gold in the firelight. Her eyes seemed to grow and grow and drown him.
"Um...."
Suddenly his brain was disconnected from his tongue.
"....er..."
As she knelt at his feet, smiling up at him.
"...it...it's still early...go back to sleep...."
He was turning away to leave. A flickering slideshow of death and destruction flashed before her eyes.

I'm so cold...!

She let the fur slide off her bare shoulders.
"Please stay. I don't want to be alone."

The large cauldron was a bowl of green fire, searing white at its core.
"Dread Lord, we conjure thee..."
Hissing, the green flame threshed and twisted viciously, spitting out shards like bright dagger blades.
"...in thy name we invoke the powers of the Darkness...!"
Aiko moaned.
"AAAaaa...oooo.....hhh...!"
Gleaming in the eerie green glow, her naked body writhed and twisted in the tall chair, secured by her wrists and ankles.

His robes swirling, a menacing black shadow, the tall figure loomed over her, eyes sparking in the red-rimmed slits of his hood.

"...will you speak...?"

Panting, Aiko shook her head weakly. A black-gloved fist seized her by the hair, jerking her head back.

"Speak...!"

He gestured to his grey minions, servicing the cauldron. One raised a carved goblet and held it over the glowing green coals.

"...who is she...?"

The goblet tilted and a thick dark liquid, blood turned black in the strange light, oozed over the rim and dripped down to the greedy tongues of fire.

Aiko screamed. Her slim body arched up and out of the chair, straining against her bonds.

"...Speak...!"

The paleness of the dawn flowered into a sublime morning. The small town basked in it.

"Good morning!"

"Good morning!"

It was a new town, a picture postcard town set like a jewel in a green oasis, the product of elaborate irrigation that conquered the desert.

"Good morning!"

It was called Paradise Gardens and was at the cutting edge of property development, an opportunity for the youthful and optimistic, with ambitions to step out and make their mark. First homes to raise a young family in, designed to evoke the cozy communities of a bygone and more neighborly age, with shady porches, manicured lawns and white picket fences; but with all the mod cons.

"Good morning!"

Down a neat grid of streets lined with small but perfectly proportioned trees, the morning tinkled with birdsong, and the bell and cheery greeting of the mailman on his bicycle. In every house the kitchen hummed with activity, eager for the day: housewives bustling to feed their chattering children, while assisting husbands fumbling with their ties and forgetting where they left their briefcase. All to a merry soundtrack of eggs and bacon sizzling, coffee percolating and toasters popping.

"Good morning!"

Where you turned off the desert highway there was a bold signboard: Welcome to Paradise Gardens and the New Frontier! In its shadow, there was a smaller sign, an arrow pointing the way: DRY GULCH—HISTORIC GHOST TOWN.

In 1892, when they built the town, they called it MOTHERLODE because there was said to be gold running in rich veins through the wrinkles and folds of the low scrubby hills all around. And no matter that it was parched almost all year round; they would drill down to water, which the geologists swore was there, in a bottomless underground lake.

For a while, the town boomed. First the miners, then the suppliers and saloonkeepers and good-time girls. And it was one long party, for a while.

But then the water ran dry and the drills broke on solid rock way down. And what gold they were finding now wasn't worth the effort. So, by 1902 the town was abandoned, left to be swallowed, digested slowly, by the desert.

Only the tumbleweed moved down Main Street and its buckled, collapsing boardwalks. And the structures that flanked it, the saloons and stores, were gutted shells with dunes of windblown sand ramped up against them, weighing on them until they collapsed.

Historians and Frontier buffs, photographers and film crews visited occasionally. Hippies made camp there before moving on in their search for whatever it was they were looking for. Motorcycle gangs hid out there. It was rumored that the loot from old robberies was stashed there.

A tourist company had once bussed excursions all the way out there and some of its faded signposts were still dotted around. Boot Hill said one of them. A few scraps of fencing still marked the extent of the old graveyard, on a slight plateau, just outside the town; and tall, teetering gateposts now missing the crossbar from which, or so legend had it, someone was lynched in 1895.

The wind had long since sandblasted the inscriptions on those wooden markers that were still standing. The gravesites were eroded and barely discernable. It was an empty place, under a vast blank sky, flayed by the raw, gusting wind.

Something moved; something big and dark, rolling up the shallow slope onto the plateau of BOOT HILL. Its presence was a low dark vibration that stirred the scraps and grit which carpeted the ground, making the sand shiver and shimmer as if charged by strange electricity.

Diluted by the glare of the great blank sky, pale green beams traversed the ruined cemetery, raking slowly across the low mounds and leaning headstones.

With a crack, a wooden cross split down the middle. At its base the earth seemed to swell and then begin to pulse, first slowly, then faster and faster. The gritty crust cracked open. Grey fingers clawed upwards, seeking the light; a naked arm, with dry dead skin shrunken to the bone, a clutching hand, bones protruding from the fingertips.

"What...?"

The mailman squeezed the brakes, slipping his feet off the pedals and planting them on the ground.

"What the heck...?"

He felt it in his chest before he heard it. A dull compression pressing on his ribcage.

"Hey! Willya look at––!"

It was black, a low slung gleaming black beast sliding down the quiet street towards him. A deep dark rumble preceded it, making the tarmac quiver beneath the mailman's feet.

Mesmerized, he stood astride his bicycle in the middle of the street, jaw dropping.

"Gol-leee!"

Its eyes flared with green fire.

"YAA-GG-GHH-HHH...!"

The bell and the bicycle frame melted. The mailman was melting, dissolving, his face dripping from his skull.

The sound was drowned by the merry breakfast symphonies.

"...GGGHH...HHH...!!!!"

The beast maintained its stately progress through the town. Its growl seemed to swell till it loomed over the rooftops like a grumbling thundercloud. In the kitchens puzzled faces tilted upwards.

"Funny, they didn't forecast rain..."

Darkness came with it. The light and color drained from the blue sky and the green grass and the trees and all became monochrome and lifeless. A chill wind made the grey grass shiver; the leaves turned grey, curled up dry and brittle and fell away. Bare branches rattled.

"...help us, oh Master...!"

The green glow was pulsing, the white heat a heartbeat at its core. Clustered within its eerie pool of light, shoulder to shoulder in a ring around the cauldron, cloaked figures were conjuring.

"...help us as the Power grows..."

Aiko's head lolled forward, her long blue-black hair falling over her face.

"Enough...!"

Her body was falling slackly out of the tall chair, suspended by the ropes on her wrists and ankles.

The tall black shadow cupped his hand beneath her chin and tilted her face upwards. Her eyes were wide open, staring sightlessly, her lips moving but making no sound.

"...She will never talk..."

The black robes swirled, hissing on the stone floor, as the tall figure turned and made for the door.

"...But she will serve her purpose...she will bring the One to the Master...!"

The pale finger of dawn probed a crack in the tent flap. Its rosy shaft crept across and tickled Cat's toes, peeping from beneath the fur blanket.

Murmuring, she quivered, flexed her shoulders and rolled over. Opening her eyes, she yawned, arching her back. Beside her, her lover frowned, grumbling in his sleep. Propped on her elbow, Cat gazed down on him. She was mellow, all warm honey inside.

The memory of the night made her smile. He was a mighty lover. He took her as a conqueror that was magnanimous in victory and, for once, Cat had let herself be conquered and abandoned herself to the tides of ecstasy. And afterwards, she curled up and cried quietly, like a little girl, and he wrapped her in his arms and they fell asleep together.

In the soft infiltrating light his profile had nobility.

Oh God! You're beautiful!

A hard glitter jarred in this soft-focus scene; the plastic chrome of a small transistor radio. Cat sat up, the blanket slipping from her bare shoulders. She flicked the switch.

Cool...!

A throbbing bass and golden horns, a dark brown voice singing about sweet love.

"Hmmm...mmphh...!"

His eyes popped open as he jack-knifed upwards. The revelation of his chiseled torso made her ache for him all over again.

"Hey...."

Unable to resist, Cat smoothed her palm across his chest, on around his broad shoulder and up and over the flexed bicep, as hard and smooth as stone.

"...I might have known you were a Soul man..."

Her heavy breasts quivered as she swung towards him with a subtle shimmy of her shoulders. In the pale light she seemed to glow like pink gold. All of the sounds and sensations of a night of passion came back in an intoxicating rush. He was reaching for her and Cat was groaning softly, deep in her throat, arching her back, thrusting towards him.

"HEY...!"

The tent flap was wrenched open and the low sun was blaring in right at them, making them blink and shield their eyes.

"...WAKE UP...!"

Two young men stumbled into the tepee, falling over each other. Their long black hair was falling around their eyes and they'd obviously dressed in haste, shoeless, shirt-tails flapping, one with his fly buttons undone.

Scuffing to a stop, they stared, bug-eyed, at Cat's glorious, golden nakedness. Their minds went blank.

"Ah...ah....."

Cat just sat and glared at them. Her lover quickly replaced the fur around her shoulders.

"Well?" he snapped. "What is it?"

The young men gulped.

"Free Town...!" one gasped. "Free Town!"

Cat's blood ran cold.

Uncle John!

She jumped to her feet, clutching the fur cape to her.

"What? What's happened?"

The boy stammered and she grabbed a fistful of his baggy shirtfront and shook him furiously.

"Hey, baby...cool it...."

Their leader was at her side, his hand on her shoulder. She was oblivious to his nakedness now, her mind swamped by visions of black horror.

"Hey man, what's happenin'?"

Selena was worried. This didn't sound like him. He sounded like he was losing it.

"Dunno, I just dunno...," John Warburton's voice was fractured, distracted. "They're all gone...all gone...!"

The frequency distorted and his voice faded behind a wall of static. Cursing, Selena reached across her desk and tweaked the knobs.

"Repeat please, Big Daddy..."

He surged up again as the interference retreated.

"...all gone...the girls...in the night...every last one of them...all gone...!"

The dead walked the streets of Paradise Gardens.

Hungry for living flesh, they clawed down the doors and tumbled through shattered windows, clambering over each other to get at their victims. They swarmed over the families cowering in their lounges and kitchens, red in tooth and claw, stripping them to the bone.

Triumphant, the dead paraded, flaunting the skins of their prey as capes and banners, wearing their flayed faces like masks.

The lover was a war chief now.

"Get the guns!"

The war ponies were battered old pick-ups; the lances and bows were lever-action carbines. Engines revved, pale grey exhaust fumes flavoring the churning dust.

"Let's go!"

He was tall and proud and Cat just stood there and admired him. His eyes shining fiercely, he held out his hand.

"Come on!"

A motley convoy bounced and banged precariously, rolling over the rough terrain. Bone was jolted, teeth rattled.

"Jeez!" yelled John Warburton, hanging on, grabbing the M-16 rifle to stop it sliding off his lap.

There were Army-surplus Jeeps, their olive drab and GI stencils faded; grimy dirt bikes buzzing like angry wasps; pickup trucks scarred with dents and scrapes and rust. The young men of Free Town were scouring the desert, in search of their lost women.

And with the army of the dead came the black beast and in its wake a vast darkness....

The convoy came up and over the ridge that overlooked Paradise Gardens.

"What...!"

The Jeep slithered to a stop in a spray of dirt and debris. John Warburton jumped out and stood rooted, his jaw dropping.

"What the hell?"

The shadowed recesses of the crypt were alive with slithering whispers and the snick and scuffle of tiny claws. Coils of oily vapor slid like snakes up the slimy stone, twisting upwards from torches set in iron brackets bolted to the walls.

"Master...."

A solitary figure knelt at an obscene travesty of an altar, made of screaming skulls and demonic masks warped with perverted lust, below a twisted crucifix set upside-down, fashioned from human bones.

"...as we obey your will our power grows..."

Behind him, there was a muffled groan. A naked girl dangled by the ankles, her hands bound behind her back, long blonde hair trailing down to the mossy flagstones. A ragged gag was stuffed in her mouth and her pretty face was contorted, now ugly with pain and fear.

"Mmmm...mmmm...!!!"

The figure at the altar rose. It was tall and broad-shouldered, cloaked and hooded in black trimmed with scarlet. With hands sheathed in black gauntlets each decorated with a crimson pentangle, it seized two objects from the altar: a curved dagger and a golden chalice.

"....mmmmm...mm...!!!"

The dangling girl squirmed on the end of her chain. Her body gleamed in the torchlight.

"...from the one to the many..."

Chanting, the hooded figure approached her, the knife in one hand, the cup in the other.

"...from homes to towns; and soon cities and the world...!"

Bending, the specter set the chalice on the floor. The girl's hair swirled around as she thrashed in terror. Her screams muffled by the gag.

"...this world and all worlds shall be thy kingdom, oh Master...!"

The words blurred into a weird incantation, whispered softly into the writhing girl's ear. Instantly, she jerked and stiffened and was completely still, her body swaying slightly on the end of the chain.

The gloved fingers hooked into her hair and pulled her head back, exposing the pale curve of her throat.

The radio crackled into life.

"Uncle John...? This is Cat, where are you...?"

He grabbed the handset.

"H-hey, P-P-P-Princess...what's happenin'...?"

"We're on our way, Uncle John..."

There was a pause, nothing but the sizzle of static.

"Uncle John...? Are you alright...?"

Cold shivers ran down John Warburton's spine. He jerked himself together.

"Uh...we're just outside Paradise Gardens, Princess...but you're not gonna believe it...!"

Selena slapped her palm down, a moment of decision.

"Okay!"

She pressed a red button below the lip of the desk top and a concealed control panel rose up from the smooth surface, jeweled with dials and switches and a rainbow of twinkling lights.

"Let's do it!"

At the flick of a switch, a panoramic map of the world came alive. The USA lit up and then expanded until it filled the frame. And then a single state was selected and it in turn grew and dominated the screen; and finally a desert, with its highways and side roads and scattered small towns.

Selena rose and stood with hands on hips, surveying the luminous chart. Then she bent across the desk, her body thrusting towards a chromed, futuristic microphone on its short stand.

"Strike Force Alpha to red alert! Mission status...!!!"

Cat was jumping out before the wheels stopped turning. Wide-eyed, she threw herself into her Uncle's mighty arms.

"Oh, Uncle John! It's so good to see you!"

She almost knocked the breath out of him and he took a step backwards, squeezing her tight.

"You too, Princess...we were getting worried..."

She didn't notice how pale he was, or the strained young faces all around him. Smiling, she detached herself and turned to make the introductions.

"Uncle John," she said breathlessly. "This is Tom...Tom Ahiga...it means 'he fights'..."

As his war party disembarked from their vehicles, their leader strode forward. Shouldering the M-16, John Warburton came back down from the ridge and advanced to meet him, extending his hand. They shook solemnly and stood silently, appraising each other.

"Yes," said John Warburton. "You look like a fighting man."

"And you, sir," Tom Ahiga replied. "And I think we both seek the same thing, a great evil in the land."

Cat came bustling up between them, her face bright and full of stories. For a moment, the color returned to her Uncle's cheeks, remembering the little girl, always eager for adventure.

He put his big hands on her shoulders.

"Not now, Princess, not now..."

She saw a rare chill in his eyes, which were always so merry. It sobered her instantly as a cold fist clenched inside her.

"Uncle John, what is it?"

He turned away from her, striding back up to the shallow crest. "That great evil you speak of…I think we've found it…"

CHAPTER 13

THE GATES OF HELL

"Oh my God...!"

Seen from the crest of the ridge, Paradise Gardens was a great black stain on the land. A festering scab, a suppurating sore. Thick, sulfurous yellow vapors oozed like pus from cracks in its streets and sidewalks. The skin of its houses was bubbling and peeling and falling away in twisted black flakes, their smashed windows like eyeless sockets, gouged out and ragged.

Cat's eyes got wider and wider. Her jaw dropped. Gulping, she struggled to speak.

"Wha...what...?"

Screams.

A door banged open, hanging on a single hinge. A woman ran out onto the short, tiled driveway, her floral housecoat flapping around her ankles, her hair in curlers. Her eyes were bulging with terror, shrill shrieks spilled from her gaping mouth.

Grotesque figures were spilling out of the doorway and the shattered ground floor windows, shoving and squeezing and squirming and climbing over each other, as the screaming woman stumbled and fell on her hands and knees.

Oh...

They were grey, their hair lank and colorless, framing faces like grinning skulls, parchment skin shrunk onto the bone. Hung in rotting rags, their forms were emaciated, skeletal, wrapped in twists of desiccated sinew and shreds and tatters of skin.

Their lipless mouths emitted guttural growls and rasping yelps. Like pack animals closing for the kill, they came swiftly, lurching and jerking on splayed legs, arms outstretched, talons grasping. As the woman rolled on the ground, screaming, they covered her in a writhing pile, broken teeth clashing, ripping and clawing with nails that had grown in the grave.

The screaming was muffled and then choked off. A red spray fountained; raw chunks were tossed up and squabbled over wildly in a frenzy of snarling.

...shit...!

Cat was paralyzed. Beside her, Uncle John hefted the M-16, raising it to his shoulder and then letting the muzzle drop, his head spinning.

One of the creatures lifted its head and in their deep skull-like sockets the dull yellow orbs of its eyes rolled around and saw them. It opened its jaws wide and gave vent to a piercing howl. Instantly, the others were rising from the bloody horror and were crouching, alert, looking up at the ridge.

"Go! Go! Go!"

The whirling blades clattered, exhaust fumes making a grey haze.

"On the double!"

In single file, ducking low beneath the wash of the twin rotors, they lined up to board the camouflaged choppers, long, low-slung transports, poised on their insect-like undercarriage.

"C'mon, pick it up there!"

Slide doors slammed shut. The beat of the engines quickened. Lift off.

"FIRE!"

Tom Ahiga worked the lever of his Winchester.

"OPEN FIRE!"

John Warburton wrenched back the cocking handle. All around him, there was a rattle of semi-automatic fire.

In a bunch, the creatures were advancing down the path. They were crossing the burnt brown and black stubble of the front lawn, onto the broken sidewalk, crossing the street, their rotting feet sticky on the bubbled tarmac.

"POUR IT ON!"

They were coming up the shallow slope. Cat stood dumbly, looking at her empty hands.

"Here, Princess!"

Taking his hand off the trigger, her Uncle ripped open the flap and plucked a big .45 automatic from the holster on his belt.

"Catch!"

He tossed it to her. She caught it deftly, worked the slide and started shooting.

The firing built to a crescendo, as the young men from Free Town and the war party stood shoulder to shoulder on the crest of the ridge.

Caught by a hailstorm of lead, the creatures rocked and staggered. Scraps and bits flew off them. An arm was severed. One lost both its legs but kept on coming, shuffling on its stumps.

"Fuck!"

The slide stayed open, the magazine empty. Nimbler than the rest, one of the creatures was almost on her. Cursing, Cat lashed out viciously. The thing's face crumbled and caved in but it still raked at her, its claw-like fingernails snagging her hair.

Yelling, Cat hit out again and again and this time the head came clean off its shoulders. Cat stumbled backwards as the creature fell, clutching at her legs.

"Aw, hell...get off me willya...!"

Then Tom Ahiga was stepping up to her side, swinging the Winchester like a baseball bat, with a force that lifted the headless horror into the air and sent it pin wheeling away down the slope, arms and legs flailing.

Cat grinned at him.

"Thanks!"

He glared at her with eyes blazing with the fire of battle. And then Cat was off and running, jumping into the back of one of Free Town's old Army Jeeps, ripping back the bolt of a big .50 cal.

Have some of this, motherfuckers!

She kept firing until the long belt fed through and was spent. Halfway up the slope, the creatures were disintegrating, reduced to scraps and tatters and to powder. What was left was barely recognizable, bits of bone and ashes scattered on the ground.

Wild-eyed, Cat was still gripping the handles, still squeezing the trigger. John Warburton tapped her on the knee.

"You did it, Princess. You can stop now."

Panting, Cat shook herself together and jumped down. His face pale, her Uncle stared at the debris littering the slope. He shook his head slowly.

"Just what the hell is going on...?"

Tom Ahiga was staring at her, amazed. Grinning, Cat just shrugged, strolling blithely by.

Then someone shouted.

"Oh no!"

"LOOK...!!!"

In the crowded studio, the bustle of preparation was quelled in an instant to a pin drop silence taut with keen anticipation.

"Okay," said a quiet voice of authority. "Are we all ready?"

Nods all round. A double thumbs-up from the engineers at their panels.

"Then we go in...three..."

"E.T.A. in five-o-three..."

They flashed across the vaulting bright blue vastness of the sky, as the baking desert flowed by beneath them.

There were crackling spasms of radio chatter, kept to a minimum. They flew low, rising and falling with the contours of the terrain, the long ripples of a series of saw tooth ridges, the undulations of low hills.

"Close up, Blue Two, keep it tight..."

"...two...one....."

The director gave the signal. On the desks the monitors glowed and came alive, banks of them all with same display, a man's grave face, waiting patiently.

Sat next to the director, the interviewer intoned into his microphone.

"Ladies and gentlemen, we now take you live for an address by the man who has been referred to by no less than the President himself as the spiritual father of the nation, the Reverend Thaddeus P. Calhoun..."

Oh Jesus...!

A pillar of dust towered into the sky, dulling the sun which became a blank disc showing dimly through it.

Cat's blood froze. She gripped Uncle John's arm, down to the bone. Mesmerized, he hardly noticed.

Tom Ahiga was thumbing brass cartridges into the empty Winchester. He stared numbly, the slug slipping from his fingers. His lips moved, whispering a prayer in his people's ancient tongue.

Behind him, his war party, bunched together, took a collective step backwards. The young men of Free Town just stood dotted around, gaping.

We've had it...

A grey tide was rolling across the land. It came over the shimmering horizon and swept towards them. There were hundreds of them. In their coffin rags and tatters of rotting flesh, their bones held together by shrunken sinew.

"Aw...!" bawled John Warburton.

The pale yellow orbs of their eyes bulged from the sockets in their skulls. Broken teeth chomped and clacked in anticipation. Some brandished sticks and clubs and even axes. Most were grasping with fingers of rotten flesh falling from the bone, flaying the air with their discolored claws.

John Warburton wrenched his arm from Cat's crushing grasp. Gasping, she lurched backwards. With a hand on her shoulder, Tom Ahiga steadied her. Scraping the hair from her eyes, she looked at him desperately.

The fire reignited in his fierce eyes. He held the Winchester up high.

"Circle the trucks!" he shouted, drowning a fearful muttering all around.

For a moment, they all just stood and stared at him. Then at the fast moving wave that spilled on towards them. Then back at their leaders.

"Yes!" echoed John Warburton. "Now! Make a circle!"

Cat was off and running, leaping into the cab of a battered pickup. Engines revved, wheels span in a spray of dirt and small stones, then bit into the gritty surface. A dome of pale dust hung over them as the trucks and Jeeps and other odds and sods, engines grinding, jerked forward and back, some banging and scraping together, scrambling to get into formation.

"C'mon!"

The Reverend's face was calm, his tone mellow. But his words were fearful and spoke of evil and the judgment to come. His voice flowed from their TV speakers and wrapped around them. In living rooms across the nation, in seedy tenements and fine mansions, the fear radiated, infecting all those who heard him.

The dust drifted away. The engines fell silent. Wide-eyed, with anxious faces, the young men waited, weapons bristling, behind their makeshift barricade.

John Warburton's breath hissed out slowly through clenched teeth. He rubbed his big hand over his face, smearing the greasy film of sweat. At his shoulder, Cat's face was taut and pale. She was struggling to focus, fumbling with the magazine of an M-1 carbine, cursing and then slapping it in.

They were close now. They could hear them, the flap and rustle of their rags, the clicking of their claws, the clashing of their bony jawbones. The lustful groaning, the shrill barks and baying, the sound of the pack on the hunt.

Tom Ahiga filled his chest with a great lungful of air. He breathed long and slow and deep. Cat turned to look at him and he held her gaze.

They could smell them now. It washed over them and made them flinch, their faces contorting. The smell of death and decay.

John Warburton cocked the M-16. The sound was very loud.

"Hold steady, boys! Hold steady!"

The boom of his voice put steel in the spines of the young men of Free Town. Lined up beside them, the war party was chanting the words their ancestors had taken to battle with them.

Cat looked deep into Tom Ahiga's eyes. She smiled.

"We don't stand a chance, do we?"

He smiled back at her.

"It's a good day to die…"

Another sound. Above all the rest, high in the sky.

"Hey…?"

A droning sound, like a swarm of bees, approached. A whirring, like great wings. A clatter of whirling metal.

"Target acquired…"

"I'm going in…"

The small attack 'copters came in low and fast, up and over the humps in the land. Spitting fire, they strafed the advancing tide, the streams of tracer carving great furrows in the grey mass.

The passed over, then soared and wheeled and came down again, the rattle of their guns sounding thinly through the churn of the rotors. The effect of their guns was like a vicious hailstorm in a field of corn, battering it down and thinning it.

"Okay Red One, we're coming in now…"

The heavy twin rotors were slung with pods each housing a dozen missiles. They measured their distance and took station, three of them, in a line abreast, and hovered there.

"Let 'em have it!"

The pods loosed their arrows with puffs of white smoke. Lances of fire, the missiles fanned out and spanned the seething sea of grey. Great boiling bubbling eruptions of flame, deep orange laced with black, smothered the target. And when the bubbles of fire had risen and were faded by the glare of the sky and had evaporated till there was nothing but a faint smudge high above; then there was nothing left, just a vast mound of charred black and twisted and crackling things.

Nobody said a word.

Dumbfounded, they stood and watched the choppers land, on the flat plain a little way off.

The dust settled. The engines scaled down and the whirling rotors slowed. The slide doors slammed open.

"Looks like we got here just in time!"

And then Cat was laughing, running, arms outstretched.

"Selena!"

She looked fantastic, swaggering in her pale-sand combat fatigues, criss-crossed by belts of ammo pouches, hefting an M-16.

"Hi, Cat..."

Cat's arrival rocked her back on her heels; now they were both laughing. Arm in arm, they marched towards the circle of motley vehicles.

John Warburton came out to greet them.

"Hey, Mama..."

Their embrace was powerful, the kiss lingering. Cat stood back, grinning.

"Hey," her laugh was breathless, her voice shrill with release and relief. "You guys...!"

Tom Ahiga emerged and Cat made the introductions. He shook Selena's hand respectfully. He tried hard to keep his eyes fixed firmly on her proud face and not devour her spectacular shape. Selena simply let her fierce eyes roll all over him.

"Oooh, Cat, you do have fine taste. He's beautiful!"

Tom Ahiga was actually blushing, and gathering behind him, the war party were smothering their grins.

And then they had other distractions, as Selena swiveled to signal to the helicopters.

"Hey...!"

The big twin rotors disgorged their passengers.

"Wow!"

Girls, all clad identically in crisp desert fatigues. Slim, fit girls, moving lithely, hefting their weapons lightly, professionally. Spreading out, taking post, ready for action.

Cat looked hopeful, and then her face clouded with disappointment.

"Aiko?" Selena asked softly.

Suddenly, Cat's eyes were brimming with tears.

"I lost her," she murmured. "It's my fault."

Reaching out, Selena stroked her golden hair.

"Don't worry, sweetheart, we'll find her."

And then she was all business. She stepped out briskly, past the barricades, and stood gazing out at the mound of charred and smoking wreckage.

"Now, just what the hell is goin' down?"

John Warburton frowned, shrugging his broad shoulders.

"Beats me, Mama. It's like Hell's been let loose on the world."

Selena surveyed the young men of Free Town, who stood looking all around, white-faced, their eyes wide with shock and horror.

"I think you'd...?" Selena suggested.

John Warburton nodded. He stepped forward, the M-16 cradled in his mighty arms.

"Gentlemen…!"

He was their commander and, marveling, Cat saw him transformed into the fighting legend who had gone into South-East Asia with the first Special Forces advisers sent by President Kennedy in May 1961.

"…well fought! I'm proud of you…!"

He issued them their orders—some to remain to stand sentry over part of the assorted convoy; the bulk to return to Free Town, to guard it against any further assault. And Cat saw their backbones straighten, the sinew stiffen and the fire glow in their eyes again.

"That's my main man!" Grinning, Serena saluted him.

John Warburton frowned.

"Truth is," he replied. "They're spent. They can't fight any more. They're willing, but they're not soldiers."

His eyes were brimming, welling with a deep sadness. And now Cat saw the terrible ache of disillusionment that had caused him to turn his back on war and the dirty politics that made it; and then on to a mighty business empire, taking his riches to found the haven of Free Town, to seek an oasis of peace and harmony in a corrupt and conflicted world.

"They didn't come to me to fight and die…"

And now tears were rolling down his cheeks and Cat sprang forward and threw her arms around him, holding him tight. She was crying too, her shoulders shaking.

Smiling gently now, Selena stroked her palm across his broad shoulders.

"No sign of your womenfolk?"

Breathing deeply, he kissed the tears tenderly from Cat's cheeks and released himself from her embrace.

"No, nothing. We hoped to find some sign between Free Town and Paradise Gardens. But nothing. Not even the town. Nothing. It's gone."

"Paradise Gardens?"

"All gone."

"Shit, this is getting heavy, man."

From the crests beyond the seeping scar of Paradise Gardens, the black beast was watching. Its green eyes blazed with a searing fury.

In the glowing tepee, they drank the potion that the Old Man gave them.

"F-f-far out…!"

It was a dark brown concoction, with a glow of mellow gold at the heart of it. As thick as liquid honey, bittersweet, with a tingling aftertaste that was like sparks dancing on the tongue.

They sat in a semi-circle by the fire: Cat and Selena and Tom Ahiga and John Warburton. Across from them, the Old Man's face seemed to float in the flames, a mask of amber, eyes closed, his lips moving as he murmured an old evocation, his voice the merest wisp of a whisper.

"Oh...wow, man...!"

The Old Man lifted his hands, so thin and frail that they were transparent, translucent, in the firelight. As he did so, the flickering flames became rainbow butterflies.

He was leaning towards the fire, passing his hands over it and through it slowly. The others watched, wondering. Cat reached out, wanting to touch the butterflies. Tom Ahiga seized her wrist.

"Don't!" he hissed. "You'll break the spell."

And then, abruptly, the Old Man was sitting bolt upright, silent, his hands folded in his lap. His blanket robe had slipped from his narrow shoulders. Tom Ahiga stood quickly, went across and replaced it gently.

"He knows," he said. "He knows."

At night, phantoms walked the streets of Dry Gulch.

They swore they could hear the ghostly tinkle of a piano and the clink of glasses in the gutted saloons. The tinny creaking of bedsprings in the cobwebbed bedrooms of the town brothel. A faint echo of pistol shots and just a hint of gun smoke.

The Moon slit through a thin veil of cloud and its light poured down like silver. The Old Man stopped and lifted his hand.

At his shoulder, Tom Ahiga mirrored the gesture, forcefully, clenching his raised fist.

On the ragged, crumbling fringes of the town, they fanned out in a long and shallow cleft in the ground, hunkered down where the Moon could not find them. The Old Man was in the lead, with Tom Ahiga keeping tight to him. Then came John Warburton, and Cat pressed up close to him; the young men of Tom Ahiga's war party; and Selena with her squad of girl commandoes.

Gun barrels gleamed, cartridge belts glittered, in the half-light of the trench. Their eyes showed dully, wide with tension and keen anticipation, as they all gazed upwards, waiting for the Moon.

It seemed to take forever. Cat's mouth was as dry as dust. Licking her lips, she swallowed hard; it was like swallowing a rock. Her Uncle slid his brawny arm around her waist and gave a little squeeze. Cat smiled weakly and let her head dip briefly onto his broad shoulder.

Tom Ahiga was looking at her. He put his hand on his heart. Cat's smile warmed; she gripped her carbine tighter.

At last, the Moon cooperated, slipping back behind the veil. The Old Man lifted his hand again, waving them forward.

Spread out, guns held at the ready, they advanced with swift caution across the broken ground on the edge of town. They swerved to negotiate tumbledown sheds, stepped nimbly over toppled and teetering rail fences.

At a silent signal they split, Selena's girls flanking to the left, the war party with Uncle John and Cat to the right. On silent feet, they doubled the pace, loping down narrow side streets, strewn with scraps of refuse, skipping around the old tin cans.

And then they were poised in the shadows, beneath the remains of the sagging wooden awnings, on the boardwalks, either side of Main Street.

The Moon slid out again, but its baleful glare could not find them, pressed against the flaking walls of the houses. Frowning, Cat glared back at the Moon. Her heart was pounding, her palms slippery on the wooden stock of the gun.

Come on! What's the matter with you...?

She was angry with herself. This wasn't like her. She was always cool as ice, going into action. Not like this, not wound up tight like this. But this was different. Now she was up against something she just couldn't get her head around.

This is a bad trip...a bad, bad trip...!

For a second, she wanted to wake up and find out it was all just a dream. Then she saw Tom Ahiga's powerful silhouette up ahead and when he turned to look to the Old Man, his strong profile. And close by there was the reassuring presence of her Uncle. She swiveled to glance at him and John Warburton rolled his eyes and grinned at her.

And then she was on the move, as the Old Man set off without warning, covering the warped boardwalk with a speed that took them all by surprise.

In the crypt, the girl's body was a pale glimmer in the shadows, hanging limp and bloodless. Her dead flesh was tinted by a strange luminescence, radiating from a brazier heaped with glowing green coals.

The hooded figure glided across the flagstones, approaching the brazier on its tripod stand. In its hand was a weird chalice fashioned from black stone, embossed with dragons clutching skulls in their claws.

Murmuring an eerie incantation, the black-cloaked apparition was slowly tipping the contents of the chalice onto the coals. The girl's blood, thick and coagulating, was dripping down like syrup.

The glowing green coals flared into writhing tongues of flame. Images formed in the flames.

The rails were dull and corroded by decades of disuse.

The Old Man was leading the way, in the narrow space between the rails, treading on the wooden sleepers. He was murmuring, his voice a low melodic drone, making spells, wafting with his hand as though he was casting seed upon the ground. In his other hand he twitched a crooked staff, decorated with feathers and eagle's claws and rattles cut from snakes' tails.

And then the Old Man halted and was pointing, the staff jabbing like a spear.

"Here we go..." muttered John Warburton.

The rails ran for about a mile, to a cluster of low hills huddled together, grey domes in the half light. Their slopes were wrinkled and parched, like old fruit left to shrivel and rot.

The earth was grey, the dark sky the color of lead. The sight of the dead hills made Cat shiver. Beside her, Tom Ahiga was frowning.

"They sucked the land dry," he whispered. "These white men with their sickness for gold."

The snake rattles jangled as the Old Man marched on, brandishing his staff. He caught the others by surprise again and they had to jump to catch up.

And now the Old Man was pointing again, thrusting with the staff.

"Hey..." breathed John Warburton.

The rails vanished into a black gash in the hillside; the mouth of a man-made cave, framed by stout timbers. The rough ground nearby was strewn with the rusted relics of past activity: a rail wagon made of riveted steel plates, tilted on its side; heavy hammers and pickaxes; dented miners' helmets and lamps with their dusty lenses cracked; even a pair of steel-capped boots, the leather dry and cracked.

The Old Man squatted down and sat cross-legged on the ground, beside the entrance to the mine. He laid the staff down in front of him. From a shoulder bag made of tanned leather he produced a handful of pottery shards with strange symbols etched on them. He cast them down on the earth at his feet and passed his hand back and forth over them, then scooped them up and did it again, his lips moving silently, his eyes clouded, far away.

"He will go no further," said Tom Ahiga, his war party standing ready at his shoulder. "He will stay here and make magic to help us."

Cat couldn't shake the cold from her bones. The steel of the gun was so cold it almost burned her hands.

Selena stepped up close to her and her presence was warming.

"Do your thing, Old Man. We're gonna need all the help we can get."

One fierce glance and Selena's girls were fanning out, watching their backs as they inched forward warily, advancing on the blank black mouth of the mine. And then they were all gone, vanished into the heart of darkness.

CHAPTER 14

MONSTERS

The darkness sucked them down and down. It retreated before the bright splash cast by their flashlights, taunting them.

"Jeez!" John Warburton panted. "Just how deep does this go?"

The walls of the mine shaft were craggy and crumbling. Old beams sagged and creaked fitfully, as they passed by. This prompted a fine rain of dust that trickled down in strands and floated like a veil, bigger bits pattering on the uneven ground.

Grimacing, Cat raked her fingers through her long hair, combing out the grit. It was hot and airless in the tunnel and her face, stark in the harsh light, shone with perspiration.

At her feet, the rails were rusted and broken, the wooden sleepers dried out and crumbling. Cat stubbed her toe and stumbled, cursing loudly.

"Ow! Shit! Damn it!"

Tom Ahiga moved close and put his arm round to steady her.

"Sssh...," he admonished softly.

Cat leaned readily into his strong embrace, letting her head tilt back onto his shoulder. Selena rolled her eyes, shook her head and smiled. Cat blushed fiercely and detached herself abruptly.

"Sorry..."

Uncle John was grinning at her.

"Ready?"

Cat pouted, angry now.

"Yes, yes," she hissed. "C'mon, let's go!"

Chuckling, John Warburton led the way, the others close behind.

"Spread out..."

They divided to the left and right, hugging the tunnel walls; Tom Ahiga, Cat and the war party; Uncle John, Selena and her girl commandoes. The steel of their guns gleamed, mirrored by the cold determination in their eyes.

As they advanced, the beams of their torches seemed to make the ragged walls of the mine shaft move, shadows writhing in every cleft and fold as the raking beams flushed them out and banished them.

Behind them, a shadow suddenly and silently separated itself from a deep scar in the wall. It expanded upwards and outwards and spread itself like great black batwings. And fell like a cloak of darkness, enveloping the young man who brought up the rear of Tom Ahiga's war party, stifling his shout to a sound too faint to be heard even by the man walking a few feet in front of him. Then the black shadow was gone, shrinking back into its niche in the wall, and the young warrior was gone with it.

They pressed on. Within the next few hundred yards the black shadows came to life twice and took away another of the war party and one of Selena's girls. For an instant, her eyes were huge and terrified, glaring out of the spreading stain of darkness. Then they were gone, snuffed out.

"Hold it..."

John Warburton raised his arm, fist clenched to signal a halt.

"Listen..."

They strained to hear but heard nothing. Brow furrowed, Cat concentrated, but then stepped back, shaking her head.

"What...what is it...?"

"There! Can't you?"

"Yes...yes!"

It was as much a feeling as a sound, a faint pulse, deep down.

"Drums?" suggested Tom Ahiga.

"No," said Selena. "It's too..."

"Too mechanical," John Warburton finished for her.

"Machines?" said Cat. "But this mine hasn't been worked for years. It's been––"

There was an exclamation of surprise.

"Hey!"

At the back, young warriors stood staring in confusion.

"Where's Long John?"

"And Billy Jack?"

Selena was striding back down the line, her eyes flashing an alarm.

"And Lina! Where is she?"

A chorus began calling out the names, till John Warburton hushed them. In the sudden silence, the distant dark pulse throbbed dully, somewhere deep underground.

Icy fingers played up and down Cat's spine. Tom Ahiga saw her shiver and stepped up close. As tall as she was, she looked up to him, into his calm brown eyes. She summoned up a pale smile.

"What are we up against?" she whispered.

He took a deep breath, squaring his broad shoulders. Before he could speak, Selena came marching forward, a Fury ready for battle, a fierce fire blazing in her eyes. She turned to face John Warburton, who brandished the M-16, like a toy in his ham-like hands.

"Let's go!"

205

The great crypt was an ancient place hewn of black stone, or that was how it was meant to appear. It was in fact a recent, secret construction. Its smooth walls, curving upwards to form a hollow dome, were clad with gruesome tapestries—hideous beasts and grotesque demons, flaying and burning and dismembering their shrieking victims—a ghastly panorama of Hell.

Stone steps climbed to a lofty summit, bathed in a cold pale glow cast by tall candelabra. On high, there was a mighty throne, carved from an exotic black wood, encrusted with snakes and grinning skulls.

The throne was occupied by a tall broad-shouldered figure hooded and cloaked in black and scarlet. From its lofty heights, it gazed down upon two acolytes, in robes of humble grey, cowering on their hands and knees at the foot of the steps.

"Speak...!"

The disciples flinched, their shoulders bowing lower till their noses were almost touching the floor. They did not dare to look up.

"t-t-the...harvesting p-p-p-proceeds..."

"b-b-but the process is...slow..."

The hooded figure soared to its feet, the black robes swirling. He cut his stammering minion short with a slashing gesture of a gloved hand.

"Enough! I want no excuses!"

His shadow cast a chill over them.

"The Master grows impatient. He is displeased with us. He longs to rise up and claim his kingdom and he will tolerate no delay...!"

They were shivering visibly. Another gesture dismissed them.

"Be gone from my sight! And redouble your efforts! Press on! Press on...!"

On all fours, they scuttled backwards like startled crabs, the tips of their noses scraping the flagstones, till they reached a broad ironbound doorway at the far distant end of the throne room. There, they exited, bowing.

"And close the door behind you!"

The towering rage and majesty mellowed somewhat. The broad shoulders, draped in scarlet, relaxed.

"Now, my dear...."

A girl reclined beside the throne, on a heap of purple velvet cushions. She wore a collar round her throat, black leather studded with silver, with a slender silver chain that ran in coils to a ringbolt set in the floor.

"...how will you please me...?"

The girl was naked, save for a wisp of pale silk veiling her loins. She was lithe and supple, with small, pert breasts. Her almond eyes were slanting and her face was like that of a dangerous kitten.

"The walls are moving," said Cat.

"Cave in!" hissed Selena.

"No..." said John Warburton.

"But the walls *are* moving!" exclaimed Tom Ahiga.

Ahead of them, the wall did bulge and the bulge became a great head of black stone, with small pits for a nose and a slit for a mouth. Behind the head came a powerful shoulder and then a mighty arm extended, as the head pivoted slowly to stare at them with hollow eyes.

"What...?"

Then a leg, a pillar of stone, was stepping out of the wall and planting a huge foot on the ground. And then it was straddling the rusting rails with both feet, facing them. The span of its shoulders blocked the passage and it had to stoop slightly, its massive hands with their blunt stone talons extended and ready like a wrestler's.

"...the hell...?"

It stood and stared at them with its hollow eyes.

"Uh-oh!"

A dull cracking behind them. As they watched, dumbfounded, the strange materialization was repeated and a second stone monster cut off their retreat. Like its twin, it was humanoid in shape, but in form made of dark stone that plated it like a skin of rugged armor.

A rearguard, one of Selena's girls sprang forward instinctively and fired her carbine from the hip.

"No!" Selena shouted.

The slug made a splash of lead on the stone giant's chest and dropped harmlessly between its huge feet. The big head tilted slightly, as if studying her, as the girl lurched forward, her toe catching on a wooden sleeper.

"No..."

Dipping its shoulder, the monster swung an arm. The motion seemed slow and lazy, but the impact was colossal. The carbine clattered on the rails as the girl was swiped sideways off her feet. Limbs flailing, she flew a short distance and crashed into the rough-hewn wall of the tunnel. Her flight halted abruptly, she slid down limply, her eyes sightless, blood flowing from her mouth.

Her companions stepped forward, lifting their weapons.

"Don't!" snapped Selena. "Don't shoot! You'll bring the roof down on us!"

"And it's useless," muttered Tom Ahiga.

Seconds ticked by, in a silence stretched until it was screaming. The stone giants remained where they were, blocking the way, standing astride the rusting tracks, front and back.

"Close up," said John Warburton. "Stay out of reach."

Cat weighed the M-1 carbine in her hands. It felt useless, like a lump of lead. Cursing, she lowered the muzzle.

"Now what do we do?"

She looked at her Uncle, but he just shrugged. He was juggling a pineapple grenade on his palm. Selena's eyes flashed an alarm.

"No way," he reassured her, stuffing the small bomb into one of the deep pockets of his battle dress. "It would cause a cave-in."

"Well," said Cat. "We can't just stand here and..."

Tom Ahiga was lunging forward, shoving past her.

"Don't!"

The youngest member of the war party was barely 18. A good-looking youth with long blue-black hair that flowed down to his shoulders like the warriors of old, with fire in his veins that ignited in his eyes, eager to prove himself, to lay hands on his enemy, to "count coup" as the old warriors did.

He was gone before Tom Ahiga could stop him. Darting forward, his young face creased in a reckless grin. Laughing, he sprang and slapped his palm on the stone giant's shoulder.

"Oh God..." groaned John Warburton.

The boy landed lightly and turned to grin back at them.

"Look out!"

With astonishing quickness, the mighty stone arms reached out and clamped themselves around him. The boy's scream was choked off as they crushed him. They saw his eyes bulge, his face contorting. They heard his bones cracking.

Blood burst from the boy's gaping mouth. His eyes rolled up till only the whites showed and then his head lolled forward slowly. His thrashing legs stiffened, twitched, then dangled limply.

"Oh..." Cat moaned.

The monster tossed the dead boy aside like a broken toy. And then it was marching forward. The ground shook, each step jarring them as they all bunched together. The rails buckled and the wooden sleepers splintered beneath its weight, dust and debris raining down from the roof of the tunnel.

Cat was frozen, her body like a block of ice. The dead boy's bloated features floated before her like a hideous mask, transfixing her with its bulging eyes.

Fuck this!

Suddenly, she was boiling over, consumed by a white heat of anger. With searing clarity, she saw it, lying in the dirt by the side of the tracks.

Just what I'm looking for!

An old pick-axe, dulled by the patina of age, but still effective. Dropping the carbine, she sprang and dipped her body all in one smooth movement, scooping it up. It felt good in her hands.

They all stood and watched, open-mouthed, as she took a stance astride the tracks, blocking the monster's advance.

"Motherfucker...!"

The stone giant swung its arms like great clubs but Cat ducked and swayed lithely. With an explosive exhalation of effort, she scythed the pick-axe up and around and down, putting her shoulders and her back and her whole body into it, her feet planted, taking her strength from the ground.

"UUUNNNGG-GGGHH...!"

The sharp point of the pick impacted with unerring accuracy, right between the black blank hollows of the giant's eyes.

"UUGGHH!"

Cat struck again. And again. The monster swayed. Fine cracks radiated from the point of impact. The giant reeled back and Cat came after it, swinging the pick-axe, finding the target, again and again.

"UHH...HHH!"

"UGGHH!"

Stone shards splintered. The cracks expanded and the monster's face split apart and was disintegrating, crumbling.

"YAAAAAAHH...HHHH...!"

The giant was toppling, falling in slow motion. Its fall was like an earthquake that made them all flinch and duck as dirt and fragments cascaded down on them and the beams bowed and creaked in protest.

Behind them, there were loud sounds of cracking and crumbling. Alarmed, they jumped and span around.

"Jeez!"

The giant's twin was dissolving, collapsing into a pile of rubble. Selena stood looking down at it, shaking her head, her proud afro decorated by grit and bits. His long black hair paled by a film of grey dust, Tom Ahiga scrubbed a slime of dirt and sweat from his face.

"They must have been joined by some kind of spell."

Cat swayed, letting the pick-axe slip from her fingers. The fierce fire and color were draining from her eyes and her face, as she stared at the fallen giant. Sweat shone on her face and pricked her eyes, making her blink rapidly and rub them.

"Wha...what did I just do...?" she panted.

Uncle John slid his arm around her heaving shoulders.

"You saved us, Princess."

Everyone was smiling at her. Striding forward, Selena snatched her from Uncle John and enfolded her in a tight embrace. Cat submitted weakly.

"You were magnificent!"

Cat's brain was scrambled. Tom Ahiga was kissing her.

"You are a mighty warrior," he declared. "They will sing of this around the campfires!"

Her thoughts were reeling in confusion.

"Yes," she stammered. "B-but what did I d-d-do...?"

Sheathed in the black gauntlet, the hand stroked Aiko's long and shining, blue-black hair.

"Yes..."

It wandered over her bare breasts and felt their points harden.

"Oh yes..."

The hand roved across the flat plane of her belly, the tawny skin gleaming in the cold light, to her long, smooth thighs.

"...yes, you will please me...."

Despite the cold and her stark nakedness, and the hand invading her, Aiko did not shiver. She seemed to be in some kind of trance, her dark eyes dull and distant.

"...and you shall be the lure that brings the Chosen One to the Master...!"

CHAPTER 15

A HARVEST OF SOULS

A machine within a machine within a machine and at its core glowed a dark red pulse that was a slowly drumming heartbeat, a subterranean sound of dread and doom. The machine had sub-machines which in turn had smaller sub-machines, till it almost filled the awesome span of a high-domed cavern, its grey granite veined with glistening crystal.

Wheels and meshing cogs and mighty pistons belching steam. A whirring and clanking and the deep drumbeat pounding. The machine was tended by an army of ants, tiny figures dwarfed by it.

"Jee-zus!"

"What the––!"

The tunnel exited onto a narrow metal walkway that ringed the vast cavern and descended in a far-flung spiral down into the depths of the machine.

"Oh my God!"

In the red glow radiating from the bowels of the machine their faces looked like they were bathed in blood, the grime making streaks like black tears in a slick of perspiration.

Cat, Tom Ahiga, John Warburton and Selena stood shoulder to shoulder, framed by the mouth of the mine shaft. Weapons held ready, Selena's girls fanned out to her left. Ahiga's warriors spread out to their leader's right. At her signal, Selena's commandoes extended the circle, expanding the intervals between them till they semi-circled the great bowl below them. Tom Ahiga gestured and his young warriors moved to mirror them. Together, they surrounded the mighty machine.

They stood looking down over the polished metal railing.

"Jee-zus!" John Warburton repeated.

Then Cat shouted out loud, the sound sucked away by the deep dark frequencies of the massive machinery. She was pointing, out across the wide expanses below them.

"Look...!"

The night sky glowed redly and seemed to quiver, like a taut membrane, to the tune of a high-pitched incantation, barely audible yet resonant and piercing.

The Old Man was where they had left him. He sat cross-legged by the entrance to the mine, his staff laid cross-wise on the ground at his feet. With a sweeping gesture, he scooped up the pottery shards with their mysterious etchings. With a flick of the wrist he cast them back down so they fell in a shallow crescent in the dirt.

Head down, his narrow shoulders hunched, he bent his body over them. A shudder passed through him. He wafted both hands over the shards in the dirt, his bony fingers fluttering. He began to rock back and forth. His thin lips parted to emit an airy, wavering, keening sound that took shape and formed strange syllables in a forgotten tongue.

The swaying of his body quickened. His chanting became staccato, urgent. On the surface of the ground grains and bits of grit shifted. The shards were moving, forming a pattern.

"Look...!"

The army that tended the machine was cloaked and cowled in monastic hoods. It scuttled and scampered, small and lithe, apelike, up and down ramps and along gantries. Hands with leathery, long fingers spiked with yellow talons yanked at levers, twisted wheels and made quick nimble adjustments to flickering, luminous dials and gauges.

Fanned out on the walkway high above, the raiding party stood and watched, amazed, bathed in the throbbing, ruddy glow that radiated from the heart of the machine. The girl commandoes and the youthful warriors cast nervous sideways glances at their leaders, waiting for orders.

And then it was Selena's turn, to point and shout out loud, her voice choked by horror.

"Oh God!"

Looming over the entrance to the mine, the ragged saw tooth crest of the ridge was black against the red sky. A shape grew out of its jagged edge, a thing that crouched there, poised, sleek and brutal.

Down below, at the mouth of the tunnel, eyes closed, the Old Man was whispering an ancient incantation, an exhalation, ethereal. On the ground at his feet, the shards were still moving, some sliding, some rotating slowly.

On the ridge, two great eyes came to life, an eerie green with white heat at its core.

The shards were glowing, a deep orange, scorching the dry dirt. Sitting bolt upright, the Old Man raised his hands high above his head. He was chanting now, his voice strong and melodic. His eyes flashed open and a fierce fire blazed in them, as he stared into the sizzling green orbs on the ridge.

Girdling half the span of the deep cavern, on the far side of the great machine, there was a steel balcony bearing the weight of squat crystal columns, spread out across the huge circumference, spaced evenly. Transparent, the columns appeared to be hollow and filled with a pale mist that glowed green, then yellow and then green again.

"Oh--!"

John Warburton's eyes were wide, his mouth gaping, his face a contorted mask of anguish. Pressed close to his side, Cat clutched his arm, gripping tightly.

"Oh--!"

Within each crystal column, floating ghostlike in the luminous vapors, was a female figure, eyes wide open and yet oblivious, in a trance.

The crystal columns were domed, crowned by a bristling complexity of valves and tubes and wiring. All servicing a single larger pipeline that arched outwards and down into the bowels of the darkly pulsing machine.

"My girls!" John Warburton groaned. "What are they doing to my girls?"

Warriors and commandoes gripped their weapons tightly. Tom Ahiga brandished his Winchester impotently. Dazed, Cat fumbled with her carbine's cocking lever. Selena swayed slightly, wiping her lips with the back of her hand.

Each column was attended by the cloaked and hooded creatures. Till now, they and their fellows swarming over the machine had seemed unaware of the presence of invaders. Then, prompted by some animal instinct, one of them turned quickly and looked up behind him. In the shadow of the hood, they saw yellow eyes that were deep and sunken, a jutting snout and sharp canines, something that was part ape, part dog, a hideous mutation.

As they stood amazed, high on the gantry, the long snout parted to show teeth and tongue. A shriek, a high-pitched needle drilling sound, pierced through the drumming and droning and grinding of the machine; a shrill alarm call.

On the ridge, the green orbs flared, their white heat blinding. But the Old Man sat and stared right back at them, fists clenched above his head, his song strong and unwavering.

"Let 'em have it!"

Snarling like a wolf, Tom Ahiga worked the lever of his Winchester, shouldering it and firing, levering and firing, again and again. Jolted into action, his war party let rip with a ragged volley.

Hefting her M-16, Selena was firing from the hip, the bright muzzle flash reflected in her narrowed eyes. At her shoulder, John Warburton was pumping out round after round.

With a sound like the loud tearing of canvas, Selena's girl commandoes cut loose with their low-slung sub-machine guns, one after the other, all along the line. Spent brass tinkled on the metal walkway.

Cat raised the carbine to her shoulder. Now that she was in action, she was as cool as ice, as she selected her targets and squeezed off her shots.

The Old Man's song was filling the red sky. The dazzling green orbs were dimming; on the jagged rim of the ridge the menacing silhouette retreated.

"Pour it on!" roared John Warburton, consumed by battle fury.

Capering, clambering, swinging from rail to rail, from gantry to gantry, up ramps and platforms, the nimble creatures came at them in a howling rush, yellow eyes blazing, fangs slavering.

Rising, the Old Man plucked up his staff. Casting one final glance at the now empty ridge, he turned and vanished into the mouth of the mine shaft.

"What the--!"

The hail of bullets found its mark. In mid-stride and mid-leap, the creatures were halted, bowled over by the impact. And then, in the blink of an eye, they simply exploded, blew apart in a burst of grey dust.

Some stood and stared, astonished.

"Keep firing!"

The pulsing red glow of the cavern was suffused by a fine veil of dust, as creature after creature appeared to vanish in a puff of smoke.

"Watch out!"

A few survived the barrage and came vaulting up through the pale red mist. Clawing for the rail, they swung up and over, howling, their talons clawing.

One of Selena's girls staggered, screaming, her face a bloody ruin, then fell to be consumed by the machine, chopped to pieces.

Repelling boarders, Tom Ahiga was hammering with the butt of his rifle. Fighting hand-to-hand, his warriors were slashing with knives, using their carbines as clubs. One went down on his back, submerged by a triple onslaught. When the creatures rose from him, what was left was barely recognizable as human.

Selena vaporized all three with a short burst and then, the magazine empty, swung the M-16 like a baseball bat, as a fourth came up and over and at her. Her assailant was knocked off the rail in a backwards somersault. John Warburton fired and the creature exploded in mid-air like a clay pigeon.

"Nice!" Selena grinned viciously.

Cat rammed in a fresh magazine and was firing the carbine from the hip, side-swaying as the razor-like claws flicked her swirling hair. The bomb-burst of grey dust blew up in her face and she scrubbed her eyes, momentarily blinded.

When her eyes cleared, the railing was empty. Only the victors remained, panting, eyes burning with a fierce exultation, shaking the dead dust of their adversaries from their hair and shoulders.

Someone laughed nervously, a high fractured sound. Someone slapped a comrade on the back, raising a cloud of dust. They didn't look at the mangled remains lying twisted at their feet or scattered in ragged chunks across the milling, threshing fangs of the machine.

And then they remembered the glowing crystal columns and the reason why they were there.

"Oh God!"

"Oh, my girls...!"

On the dark desert highway the convoy's lights made a strand of glowing pearls. It was moving fast, reckless, regardless, pressing on. The odd, occasional oncoming traffic was simply bullied aside, forced to swerve into the sand and grit beyond the bounds of the asphalt, squawking in alarm.

It was a caravan of six, all the same; long, sleek tankers of plain polished steel, with no markings to distinguish them. The cold starlight gleamed on their mirror-like flanks as they hurtled onwards, exhausts booming.

"C'mon...c'mon...!"

They slung their weapons and, with the flat of their hands, searched the flawless surface of the crystal columns, seeking some kind of catch or a seam. The crystal was warm to the touch and tingled with a slight vibration.

"Damn it!"

Suspended within, veiled by the luminous yellow-green gas, the girls stared sightlessly, their arms down limply by their sides.

"C'mon, damn you...!"

John Warburton pounded on the crystal with his powerful fists.

"Uncle John!"

His hands were bleeding. Alarmed, Cat seized his thick wrists and drew him to her.

"Please...!"

She threw her arms around him. His broad shoulders were shaking. Selena stepped close and laid a gentle hand on him.

"They're gone, man," she stated simply. "They're gone."

The warriors and girl commandoes were bunched on the high walkway, looking all around nervously. His face a stone mask, Tom Ahiga was thumbing fresh loads into the breech of the Winchester. Suddenly, he tensed and looked up, eyes narrowing.

"Listen!"

"What's that?"

A klaxon blared, once, twice, a signal.

The convoy veered off the highway and into the desert. Arrow straight, it followed an invisible path, a road to nowhere, raising a pall of dust that blotted out the stars.

At intervals along the descending spiral of the steel walkway that circled the cavern there were archways, the open mouths of tunnels cut deep into the stone. They glowed amber, lit by a mysterious source that suffused the veins of crystal in the rock.

"There! Did you hear it...?"

A human sound, although barely human. A dismal wail, thin and distant, came echoing dimly out of the mouth of a tunnel close by them. In an instant, the drumming of the machine crushed it. Then they heard it again.

"The others!" John Warburton exclaimed. "They must still be alive!"

He was off and running, with surprising speed for a man of his bulk. Cat sprang after him, hot on his heels, having to work to catch up. Selena shot a sideways glance at Tom Ahiga and then the rest were all piling in after them.

"C'mon!"

The glowing tunnel wound on and on. They were running flat out, the pounding of their boot heels and the rasp of their panting breath a sound that seemed to swirl all around them.

"Watch out――!"

A figure was stumbling towards them. On bare feet, a young woman, still clad in the short night-dress she had worn when the phantom night raiders came for her, now smudged and tattered. Her hair was tangled, her face streaked with tears.

Slinging his rifle, John Warburton scooped her up as she swayed and fell, cradling her in his strong arms.

"Oh, Papa John…," the girl sobbed. "Papa John!"

Selena barked an order and led her commando squad forward, stepping out briskly, submachine-guns aimed from the hip, ready.

Cat was stroking the sobbing girl's hair, smoothing it from her face.

"It's okay, baby, it's okay…"

They sat her down gently, propped against the wall of the tunnel. Tom Ahiga detailed two of his men to stand guard over her. Then Cat and her Uncle John were gone, vanished round a bend in the tunnel, chasing Selena and her girls. Tom Ahiga led the rest of his war party after them, following more cautiously, keeping a wary eye behind them.

The sky was starless now, fathomless and black. The desert was grey and lifeless, nothing grew here, nothing moved.

Even sound was stifled here. The boom of the exhausts was muffled, as the fleet of tankers first halted and then began to maneuver, a kind of slow ballet that finished with them splayed out in a wide circle, like the spokes of a giant wheel, their tall cabs facing outwards.

In the center of the circle, the hub of the wheel, the earth began to move.

"Christ!"

The tunnel became the entrance to a cave; a cave which had been fashioned into an enormous cage, with massive bars of dulled iron that spanned floor to ceiling. Here the light was dimmer and in the gloom beyond the bars they could make out the pale glimmer of faces, with wide frightened eyes and mouths that opened to emit cries of relief and welcome.

"Oh, Papa John…!"

"Papa John…!"

The desert's crust began to bulge. Then it split and crumbled and there was a dull gleam of metal in the expanding cracks.

A shallow dome rose out of the earth. Its surface gleamed darkly and appeared to be seamless. But then hatches slid back and flexible transparent tentacles came snaking out, slithering towards the attendant tankers.

At the tail of each truck a panel sprung open to reveal a complex socket, designed to accept the probes that were now extending at the end of the seeking tentacles. And then the marriage was made and consummated as a flow that was now green now yellow ran through the tentacles and into the dome.

Selena's girls made short work of the locks, with a small charge of plastic explosive brought with them in their backpacks. With the imprisoned girls cowering as far back as they could go, hands pressed to their ears, it blew with a loud crack; there was a gust of smoke and the tall bars creaked open.

"Okay, let's go!"

They were off, back the way they came; down the long winding tunnel. Then up and round and round the spiral walkway, up above the machine, its pulse becoming uncertain and erratic now that it was no longer tended by its demonic slaves.

They saw the mouth of the mine approaching, a fuzzy pale wash of moonlight. John Warburton checked his walkie-talkie and saw he was getting a signal now. He began to speak into it urgently

"Red Leader to Baker Charlie...come ahead...come ahead...!"

The dome was glowing now, yellow then green then yellow again.

Shivering in their skimpy nightclothes, the women of Free Town emerged from the mine shaft and stumbled into the chill desert night.

"...we're right on you, Red Leader..."

The voice crackled from John Warburton's walkie-talkie. Distortion added to its edgy, anxious tone.

There were headlights on the ridge above, the gunning of engines. And then burly Jeeps were bouncing down the teetering slope, at speed, rocking precariously, raising dust.

"Whoa!"

The Jeeps slid and skittered to a halt and the young men of Free Town were jumping out, with angry faces, rifles in their hands. John Warburton stepped forward, hands raised to halt them.

"It's okay, it's all over!"

They gathered round him and their shoulders sagged as he told them of the dead girls in the crystal columns. Then their faces lightened as they saw the large crowd of survivors, staggering towards them, arms outstretched.

There was noise and motion up on the ridge, three pickup trucks pulling up, not nimble enough to make the precarious descent.

"Okay, let's go!"

Cat was ushering the girls up the steep slope. One fell, the strength gone from her legs. Cat gathered her up and carried her in a fireman's lift across her strong shoulders, her stride making short work of the steep gradient.

"That's my girl!" said John Warburton proudly.

The harvesting was done. The glow faded and the strange dome was dull again. The cables detached and slithered back within their confines; the hatches slid shut and the smooth surface was seamless again.

Exhaust stacks throbbed, engines gunning. Yellow headlamps flared into life. With a kind of peculiar grace, the tankers reprised their slow ballet, circling and then forming into line. Then they were back on the blacktop, the long ribbon of the highway, the strand of tail-lights receding with distance.

The silence stretched tautly. Then a low rumbling was transmitted through the ground, grits and bits stirring. A frequency so low it could be felt rather then heard, although there was nothing alive in this grey wasteland to feel it.

A black shadow detached from the surrounding darkness, a piece of the darkness, taking shape and now approaching the dully gleaming dome. As it rolled forward, with a deep dark growl like a beast of prey, it revealed itself in the dimness to be a brutish all-black Boss Mustang, its tires crunching through the brittle crust of the grey desert.

The eerie green eyes were glowing dimly, their glare subdued, as the beast slowed to a halt. Once again, a hatch was sliding back on the slope of the dome. A slim tentacle came uncoiling out, seeking the sculpted flank of the black monster.

They were mated. The dome was glowing again. Bright beads of yellow and green were pulsing along the length of the cable. The light in the green eyes intensified, surging, the white heat at its core reviving.

CHAPTER 16

DRUMS OF WAR

"Now just what the hell was all that about?" asked John Warburton.
"Hell is right," said Selena.
Tom Ahiga just shrugged.
"It's the end of the world," pronounced Cat gloomily.
She stared into the twisting flames of the campfire, then lifted her eyes as though they weighed a ton, to meet the steady, searching gaze of the Old Man.
"I know," she sighed. "I've seen it."
All around them was a hive of activity. Within a protective circle, not of covered wagons but a rag-tag assortment of veteran pickup trucks, VW camper vans, cars that were new in the 1950s, some attached to faded caravans with dusty windows. Young men stood on buckling tin roofs, cradling rifles in their arms, watching the dark desert all around them. Others were hustling and bustling, packing, helping their womenfolk fetch and carry. Children ran about, getting under everyone's feet, were scolded tenderly.
Cat heard none of it. Her head was full of screams, her eyes saw only horrors.
"I saw it all..."
Despite the proximity of the fire, Cat shivered. Tom Ahiga tugged off his denim jacket and draped it over her shoulders. She turned her head to smile bleakly at him.
"...the end of the world..."
The Old Man was wrapped in a blanket of many colors and patterns, the colors of the earth and sky. He produced a small leather pouch from beneath its folds and cast the shards on the ground at his feet. The strange markings seemed to glow in the firelight.
He took one and flipped it deftly onto the back of his hand. Then he scooped them all up, faster than their eyes could follow. He let them slide back onto the ground, dealing them out like a hand of cards.
"And how can those save us?" Cat exclaimed bitterly. "What good are magic tricks!"
Tom Ahiga glanced at her sharply and Cat hung her head.
"None at all, child..."
He was smiling at her. And suddenly, they were alone, sitting side by side in a desert that was like a mirror, reflecting the spangled starry

canopy of the night sky, so they seemed to be floating in a sea of stars. And the fire was a display of rainbows, flowers and butterflies.

The Old Man's voice was everywhere, of everything, mellow yet incredibly powerful.

"My magic lets me see and know all things," he was saying. "But it can only protect us here for a little while..."

The stars were swirling slowly beneath her feet. Then they churned abruptly into a milky froth from which drowning faces screamed at her. Cat gasped, a fist clenching in the pit of her stomach. She felt dizzy. The screams needled thinly in her skull. She was falling.

"Oh--!"

The voice chanted softly, briefly. The moment passed. The stars were twinkling again, sharp and bright.

Cat was breathing deeply.

"Oh God...!"

The voice was close by her now, whispering in her ear.

"Only one can stop it."

The drowning faces flickered, faded.

"...one...?" she mumbled. "...stop....?"

A warm breeze took the screams away. They became the fluttering of the butterflies.

"Only The One can kill the Beast."

A white light flashed behind her eyes.

"The One?"

Oh no! No!

"The One?"

The One!

"Me!"

And then time ran backwards and she sat by the fire in the bustling campsite.

"Now just what the hell was all that about?" John Warburton was asking.

"Hell is right," said Selena.

The City by the Bay liked to boast of its thrusting modernity. Its skyline, approached across the shining water, was spiked with glittering towers, like a magic castle of the future.

But the City had an older soul. Wooden houses and mansions from a pioneering age, from its first flush of vitality. With high porches and baroque gables, built on steep hills that went up and down spectacularly like a roller coaster; the movie companies liked to shoot car chases there. Its population was bohemian, affirming an alternative to the brash materialism represented by the steel and glass towers, declaring its own counter-culture. The rainbows and peace flags in their windows proclaimed it.

The old church perched on the crest of the highest hill, commanding a panoramic view of the City old and new, the sweep of the Bay and the sea beyond till sea and sky merged on the glowing horizon.

No one paid much attention to the regular comings and goings at the old wooden church lately. In this way-out community a group in funky robes attracted little comment.

So no one paid a second glance when an unmarked black van rolled up slowly and parked on the steep incline. Or when bulky figures hooded in grey got out and moved swiftly to the church doors, in a bunch, ringed around a slimmer form robed in white, its face hidden from view.

A passing pot-head grinned and bobbed his shaggy mane, flashing them a peace sign.

"Hey! Right on!"

They ignored him. The doors slammed shut behind them.

"Uh...okay...that's cool...."

He might have noticed that the slim white-cloaked figure was walking robotically, mechanically, held up by a tight grip on its arms, propelling it forward.

"I don't like it," said Selena.

"Now don't you worry," replied John Warburton.

"I don't like you going back alone without an escort."

"I'll be fine."

With deceptive ease, the big man swung his imposing bulk onto the seat of his Jeep. He propped the M-16 beside him.

"Take a squad of my girls with you."

Starting the engine, he grinned at her.

"As much as I'd enjoy their company", he chuckled. "I'll be fine, don't you worry."

Selena frowned.

"I wouldn't be me if I didn't worry."

Frowning, she stooped to plant a firm kiss on his lips.

"You take care, Big Man."

Cradling her handsome face in the span of his palm, he returned the kiss gently.

"You too, Mama…"

Spinning on her heel, Selena marched away towards the parked helicopters and the group of girl commandoes waiting by them.

"Mount up!"

The girls sprang to board the choppers. Engines throbbed, the rotors churning slowly at first then blurring.

"Woooo-eee!"

With a wave of his hand, John Warburton gunned the motor. As the streamlined 'copters rose above him, followed him briefly and then wheeled away in tight formation, the Jeep was a rocking rocket speeding across the desert, trailing a plume of dust.

The wooden church was painted white when they arrived, discolored and flaking with age. Over the months since their arrival the grey-robed newcomers had transformed it. Now it was a deep blood red, the pointed arches of its windows picked out in purple.

So now it fitted right in, and was hardly noticed.

But if anyone had bothered to give it another look they might have identified another change.

A darkness, below the blue sky. A black stain on the very tip of the wooden steeple. And every day, almost imperceptibly at first but then a little bit quicker in recent weeks, the stain was spreading downwards.

The survivors of the war party stood at a respectful distance, giving Cat and her lover some space.

"We're leaving," he said.

Their vehicles were parked in a long line; faces at the windows, roofs piled high with baggage.

Cat sighed as she blinked back brimming tears.

"Yes…."

He put his hands on her shoulders and she moved in tight to him.

"We're going to the mountains," said Tom Ahiga. "To make a last stand if we have to."

Leaning back, he looked into her eyes. She looked back at him, her vision blurred.

"Come with us," he said softly.

Sucking in a deep shuddering breath, Cat shook her head slowly.

"I can't," she whispered. "The Old Man said I have another destiny."

Tom Ahiga frowned.

"Destiny? What's that?"

She hung her head, leaning on his broad chest.

"We make our own destiny," he said. "You have choices."

With enormous effort, she released him, she couldn't look at him.

"No..."

She was walking away.

"...I don't...."

Flying fast and low, the sleek choppers formed a shallow arrowhead.

"KEEP IT TIGHT, BLUE TWO"

Flipping up her helmet mike, Selena scanned the faces of the girls who sat facing each other along the slim fuselage, their faces ghostly in a pale light.

She nodded to them, grinning to keep their spirits up. Some managed to return a weak smile. The others kept their faraway stare, trying not to see the faces of their dead comrades.

The desert flashed by below them, vast and empty. No sign of life to be startled by their passing.

"YOU TOO, RED ONE, CLOSE UP––!"

"What's that?"

Sat beside her at the controls, the pilot's voice crackled in her headphones.

"Down there—at three o'clock!"

Alarm shone out of the girls' wide eyes, bright in the half-light.

"What––!"

Coming in at them from the flank. A dark tornado, a twisted, writhing column, like smoke, rising from the desert floor.

"Look out!"

It seemed to bend, to pause and identify. Then it swayed and lunged forward, uncoiling like the lash of a whip.

"LOOK OUT RED LEADER...!"

The tornado singled out the lead chopper. Wrapping it in its coils, it sucked it up into a grey sky, the rotors splintering, its engine grinding. Then it dashed it to the ground.

"OH GOD!"

As quick as it came, the dark twister was gone and the sky was blue again. The squadron circled the charred black splash on the ground, ringed by a spray of jagged metal and licking tongues of orange fire.

They descended through a haze of oily vapor.

"No one could have got out of that alive!"

Disembarking, tumbling out of the sliding doors, they sprinted over to the stain of smoking mangled wreckage. Frantically, they searched about, reeling, hands covering their mouths, staggered by the sight of twisted black things that were once their former comrades.

Scarcely able to look they counted. Confused, they steeled themselves and counted again.

"Hey…?"

"This isn't right."

"There should be eight…"

"…six and the pilot and co-pilot…"

"I only count seven!"

"Me too!"

They forced themselves to look closer. To touch those things and turn them over and peer closely at the blackened horror that was only minutes earlier the faces of their friends.

"Oh God…!"

One turned and lurched away, vomiting. Then another.

"Hey…?"

"Selena!"

"It's Selena!"

"Where is she…?"

They were back in the desert that was a mirror reflecting the stars.

"Yes, you are the Chosen One…"

The Old Man's lips were motionless but his voice was everywhere. It filled the sky and resonated through the ground.

Cat shivered. The flames of their fire were pale and colorless and cast a thin cold light. She shivered again, tugging a blanket tighter across her hunched shoulders.

"I don't know what it means…"

The Old Man cut across her fear and confusion with a curt gesture of his hand.

"You need know only that you are the One."

The flames took on a greenish tint. The cold intensified, making Cat flinch, her hands clutching the blanket to her throat.

"The Beast has chosen you."

"B-beast…?"

He continued remorselessly…

"His creatures are preparing an ambush for you."

…ignoring the desperate pleading in her eyes.

"And you must fall into the trap."

"T-t-trap…?"

"For your path is chosen."

A heavy curtain of weariness descended upon her. But Cat managed to smash through it. Rising to her feet, the blanket slipped off of her shoulders.

"Chosen!" she cried out. "Chosen! Who chose me? And what if I don't want to be chosen!"

Tears made shining tracks on her cheeks, pale in the thin light.

"I can't save the world! If we're all going to die then I want to be with my friends!"

Suddenly the fire was changing color, the green tint banished by pale gold. And the Old Man was smiling.

"That's good, summon up the blood. The power of love."

And his voice was only him now, simple and direct.

"You will see your friends again."

The gold of the fire was rich now and molten, warming her.

"For you are their Chosen One also..."

And Cat was golden, glowing.

"If not for the world then for your friends..."

She was warm now and powerful. The power of love.

"Yes," she said softly. "I know what I have to do."

"I can't get no..."

John Warburton had customized his Jeep with an 8-track and speakers. The raunchy beat rolled along the dusty highway.

"...satisfaction!"

His palm, big as a dinner plate, marked time on the metal dashboard.

"I can't get no..."

Cat was right, Otis Redding's version was better than the original, any day.

"...satisfaction!"

So absorbed in singing along, he didn't see the movement in his mirrors. He didn't see the dark column forming in the desert, the sinister tornado swaying and twisting as it came after him.

"...satisfac...!"

Empty, the Jeep bowled along for a few seconds then veered off the hardtop onto the gritty crust of the desert, overturned, bouncing and rolling till it came to a stop, on its back, wheels spinning.

Home...

The old pickup was held together by rust. It wasn't what Cat was used to. She was used to moving fast and its arthritic pace had frayed her nerves. Worse yet was its lack of a sound system. Her world moved to a funky beat and she missed her sounds sorely.

Home at last...

The cab door creaked open halfway, she had to shove it the rest. She stepped out onto the sand of the beach. Her beach. Her sand.

What the––?

Normally, she would have kicked off her shoes and run barefoot through the sand, enjoying the sensation of it squeezing between her toes. But this was no longer a beach of sand. Her feet were crunching in a brittle grey ash.

"What the––!"

The perpetual blue sky that she lived under was gone. Now it was the color of lead. And the glittering ocean that she swam in, that frothed like champagne, rolled in sluggishly in waves of black tar.

The beach swept away in a long and curving horizon. Beyond that horizon, where the city was, the dull sky was smudged with smoke.

Cat's beach was a cold place now, the chill piercing the thin stuff of her tie-dyed T-shirt. She reached into the cab and retrieved a short stonewashed denim jacket.

"Hell on earth..."

Her eyes bleak, she surveyed her grim surroundings. Squaring her shoulders, she patted her jacket pockets, making sure her car keys were there.

Oh I hope you're right Old Man...

The old church was black now. Its wooden walls were crusted and bubbling. And the blackness was spreading out from it, down the hills on all four sides, along the rollercoaster streets and sidewalks, up onto the front porches.

The leaves on the trees withered and crumbled into ash. The color faded from the peace flags and psychedelic curtains. The cheerful old houses, daubed in every color of the rainbow, became cold and grey.

The windows of the houses, once warm with light, became cheerless, blank black eyeless sockets. The melodic carnival of music that always wafted from them was choked by moans of pain and horror and then the dismal wailing of the dead.

"Aw Jeez...!"

The interior of the church was bathed in a spectral green glow. Its wooden pews and pulpit were smashed into fragments that were heaped in the corners. The vacated space was filled by a new kind of altar.

"This is some heavy shit, man!"

A giant four-spoked wheel laid flat on the floor. Three of the four spokes were occupied. Bound hand and foot: John Warburton, Selena and Aiko.

"Aiko! You okay?"

Eyes glazed, head lolling from side to side, she was mumbling fitfully. Gritting her teeth, Selena tugged with all her might on the ropes that bound her.

John Warburton heaved a heavy sigh.

"Save your energy, Mama, it's no use..."

Lifting his head, he glared at the ring of grey-robed figures, standing sentry on the big wheel.

"Motherfuckers...!"

Selena eyed the broad beam of the wheel's fourth and empty spoke.

"Looks like they're waiting for someone."

Then light flared in Aiko's dull eyes. Words spilled from her twisting lips.

"...the One...is coming...!"

Cat stood on the beach watching the pillars of smoke rise above the horizon. A chill wind gusted along the shoreline where the black surf rolled onto the grey sand.

Shivering, she buttoned her jacket up to her chin. In the dead light coming from the leaden sky she looked very pale. Her eyes were desperate.

Aw, this is freakin' me out...!

She heard tires crunching up behind her. Alarmed, she turned quickly.

No way!

Her hand flashed to her waistband, came up pointing the brutal blue-black .45 automatic.

No fucking way!

It was a familiar VW Beetle with surfboards strapped to the roof. But its psychedelic paintwork was eroded by dull, dark corrosion.

The VW rolled to a halt some 50 feet from her. Cat stood amazed and watched as the doors swung open and the occupants jumped out.

No it can't be!

But it was, she recognized them, the kids who had sported with her dune buggy, what seemed like a hundred years ago, when the sky was pale gold and the sea was like pink champagne.

It was them but they were not themselves anymore. They were grotesque parodies of themselves, the putrid flesh dripping from their grinning skulls, mere skin and bone, held together with twists of rotting sinew.

Paralyzed, Cat watched the things that once were laughing, playing teenagers, such a force of life, as they took down the boards from the roof of the corroded VW. Tucking them under their skeletal arms, they ran down to where the black surf sucked at the grey sand.

"Oh--!"

They were surfing. They were actually surfing. They were riding the boards, on the slow sluggish black swell. They were making the moves, striking the poses, as the rotten shreds of flesh fell from their bones.

They saw her. With dull yellow orbs rotating in their sockets, veiled by the lank remnants of long hair that still clung to their skulls.

Cat raised the automatic.

"Oh....!"

She couldn't do it. Her face taut and anguished, she shoved the gun away. Dashing to where the pickup was parked on the tilting grey sand, she threw herself into the cab and slammed the door shut. The engine grated and coughed into life. The tires churned briefly then got a grip.

Cat hurled the pickup back onto the highway, slewing sideways, tailgate weaving from side to side and then was barreling off into the distance, heading towards the towers of smoke.

Suddenly, hot tears blurred her vision. She slammed on the brakes and sat there with her head down on the wheel, shoulders shaking, sobbing violently.

"Aw, ya gotta be kiddin'...!" said John Warburton.

A huge bronze cauldron was bubbling. Ringed around the four-spoked altar and the three figures bound to it, the grey-robed acolytes were chanting, hands raised in adoration.

"...this is like a bad B-movie!"

Presiding at the cauldron was a tall, broad-shouldered figure whose cape and cowl were black satin trimmed with scarlet.

"That must be the Big Boss Man," observed Selena.

Stretched out between them Aiko stared sightlessly, mumbling softly.

"...the One...is coming...."

John Warburton frowned, his walrus moustache bristling.

"What's she talking about?"

The tall figure was making elaborate commanding gestures with his gloved hands, passing them through and around the heavy glowing green vapors that rose from the bubbling cauldron. He was sculpting with them. Fleeting images were formed.

And suddenly Selena was grinning broadly.

"Don't you worry, Big Daddy, we got nothing to worry about!"

The chanting stopped and the tall figure ceased its conjuring. In the sudden silence they all stared at her. The eyes in the slits in the hoods glared at her. Selena was grinning right back at them.

"Nothing at all!"

CHAPTER 17

THE ONE

Home...

Cat was picking through a mound of charred wreckage piled high on the beach; a few burnt timbers still standing upright, and the cliff face scorched all the way to its grassy crest.

But she was seeing something else. Her mind's eye was remembering:

...The beach house was a bright white one-story affair with a sloping roof that shaped it like a blunt wedge. It stood on stilts, all the way back from where the rhythmic tides lapped at the sandy shore, up against a rust-colored cliff topped by a thatch of tall grasses.

A balcony with a wooden rail ran all along the front of the beach house. There was a white plastic table and chair on the balcony.

Inside, the beach house was simple and sparse, woven mats on the bare wooden floor, a few large cushions thrown down casually here and there. Beaded curtains masked a small, functional galley and a bedroom bare except for a tall wardrobe and a Japanese-style bed on the floor. Posters on the walls advertised bygone jazz festivals. A portable TV stood on a stool in the corner, covered in dust. The telephone was on the floor, with the receiver off the hook.

A tangle of cables was connected to a hi-fi deck and its twin speakers, spread wide apart in opposite corners of the main room. Mellow funk oozed from them, the horns like spooned honey. With the joint in her hand, the blonde woman came dancing in from the balcony, making her hips swing slowly from side to side. She hip swayed and bellied around the room, laughing as she surfed on the mats, sliding on the polished floor....

She ached so bad inside that she thought she was going to break in two. It was like that every time she went back to look at it and she wondered why she did it.

"Oh, Daddy...."

It had been sacrificed a year ago—was it really a year ago? *Am I really a year older?*—a burnt offering to serve the cause in a struggle against a different evil than the one she was up against now. But in that struggle she had seen her own estranged father exposed as a force for evil; and it was his own brother, her beloved Uncle John, who had stopped him with a bullet through the heart.

If only that heart had contained an ounce of love for her. If only....

Oh, Daddy!

She shook herself, scrubbing away the tears.

Now's not the time...

She strode out straight and purposeful, up and down over the blackened pile of rubble.

I've got things to do...

The broad steel shutters had been well camouflaged, partly by the dark staining of the fire, partly by her own subtle touches.

"Okay..."

Cat tugged the netting aside. She produced the little silver remote from the hip pocket of her bleached jeans. She pressed with her thumb and a red pin light was blinking. With a hiss of well-maintained hydraulics, the steel doors slid aside.

Long tubes of neon lit up the cavern of her secret garage, cut deep into the scarred cliff face.

"Hi gang...!"

She smiled, the tension seeping out of her shoulders. She was amongst friends.

"Hello baby..."

The red Olds 442 with its racy white trim.

"...Hey sweetheart..."

The blue Chevy Chevelle SS with its blunt prow like a battering ram.

"Heya!"

The bright little pert Dune Buggy; and a Daytona orange Dodge Charger 500 up on blocks with its wheels off, its body shell a patchwork of grey primer.

"Aw, I'm sorry, babe, I will get to you one day, I really will..."

But her heart was reserved for another, parked in a special place all of its own.

"There you are...!"

A yellow T-top Corvette ZL-1, contoured like a shark, its vicious jaws traversed by a broad black stripe that tapered dramatically as it raced rearward over the dramatic front wheel arches. It was low-slung, sleek and menacing; in their chrome sheathing, gleaming side exhausts proclaimed extravagant power.

"Oooooo...!"

Cat smoothed her palms over the machine's lean and muscular flanks; she spread her body across it.

She leaned into the open black cockpit, savoring all those familiar fast car smells.

"...Mmmmmm....!"

Cat loved to recite the blurb from *Motor Trend*:

"...The baddest car on the block—only three of a kind—the Corvette ZL-1; the fastest production car ever produced. Boasting an all-aluminum big-block 427 advertised at 430 horsepower but underrated purposely to keep them off the streets and out of the hands of unskilled drivers. More like 525-plus and in racing trim, as intended, more in the way of 560 to 585 stomping ponies! This baby demolishes the quarter mile in 12.1 seconds at 116 mph and can hit 200. All in a package that cost an extra $4,000 and climbing..."

Cat smiled. Small change, thanks to her $5 million trust fund.

Thank you Uncle John!

And then she was all business.

"Okay, baby, we've got work to do!"

A room at the rear of the garage was a polished steel strongbox. Neon strip lights lit automatically as she entered, her movements making crazy, jangling reflections.

"Hmmm......."

Racked securely on the wall there was a lightweight .25 Colt automatic carbine, fitted with a sniper scope; a stumpy Ingram submachine-gun; a Remington pump shotgun with folding skeleton butt; and a government-issue M-16.

She walked past these and the steel shelves packed with cartons of ammunition, the stack of wooden boxes stenciled with military specs and codes that denoted smoke and gas and fragmentation grenades. She ignored the compact, portable rocket launcher and its attendant missiles.

She reached a steel cabinet mounted on the far wall and opened it, decoding the combination lock briskly.

Then she paused, her brow furrowed, frowning.

No...

No, not the blue steel Smith & Wesson .357 Magnum; nor the .45 Colt automatic; or the 9mm Beretta. Not even the chromed Walther PPK, with its pearl grips.

No, I won't need any of those; these weapons are no use...

The blue steel reflected in her eyes. Sucking in a deep breath, she slammed the cabinet shut.

...I am the weapon!

The blackness spread out from the old church on top of the hill. It fanned out, up and down the rollercoaster, branching out from the main streets into the side streets but always moving downwards, towards the proud towers of the city by the Bay. In its wake it left a stain of foul corruption.

Like a dull mirror high above, a shadow spread across the sky, casting a sudden chill over the city that had been basking smugly in its welcome sunshine.

The glittering waters of the Bay lost their sparkle. Its busy traffic of tugs and toiling freighters, fishing boats and nimble pleasure yachts was becalmed, stuck fast in a lake of lead.

The darkness was climbing the towers, entwining round them like a poisonous black vine, twisting tentacles, coiling snakes.

The yellow Corvette was a streak of light in the gloom cast by the shadow in the sky.

Go baby go...!

The twin side-exhausts played a raw fanfare as she rocketed onto the coast highway. The needle was nudging past 90 in the blink of an eye and the race-tuned ZL-1 could double that and more.

Cat's fingers flexed on the stick-shift, ready to give her the gun.

Shit!

Alarmed, she eased off rapidly, braking hard. Protesting, the 'Vette's tail tried to twitch out from under her, but Cat deftly reined it the speeding car.

"Whoa, baby..."

What the fuck...?

The highway had become a cluttered obstacle course. Coming and going, obstructing every lane, cars and trucks had come to an abrupt stop, skewed sideways, pointed in the wrong direction. Others were still rolling, slowing down to a crawl, going nowhere, crossing lanes and crunching into each other.

"This is crazy!"

Ahead of her, a Mack truck rode up onto the crumpled wedge of a small compact, tilted over and crashed onto its side, skidding along with a screech of rending metal and a shower of sparks. The compact blew up in a ball of oily black and orange flame.

"Aw hell...!"

The mangled bulk of the big truck was bearing down on her.

"OH SHIT....!"

Reflexes, fine-tuned on the race track, kicked in instantly. Lithely, the Corvette side-swerved and flicked between the oncoming wreck and the blazing shell of the compact.

Thank you baby...!

Ahead of her was a crazy weaving slalom course marked out by the scattered vehicles stalled at random intervals as far as the eye could see. It tested Cat's skills, the keenness of her edge, but she relished the challenge, taking it fast and smooth.

"Wooo..."

She was starting to enjoy herself.

"....eeeeeee...!"

And then her CB radio crackled.

"Come to us, Chosen One...!"

In the distance she saw the towers of the city, dwarfed by looming pillars of smoke.

"...He is waiting....!"

And she heard other voices—voices she recognized...

Uncle John...!

Calling out to her...

Selena...Aiko...!

She felt a sudden chill, a darkness, a great weakness draining her. Her vision blurred. And then she heard the Old Man's voice and a warm golden light banished the shadow from her eyes.

In the city the eyes of the people wherever they were—on the crowded sidewalks, in their offices, on the subway, grabbing a cup of coffee in a café—became lightless and lifeless.
Their thoughts all merged to become a single thought:
"Heed the call of the Master...!"

Her rear-view mirror was filled with black. Something was coming up fast behind her.
"Hey...?"
A horn sounded but not like any sound she'd heard before. A clarion call coming from a very dark place.
"Hey!"
It bulled and bullied its way past her and Cat had to react quickly to avoid being shouldered off the highway.
"HEY!"
A black Boss Mustang with black blank windows. Moving with supernatural speed and agility, making light work of the stalled obstacles in the road.

Oooo, you're a mean...

Cat's competitive instincts were inflamed. Ever fiber of her being urged her to launch off in pursuit.

...motherfucker!

And then the golden warmth was soothing her.

No, that's not part of the Plan...

She looked back at herself in the mirror.

...not yet....

The tall one's eyes were slits of fire. A curved dagger flickered brightly, drawn from the copious folds of his sleeve. The black and scarlet of his robes shimmered as he advanced angrily on the figures bound to the spokes of the altar.

"Puny mortal...!"

He passed the blade close to Selena's face and then laid the edge on her throat.

"Fear the judgment of the Master...!"

Selena heard John Warburton chuckle, deep in his barrel chest. She saw the cloaked shoulders stiffen.

"I ain't worried," she drawled. "You'se the one gotta worry, man..."

The knife drew back, quivering, poised above her.

"The Chosen One will come when the Master calls—and bring with her the Day of Doom!"

Uncle John guffawed loudly.

"Oh, she's comin' alright...!"

Warmth was returning to Aiko's face. Her eyes came alive. She was smiling.

The yellow Corvette weaved its way down the canyons of the city.

This is some bad trip!

It was a perilous ride, dodging the stalled buses, trucks and cars tumbled all about. Looming above, the tall towers were dulled and corroding, wrapped in a web of creeping black vines, snaking their way to the top, cracking the windows and probing inside. Strange winged creatures circled the crowns of the skyscrapers, black against a leaden sky, their raw reptilian cries echoing downwards.

"Oh...!"

A delivery truck was sliding towards her sideways, its driver slumped over the wheel. There was only one way out. Cat swerved the 'Vette up onto the sidewalk.

"...shit!"

The sidewalk was crowded; figures with grey faces and dull dead eyes. Men in business suits carrying briefcases, women with shopping bags.

This can't be real....

Walking, jostling, and bumping up against each other, wide eyes seeing nothing.

...I must've dropped some bad acid...

They seemed to sense her. Arms outstretched, fingers clawing, they assailed the yellow Corvette, their bodies spilling off its smooth shark-like angles. Their gaping faces screamed silently at her through the acutely angled windshield.

...I'll come down in a minute...

Her stomach turning over, she heard them thudding off the bodywork, crunching under the wheels.

...it's just a bad trip....

Still clutching her shopping bags in both hands, the grey husk of what had been a woman was flicked up by the arrow-like front fender, rolled along the long hood, up and over the top and vanished behind.

Giving thanks that she had the top up, Cat wrenched the 'Vette off the sidewalk and back onto the street. She flicked the car around the next corner, saw a clear path ahead and accelerated down it, the snarl of the engine reverberating off the steel and glass walls of the city canyons.

Beneath her wheels the asphalt was starting to rise and bubble.

"Fuck!"

Putting the pedal to the metal, she outran a boiling black tarry tide. She was through the city center now and shooting out the other side, arriving at the foot of the first hill where the old city stood.

OH!

Braking hard, she sat and stared at the old wooden houses, now colorless and crumbling, flaking, at the trees now withered and twisted, leafless.

That dread cold weight fell on her again, that dull stupor dulling her vision. Furious, she shrugged it off.

NO!

Tires smoking, the Corvette exploded into motion. Like a panther, it sprang up and over one hill after another, roaring.

There was one hill left. She could see the old church, black against the grey sky.

"She will come! She will come to the Master...!"
Selena was laughing.
"Be careful what you wish for, man."
"Yeah," said John Warburton. "You might just get it!"

The green eyes blazed, white light sizzling at their core.

"Come and join us, oh Master...!"

The black Mustang was cruising the steel and glass canyons.

"...and claim your prize...!"

Its deep dark rumble rippled the boiling black river of the street and buckled the slabs of the sidewalk. It cracked the panoramic plate glass of the exclusive shop fronts, splintering it into pieces that flew like daggers.

The black beast made a stately progress and as it passed by, the black vines that choked the tall towers writhed and re-doubled their inexorable advance upwards. As the vines climbed, the windows high above were bursting in a spray of twinkling fragments. Bodies were tumbling out and falling like limp dummies, arms and legs flailing. They plummeted down and hit the hard ground, bursting loudly on impact.

On the crowded sidewalks, those that weren't crushed by the falling bodies or lacerated or decapitated by the flying glass formed a line along the edge of the street, standing in ranks, a guard of honor, their dull dead eyes fixed on the black Mustang as it rumbled past.

Their writhing lips were chanting. Repeating over and over again: the number that was etched in green fire on the Mustang's license plates:

"...666...666.....!"

CHAPTER 18

BLACK AND GOLD

The sleek Corvette took the last hill in a single bound, surging to the top with a roar in fine-tuned stereo from its twin side exhausts.

She didn't hesitate. Cat was up the front steps and through the church doors. Dry and decayed, they splintered, ripped from their corroding hinges, and crashed to the floor.

In a ring around the four-spoked altar, the grey-robed disciples all turned as one to face her. Their eyes glowed a baleful yellow in the deep shadow of their hoods.

The black satin of his robes shimmering, their leader rounded on his minions.

"Seize her...!"

Cat vaulted lithely over the wreckage of the doors and came striding forward. Her face was a mask of perfect serenity, her eyes cool and focused.

"She is the One!" the Leader screamed. "Seize her...!"

She was golden, glowing, empowered. Her green eyes were flecked with gold and light shone from them.

"She belongs to the Master! Seize her...!"

As Cat advanced towards the altar there was an aura of pale gold radiating from her. Sparkling, it tingled with electricity and when the grey acolytes made a move to intercept her it repelled them, sending them reeling backwards.

She gestured, the merest flick of her hand. On the altar the ropes fell away, dissolving.

"C'mon...!"

Released, her friends felt a surge of power in their limbs. Their blood was on fire.

"Let's get 'em!"

For a moment, the grey-robed disciples stood frozen to the spot. Then battle was joined.

Shoulder to shoulder, two hooded figures made a move on John Warburton. Two against one, it was hardly fair.

They came in swinging, their generous sleeves flapping. Uncle John batted the blows aside like he was shooing away flies. His huge hands seized them by the throat in a vice-like grip.

"URGH!"

"AKH…HH…!"

Effortlessly, he slammed their heads together, meeting with a crack muffled by their hoods. The eyes in their slits rolled up till only the whites showed. Released, they crumpled to the floor.

"HAH-YAH…!"

Selena was a whirling dervish. As they came at her in a bunch she cut a swathe through them, with high spin kicks and her arms scything, chopping with the edge of her hands. She sent them rolling and tumbling in all directions, a wrecking ball, bowling them over like ninepins.

John Warburton's technique was more basic, as he waded in gleefully. His big fists came crashing down like sledge-hammers, crushing bone. A right cross had one hapless victim bouncing off the wall. A mighty uppercut sent the next into orbit, leaving the ground in a backwards somersault.

"HAA-EEEE…!"

By contrast, Aiko was all grace, a dancer. Feather light on her feet, she scarcely seemed to touch her opponents. She appeared to merely brush them with her fingertips. And yet the effect was explosive, a detonation that sent them sprawling like rag dolls.

Ah, there you are…!

Two stood apart from the melee. Cat, radiant and golden. And the tall figure robed in black and scarlet. She glimpsed him, at the far side of the maelstrom, through the blur of whirling limbs and tumbling bodies.

I see you…

Her target was edging away slowly, hoping to go un-noticed. Then he sensed Cat's eyes upon him, turned and was moving swiftly towards a narrow doorway at the back of the church.

Cat could hear the voice of the Old Man, singing in her ears. Her eyes were orbs of gold.

I'm coming for you…!

At the foot of the last hill, down below the church, the black beast slowed, hesitating. The fire in the green eyes fluttered, uncertain.

There was a crack in the grey steel of the sky above that emitted a pale, glowing golden light.

The black satin hissed as the tall figure took the steps two at a time, ascending a tight spiral stairway that climbed to the top of the church tower.

At the summit there was a narrow arched doorway leading out onto a confined platform that was open to the sky. The hooded figure swayed, breathing heavily. He leaned on a low railing, broad shoulders heaving.

On all sides, he saw a great grey vista of smoking, smoldering corruption. A grim panorama, the withered hills, the blackened towers of the city and the iron waters of the Bay.

High above, the crack in the grey sky widened like a great eye opening and a golden light shone forth. It bathed the top of the church tower and the black-robed figure reeled and cried out as if scalded.

He flung out his arms, imploring.

"She is here, Master! I have brought her to you!"

Falling to his knees.

"Why don't you come...?"

And a voice seemed to answer him, from the great golden eye radiating in the sky. A quiet ancient voice that was everywhere; and inside him.

"Because she has come...."

Cat was standing in the arched doorway. She was shining, invincible. Rays of light were shining from her fingertips.

He lurched to his feet, drawing the curved dagger from the billowing folds of his sleeve.

"No!" he shrieked. "This is not right...!"

He was rushing at her, slashing with the knife.

"You should have come as his slave!"

Her golden fingers closed on his wrist. The bones cracked, his hand sprang open and the blade clattered on the boards.

With a yelp of pain, he staggered backwards. Cat seemed to glide above the ground. She reached out and ripped the tall hood from his head.

His face was pale and contorted.

You!

It was a face familiar to millions.

"You bitch!" shrilled the Reverend Thaddeus P. Calhoun. "You've ruined everything!"

His good hand was clawing for her throat. Her face a warm golden mask of serenity, Cat took hold of him and hoisted him effortlessly, up above her head.

"BITCH! BITCH! BITCH....!"

Howling, the Reverend kicked and thrashed but his struggles were futile. Cat carried him like a child, to the edge of the platform.

She held him out over the rail.

"N-NO-OOOO..."

The quiet voice drowned out his frantic screams.

"...the One..."

She let him go. Eyes bulging, mouth gaping, his needling shrieks diminished as he fell, arms and legs flailing.

"AAAAA...IIIII...EEEEEEEEEEE....!"

He fell into the overgrown graveyard at the rear of the church. There was an old slanting tombstone shaped like a broad spearhead. It received him, snapping his spine.

"AAAGH--!"

His limbs convulsed. Black blood burst from his mouth. For an instant, his bulging eyes glared all the way back up at her, a distant silhouette at the top of the tower, blazing with hate. Then they dulled and rolled up till only the whites showed, his head lolling limply.

Its deep dark growl made the ground tremble. The black beast was leaving the city.

The grey dead threw themselves at it, in front of it, groping, clawing desperately, begging it to stay. Ruthlessly, it rolled right over them, mangling and crushing them into dust.

At the top of the tower, Cat's aura was dimming. She was panting, dazed and confused. She rubbed her eyes as though waking from a dream.

She heard the voice again.

"No, not yet, child..."

"HAH-YAH!"

Aiko let the disciple's onrushing bulk do the work. With a subtle shimmy she flipped him head over heels. He came down with a sickening crack, his neck broken.

 John Warburton was enjoying himself immensely. He set up his next victim with a straight left, his fist like a battering ram; and then followed up with a smooth combination, left and right, body and head. His grey robes puddling around him, the helpless acolyte crumpled to the floor.

Close by, Selena fought grimly, her face a cold mask, her eyes steely. She fought for her dead girls and she showed no mercy. The edge of her hand came down like an axe and her opponent was dead before he hit the ground.

"You have one more thing to do..."

Cat came down the spiral stairway two at a time. Looking neither left nor right, she weaved her way nimbly through the tangle of battle.
"Go get 'em, Princess!" yelled Uncle John.
The golden glow was gone. She was herself now, fearless and determined. Two disciples had the temerity to stand in her way, blocking the door. Aiko moved to intercept them, but then stepped back, smiling.
"Yours, Cat..."
Cat went through them as though they weren't there, blowing them away like rag dolls. And then she was gone.

The steep rugged slopes of Devil's Butte were ideal for a last-ditch defense.
"We've come to the right place, my brothers..."
All around them stretched the great expanses of the desert. A grey desert now, beneath a lowering sky veined with crackling electricity. There was a darkness on the vast horizons; it was spreading, creeping steadily towards them.
Rifle in hand, Tom Ahiga addressed his young warriors.
"To make a last stand!"
At a distance, the women clutched their children to them, murmuring a soothing song. The young men breathed deeply, filling their chests and squaring their shoulders. As one, they brandished their weapons and shouted out loud:
"It is a good day to die!"

The yellow Corvette was re-tracing its route, leaving the City.

Wait for me, I'm coming...

In its wake order and color were restored slowly. The sky became brighter and the waters of the Bay reclaimed their sparkle.

By the campfire the Old Man was watching, looking deep into the flames.

"Sonofa--"

Speed streaked earth and sky, the desert highway a dusty blur beneath their wheels.

"--bitch!"

The black Boss Mustang was teasing her. Weaving, flicking and sliding from side to side, it kept its tail in her face, frustrating her.

Hey man, you're good...!

She pulled out her bag of tricks, ducking, diving, feinting left and right. But the black beast deflected all her tried and tested maneuvers.

...too good...!

Every time, it slammed the door shut. And then, with a roar it was pulling away, diminishing into the distance with an awesome surge of power.

"AW SHIT!"

It was playing games with her; slowing down to let her catch up and then pulling away effortlessly again.

"SHIT! SHIT! SHIT!"

She couldn't believe it. It was faster and better than her.

...you're not human...!

And then it zoomed away and was gone.

"Fuck!"

She braked hard. She was slumped over the wheel, shoulders heaving.

"Oh fuck...!" she panted.

Cat fumbled for the secret place under the dash. The little bottle dropped into her hand.

No way, man...

The contents rattled as she dispensed them onto her palm.

...you're not getting away from me...

The pillars of smoke began to thin till they faded away altogether. The black vines retreated from the tops of the towers. The spark of life was re-kindled in the people's eyes.

Gotya!

She was reeling it in. She had her edge now. It was growing in her sights.

You can't get away from me...!

And then it stopped. The Beast was waiting for her deep in the desert, it was straddling the blurred center line on the dusty highway.
The green orbs were lit by a slowly pulsing glow. The deep dark heartbeat was idling, throbbing, as it waited patiently.

Sitting cross-legged by the campfire, the Old Man was swaying, his lips moving. But no one could hear him. No one could see what his eyes saw.

The Corvette was a speck on the distant vanishing point. And then it was there, in the blink of an eye.

Excuse me...

The pills were kicking in. She felt better now. Her music was playing. The 'Vette was humming, and all her senses were tingling. She was flying, on a spectacular high.

...while I kiss the sky....

She glided smoothly to a stop, parked broadside on, separated by a short strip of dust-streaked blacktop. The car door opened and Cat's long legs swung out, followed by the rest of her.
She was dressed for action: a skimpy red halter top that bared her strong arms and sublimely toned midriff; raggedly cut-off blue denim hot pants and tall tan suede boots with fringes round the top. Large round mirror shades masked her eyes.
"Now there's gonna be some serious ass-whuppin'!"
With a lithe stalking stride, she approached the idling black Mustang. Its dark pulse vibrated through her entire body.

Huh...?

Bending down, she couldn't see through the tinted window, like a black mirror. Only her own distorted reflection.

"HUH--?"

"What the hell...?"

Exiting onto the church porch, they saw the great golden eye in the sky, as though bloodshot, assailed by forked lances of red lightning.

Aiko clung tight to Uncle John's arm. Selena blinked as a sudden gust blew flecks of grey ash in her face.

That's right...," she whispered. "Hell..."

"Yes..."

Tom Ahiga watched the darkness advance from all points of the compass.

"...a good day to die!"

"HUH...?"

Her world had become a whirlwind. The sky above and the grey desert all around were a spinning vortex, a hurricane. She screamed, more in amazement than fear, a thin sound sucked away and extinguished by the spinning cone of dust and cloud as earth and sky merged into one.

They were in the eye of the storm, as the vortex roared around them— Cat, her yellow Corvette and the jet black Boss Mustang. And suddenly it was very cold.

The black Mustang was changing.

"Oh my..."

The sizzling green orbs were now slanting slits of fire.

"...God....!"

Its streamlined fastback was arching and elongating. Its polished skin, like black glass, was crackling and growing broad leaf-like scales.

Chilled to the bone, Cat could only stand and watch. Her mouth opened and shut but no sound came out.

The slit eyes framed snarling jaws that were sprouting teeth and a tongue of green fire. The low-slung radials were morphing into stunted forearms with claws like curved daggers.

The Old Man scooped up his tokens and talismans and cast them into the fire.

Jaws gaping to expose its fangs and release its long tongue of green fire, it was rearing up on massive hind legs. The scales gleamed like black armor.

Cat was paralyzed, her face drained, her eyes stark and staring.

A long tail was thrashing. There were wings, expanding vastly from the creature's back, like giant leathery batwings; and the whirling vortex drew back to accommodate them as it began to thin and diminish in intensity.

The wings were billowing, slowly and yet with immense power. The dragon was rising.

Mouth wide open in a silent scream, Cat strained every muscle in her body and yet she barely quivered.

The black dragon hovered above her.

"I have done what I can..."

The desert was a grey blur below her. The rushing wind was as cold as ice, flaying her.

"...uuuhh...hhh....hh...."

She went in and out of consciousness, in a series of broken images.

"...oh...hhhh...."

Cat saw cities corrode and crumble, their streets crowded with the living dead...oceans boil and forests withered by green flame...

"AAAA...HHH...!"

And then suddenly it all came to her in terrifying clarity.

"N-N-NOO-OOO...!"

The black dragon had her in its claws, as it soared across the barren, dying desert, propelled by the measured undulation of its great wings.

Its grip was cruel and she had to strain to breathe. It turned its head on its long neck of gleaming black scales and gazed at her with a baleful eye. The tongue of green fire flicked out at her wickedly.

Cat felt its blast of scalding cold and screamed. The long tongue of flame lapped at her, making her writhe and howl with pain.

"...I have summoned the light..."

The mothers covered their children's faces so they couldn't see.

The advancing blackness was a solid mass. And then contorted demonic forms would shape themselves out of it, with glowing eyes and clutching talons, before receding again into the black tide that rolled on, unstoppable.

At its touch the ground froze and split open, ice vapor exhaled from the cracks, the earth itself gasping for breath.

Tom Ahiga cast the Winchester carbine aside. He plucked a dagger from his waistband, a broad Bowie knife with a tarnished blade, its ivory hilts yellowed by time.

He would die with his ancestors' weapon in his hand.

With his free hand he ripped open his shirt, baring his chest. His eyes were fearless, unblinking, already far away in another land.

At last the dragon's head turned away and the pain was gone. Cat saw where it was taking her. They were going to the mountains.

"...only the light and the One can banish the darkness..."

There were blisters on the Sun. The sky was the color of blood.
The desert had been as cold as ice. Here in the mountains it was a scorching blast furnace. With Cat writhing in its claws, the black dragon extended its great wings and was gliding, spiraling slowly on the rising waves of heat.
The earth rotated slowly far below her. The wall of jagged peaks stretched from horizon to horizon, a livid scar, septic and festering. The noble icecaps had evaporated and the craggy tops had split open like boils bursting to expel their poison, oozing strands of bubbling lava. The malevolent red glow laced the folds and seams of the mountainsides and formed smoking rivers in the twisting valleys.
The blasting heat scalded Cat's face and made her squeeze her eyes tight shut.
When she dared open them she saw an open wound that formed a vast crater in the top of the tallest mountain, filled with boiling lava
It was a living, hungry thing. Thirsting tongues of flame flickered greedily on the churning surface.
The dragon was descending in slow deliberate circles.
"OH...HHH...!"
She felt the talons flex. She knew what was going to happen.
"...N-N-NOOO...OOO...!"
And then she was falling.

The darkness prevailed in the old part of the city.
Their backs were to the wall.
"This is it..." said John Warburton.
Packed shoulder to shoulder on the narrow path leading to the front door of the church, their shuffling ranks stretched down the hill.
Selena smiled at him.
"Yeah, Daddy. It's been a great ride..."

She was falling...falling...falling.....
The mountains were where the sky should be and the sky was below her and then everything was the right way up and then upside down again.

...falling...falling.....
A hot wind was tugging at her, singing in her ears.
...falling.......
She was sure that she was screaming but all she could hear was the shrieking siren of the wind.

The running sore of the mountain top was a glowing red maw gaping to receive her. The savage heat radiating from it seared her skin and now she could hear herself screaming.
...falling...falling.....

In their ragged ranks, they came on; the army of the undead, with their grey flesh hanging from their bones in tatters, lipless mouths baring their rotting teeth and venting carrion breath, eyes dull balls rotating in their deep sockets.

Aiko laughed suddenly, a brittle sound.
"See you on the other side!"

And then suddenly...

OH......

Suddenly she was rising, up and away from the heat and fiery doom.

....

She was cushioned, protected, reclining on a bed of feathers. A bed of golden feathers.

..................????

No—a back, a broad back that rippled with the strong regular machinery of powerful muscles, upholstered with shimmering feathers each a gilded spear point.

The extended muscle-play powered an enormous wingspan, wings that beat slowly, at measured intervals of smooth soaring. A fan of long tail-feathers trailed behind with a flash of gold. A long neck supported a noble gilded head, with mellow golden eyes belied by the fierce sickle curve of its beak.

The great golden bird opened its jaws to emit a low and throbbing call. Flexing its long neck, it looked back at Cat and the feathers on its wide shoulders seemed to plump up to accommodate her, sitting her up and making her comfortable.

Cat saw herself reflected in the golden eyes. And she was golden too.

"…only the light…."

A grotesque silhouette against the red sky, she saw the black dragon wheeling up above them.

"…and the One…."

The black dragon dipped a wing and with a breath of green fire and raw metal croaking came plummeting down upon them.

"…you are the One…"

The two giants, the black beast and the golden bird, dueled in the red sky, performing a deadly and yet somehow elegant choreography. They wheeled and banked, looped and dived, climbed and cork-screwed, spiraling downwards competing to out-turn each other.

The raw metal croaking slashed across the deep almost sub-sonic booming of the golden bird. Despite its extreme maneuvering Cat seemed to ride the bird's back effortlessly. She was glowing again, her aura restored.

The black dragon was on their tail, green flame kindling in its long jaws. The golden bird weaved and was jinking nimbly from side to side as bolts of green fire flashed past its wingtips, straddling Cat's shoulders.

………………!!!!

She screamed, ecstatic, somehow welded to its broad back, clamped there by her strong thighs, with a strength she'd never had before, as the firebird, without warning, rocketed high into the red sky. And then, at the top of its climb, it hung there for an instant that seemed an eternity, and then flipped over and was coming down in a twisting dive, locked onto the black beast's tail.

Once again, the firebird turned its head to look back at Cat. It spoke with the Old Man's voice.

"…*you are the One*…."

The beast was flying a wild and twisting course, weaving perilously between the jagged flanks of the mountains laced with the glowing lava flow. It glared back at them with its sizzling green eyes, trying in vain to shake them off.

The golden bird followed, hard on its tail, mirroring its every move. Venting its frustration, the dragon sent a long blast of green fire back at them. Cat's glowing aura deflected it, and it evaporated as a pale and harmless mist.

A woman cried out weakly, the sound of faint hope.
"What the––!"
Exhausted, battered and disorganized, the young warriors stumbled to form ranks again.
Bruised and bleeding, sweat streaming down his bare chest and dripping from his face, Tom Ahiga struggled to make sense of it.
"What the...?"
The black tide was receding, leaving its dead behind.

Now Cat was standing, poised boldly on the firebird's shining back. Flexing her long legs, she jumped.

"HEY!"
Her hideous adversary had suddenly stopped clawing at her.
"WHAT?"
Its skeletal arms dropped limply to its sides. The twists of sinew and shreds of skin began to dissolve into dust. The scraps of flesh still clinging to the skull fell away, the dull orbs of its eyes shriveled.
In seconds there was nothing but a heap of dust at Aiko's feet.
"I never even touched him!"

Cat landed lightly on the black beast's scaly back. The fire flashing from her fingertips had become a spear of light. The dragon rolled and rocked, trying to shake her off. Her eyes blazing, the golden girl merely tossed her head and laughed, her long hair swirling like a glowing halo about her shining face.

Dazed, they sat shoulder to shoulder on the church porch steps. They stared numbly at the long trail of grey ash and bone that stretched away as far as they could see, all the way up and down the hills of the old part of the city.
For a long time no one said anything. Then John Warburton heaved a heavy sigh.
"I really wish someone would tell me what that was all about!"

The dragon twisted its neck to snarl back at her. As green fire ignited in its gaping jaws, Cat thrust the spear of light into its eye.

A ghastly shriek erupted from the beast's fanged maw. A scream so shrill that she felt rather than heard it, slicing through her brain. The pain was excruciating and for a moment everything went dark.

She was in and out of consciousness in a black flash and when her sight returned the mountains and red sky were a blurred kaleidoscope revolving dizzily, the hot wind roaring in her ears.

With the talons of its short forearms the dragon struggled to extract the golden lance from its wounded eye socket. A thick black slime spurted. From its clashing jaws the fire lashed fitfully and was then extinguished in a gust of green vapor.

Fine veins of gold were radiating from the wounded eye; the monstrous black skull was glowing from within. The vast black wings went rigid, convulsed violently and then hung flapping limply.

A bright light shone from the beast's mouth and eyes. A slow shudder ran along the great length of its body. Golden rays were radiating from beneath the black scales which were dropping away like falling leaves.

The blood red sky was paling. Groaning, the dragon rolled onto its back. And then it was toppling out of the sky, plummeting in a wild spiral, out of control.

Wild-eyed, exhilarated, Cat rode it all the way down, screaming like a kid on a fairground ride, her eyes crazy, long blonde hair lashing across her face, her arms and legs clamped around the dragon's long neck.

Uh-oh...!

On the ruptured mountain peak, the cauldron of bubbling red lava was rising to meet them.

His legs gave out beneath him.
"Awww...!"
Tom Ahiga sat shoulders slumped on the ground, weak with relief.
The women were crying and giving thanks. The children simply stared in wonder.
The Old Man's fire erupted in a rising column of glittering sparks. Invigorated, the years falling off him, he sprang to his feet, flung out his arms, shouting an ancient cry of victory.

The lava absorbed the falling dragon with great flash of red flame. The boiling surface churned in a fiery whirlpool.

Amazed, a child again, Cat was suspended on a cushion of air, the mighty updraft of the great golden bird's wings. She settled gently on its plushly feathered back and it flew away with her, back the way they'd come.

They flew over a changing landscape. Grey fields of ash became lush and green. Green leaves were on the trees again. At Paradise Gardens and a thousand other places it was as if an invisible curtain was lifted. The kitchens were humming again; the postman's bicycle bell was tinkling— "Good morning!" "Good morning!"

The golden bird returned Cat to her beach, where the sky and the sand shone again and the sea frothed like champagne, tingling her toes.

Tears of joy shining on her cheeks, she ran waist deep into the surf. Crying out loud, she wind-milled her arms, splashing gleefully.

"Oh my!"

Submerged up to her navel, Cat stopped splashing, eyes popping with surprise.

"Oh--!!??!"

On the sand, the giant bird was shape-shifting. As Cat came wading ashore, running with the incoming tide, it transformed itself.

Well, baby...

Shaking her head, eyes glowing with wonder, Cat stroked the sleek flank of her yellow Corvette.

...I never knew you could do that!

As she drove off, with the top down, up onto the beach highway, she saw the psychedelic VW Beetle and the kids surfing, gamboling on the shining sand. They saw her and waved. Her long hair floating like a golden banner, she laughed and waved back.

Coast to coast, dead children were alive again and were running back into their parents' arms. Their victims woke in their beds, what a strange dream!

In her rear-view mirror, Cat saw the Old Man's eyes smiling back at her.

The schools were lively, chattering places. Teenagers were rolling down the road again, groovin' to their music, waving and flashing peace signs as they passed the big trucks cheerfully, safely.

The traffic flowed freely and the City's arteries pulsed with life. The sidewalks were bustling as the living went to work in the shining towers; the exclusive stores and trendy cafés did brisk business.

Up and down the green hills, the old town was a rainbow again; guitars played, painters painted, poets celebrated life and took on the Establishment again.

On BOOT HILL the dead slept soundly in their graves....

The yellow Corvette slid up in front of the old church.

"Hey...!"

Cat was out and running up the porch steps. Somehow she managed to enfold all three of them in a single, warming embrace.

For an eternity, it seemed, they just hugged wordlessly, tearfully and then just stood there grinning at each other.

Finally, John Warburton threw up his hands in exasperation.

"Will someone *PLEASE* tell me what this was all about!"

Cat hugged him again, squeezing him tight.

"Oh, Uncle John," she laughed. "It's a long story!"

For a complete list of Midnight Marquee Press books and movies, visit our website at www.midmar.com

www.ingramcontent.com/pod-product-compliance
Lightning Source LLC
Chambersburg PA
CBHW071308110526
44591CB00010B/820